The Believer's Authority

by
Andrew Wommack

Study Guide

Unless otherwise indicated, all Scripture quotations are taken from the *King James Version* of the Bible.

The author has emphasised some words in Scripture quotations in italicised type.

The Believer's Authority Study Guide
ISBN: 978-1-906241-88-9

© 2009 by Andrew Wommack Ministries – Europe
PO Box 4392
Walsall, WS1 9AR, England
www.awme.net

Printed in England All rights reserved under International Copyright Law. Contents and/or cover may not be reproduced in whole or in part in any form without the express written consent of the Publisher.

CONTENTS

Introduction ix

How to Use Your Study Guide x

Lesson 1   **We're in a Spiritual Battle** 1
                 Outline 6
                 Teacher's Guide 8
                 Additional Information 10
                 Discipleship Questions 11
                 Answer Key 12
                 Scriptures 13

Lesson 2   **Whom He May Devour** 14
                 Outline 19
                 Teacher's Guide 21
                 Discipleship Questions 23
                 Answer Key 24
                 Scriptures 25

Lesson 3   **Satan's Inroads** 26
                 Outline 30
                 Teacher's Guide 32
                 Discipleship Questions 34
                 Answer Key 35
                 Scriptures 36

Lesson 4   **No Wicked Thing** 37
                 Outline 42
                 Teacher's Guide 44
                 Discipleship Questions 46
                 Answer Key 47
                 Scriptures 48

Lesson 5   **Unconditional Authority** 50
                 Outline 55
                 Teacher's Guide 57
                 Discipleship Questions 59
                 Answer Key 60
                 Scriptures 61

Lesson 6	**God of This World**	**63**
	Outline	68
	Teacher's Guide	70
	Discipleship Questions	72
	Answer Key	73
	Scriptures	74
Lesson 7	**Under the Umbrella**	**76**
	Outline	80
	Teacher's Guide	82
	Additional Information	84
	Discipleship Questions	85
	Answer Key	86
	Scriptures	87
Lesson 8	**Is This the One?**	**89**
	Outline	95
	Teacher's Guide	97
	Additional Information	98
	Discipleship Questions	99
	Answer Key	100
	Scriptures	101
Lesson 9	**Such as I Have**	**102**
	Outline	107
	Teacher's Guide	109
	Additional Information	110
	Discipleship Questions	111
	Answer Key	112
	Scriptures	113
Lesson 10	**Command Ye Me**	**115**
	Outline	119
	Teacher's Guide	121
	Discipleship Questions	122
	Answer Key	123
	Scriptures	124
Lesson 11	**Proclaim and Demonstrate**	**126**
	Outline	130
	Teacher's Guide	132
	Additional Information	134
	Discipleship Questions	135
	Answer Key	136
	Scriptures	137

Lesson 12	**Be a Witness** **138**
	Outline 143
	Teacher's Guide 145
	Additional Information 147
	Discipleship Questions 148
	Answer Key 149
	Scriptures 150

Lesson 13	**How to Pray for the Lost** **152**
	Outline 155
	Teacher's Guide 157
	Discipleship Questions 159
	Answer Key 160
	Scriptures 161

Lesson 14	**How Does Revival Come?** **162**
	Outline 167
	Teacher's Guide 169
	Additional Information 171
	Discipleship Questions 172
	Answer Key 173
	Scriptures 174

Lesson 15	**Believe and Receive** **176**
	Outline 182
	Teacher's Guide 184
	Discipleship Questions 186
	Answer Key 187
	Scriptures 188

Lesson 16	**God Has Given You Power** **190**
	Outline 195
	Teacher's Guide 197
	Additional Information 198
	Discipleship Questions 199
	Answer Key 200
	Scriptures 201

Lesson 17	**The Devil Will Flee from You** **202**
	Outline 207
	Teacher's Guide 209
	Additional Information 211
	Discipleship Questions 212
	Answer Key 213
	Scriptures 214

Lesson 18	**Law Enforcement**	215
	Outline	221
	Teacher's Guide	223
	Discipleship Questions	225
	Answer Key	226
	Scriptures	227
Lesson 19	**How the Power Flows**	229
	Outline	234
	Teacher's Guide	236
	Discipleship Questions	238
	Answer Key	239
	Scriptures	240
Lesson 20	**Cooperate with God**	242
	Outline	246
	Teacher's Guide	248
	Discipleship Questions	250
	Answer Key	251
	Scriptures	252
Lesson 21	**As You Think**	253
	Outline	257
	Teacher's Guide	259
	Discipleship Questions	260
	Answer Key	261
	Scriptures	262
Lesson 22	**Honour God**	264
	Outline	268
	Teacher's Guide	270
	Discipleship Questions	271
	Answer Key	272
	Scriptures	273
Lesson 23	**No New Testament Model**	275
	Outline	280
	Teacher's Guide	282
	Discipleship Questions	284
	Answer Key	285
	Scriptures	286
Lesson 24	**One Mediator**	288
	Outline	293
	Teacher's Guide	295
	Additional Information	297
	Discipleship Questions	298
	Answer Key	299
	Scriptures	300

Lesson 25	**The Battle Is in Your Mind** 301
	Outline 305
	Teacher's Guide 307
	Discipleship Questions 308
	Answer Key 309
	Scriptures 310
Lesson 26	**Fight to Win!** 312
	Outline 318
	Teacher's Guide 320
	Discipleship Questions 321
	Answer Key 322
	Scriptures 323

Conclusion 325

Receive Jesus as Your Saviour 326

Receive the Holy Spirit 327

About the Author 328

INTRODUCTION

Most people have a humanistic view of how life works. Even though Christians don't like this terminology, many of them function day by day with this same mentality. By only looking on the surface level, they don't recognise the spirit realm behind it all.

Humanists don't acknowledge God. As a whole, they're either agnostic or atheist – believing that everything in life has a natural, physical cause. It's sad to say, but many Christians have this same attitude. They don't realise the spiritual dynamics behind what's happening in the physical realm.

We are in a spiritual battle! Every single day, there is a battle raging in the spirit realm for the heart of each individual person, society, and the world as a whole. God is trying to draw people toward Himself and righteousness. He's trying to influence people to live consistent with Him so that His blessings can manifest in their lives. At the same time, Satan is trying to steal their hearts away from God. In an all-out battle against the Lord and His kingdom, the Enemy is pouring all the trash and corruption he can into people's lives.

Most of us – even Christians – don't recognise the intense battle waging all around us each and every day. We don't know the spiritual significance of our choices, words, and actions. We're functionally ignorant of how these things determine whether we're yielded to God and releasing His power and blessing into our lives or whether we're yielded to Satan and releasing sin and death into our lives (Rom. 6:16).

The devil can't control you outside of your will. However, your lack of awareness and understanding of the battle only works to his advantage. If you choose to believe God's Word and learn to recognise what's happening in the spirit realm, you can begin taking the proper action to improve your situation. You can cooperate with God to manifest His power and blessings.

Submit yourselves therefore to God. Resist the devil, and he will flee from you.
James 4:7

You can resist the devil, and he will flee from you. However, your passiveness and lack of resistance doesn't mean that the battle isn't raging; it simply means that you aren't winning. Satan is beating you in this area.

The revelation of God's Word contained in this book has the potential to transform your life. As you begin to understand and exercise your authority as a believer in the Lord Jesus Christ, Satan will flee, and God's power and blessings will manifest in your life greater than ever before.

HOW TO USE YOUR STUDY GUIDE

Whether you are teaching a class, leading a small group, discipling an individual, or studying *The Believer's Authority* on your own, this **Study Guide** is designed for you! Here's how it works:

Each study consists of a **Lesson Outline**, **Teacher's Guide**, **Discipleship Questions**, **Answer Key**, and **Scriptures**. Some **Lessons** also have **Additional Information**.

The teacher reads the **Lesson** aloud. While the **Lesson** is being read, each student follows along with their own copy of the **Lesson Outline**.

Once the **Lesson** is read, the teacher then facilitates a group Bible study using the **Teacher's Guide**. Simply read aloud one numbered section at a time, ask the corresponding questions that follow, and have the group answer them. Then, repeat the process for the next numbered section. For your convenience, answers are provided in parentheses.

Except for the corresponding questions and answers, the information on the **Teacher's Guide** is the same as the **Lesson Outline**. Therefore, the group should use their **Lesson Outlines** to assist them in answering the questions.

Whenever a question mentions a specific scripture, be sure to have the group look it up in their Bibles and read it together before answering the question. Feel free to interact with the group over the scriptures and points from the **Lesson** as time allows. Don't let any individual dominate the discussion, but try to draw out the quieter ones for the group conversation. As much as possible, keep the discussion centered on the scriptures and the **Lesson** points at hand. Remember, the goal is understanding (Matt. 13:19).

Discipleship Questions are provided for further study and meditation. They are designed for use as "homework," but – according to the teacher's discretion – may be helpful during the group study sometimes as well. Each **Lesson** comes with an **Answer Key**. As a brief review before launching into the current **Lesson**, the teacher may wish to go over the **Answer Key** for the previous study's **Discipleship Questions** with the group.

Some **Lessons** also have **Additional Information**. This section is geared toward the teacher. It contains resource recommendations for further study.

Scriptures from the *King James Version* of the Bible are included as another tool for reference and meditation.

For personal study, read the **Lesson** and review the **Teacher's Guide**. Then, answer the **Discipleship Questions** and check your work with the **Answer Key**. For maximum impact, be sure to utilise the **Additional Information** and **Scriptures**.

Printable files of the **Lesson Outline, Discipleship Questions**, and **Scriptures** can be found on the CD-Rom included with this book. Copies may be made for each person in the group.

Outline for Group Study:
- I. Briefly review previous study by going over the **Answer Key** for the **Discipleship Questions** (homework).
- II. Read the current **Lesson** aloud.
    - A. Be sure that each student has a copy of the **Lesson Outline**.
    - B. While the **Lesson** is being read, students should use their **Lesson Outline** to follow along.
- III. Once the **Lesson** is read, facilitate a group Bible study using the **Teacher's Guide**.
    - A. Read one entire numbered section (above).
    - B. Then ask the corresponding questions (below).
    - C. Group looks up and reads aloud each specifically mentioned scripture before answering the question.
    - D. Discuss the scripture and the answer/point from the **Lesson** as desired.
    - E. Then repeat the process by reading the next numbered section (above).
- IV. Distribute copies of the **Discipleship Questions** to be worked on as homework.

Materials Needed:
Study Guide, Bible, and enough copies of the **Lesson Outline** and **Discipleship Questions** for each student.

Outline for Personal Study:
- I. Read **Lesson**.
    - A. Read **Additional Information**, if any.
    - B. Meditate the **Scriptures**, as desired.
- II. Review **Teacher's Guide**.
- III. Answer **Discipleship Questions**.
- IV. Check your work with the **Answer Key**.

Materials Needed:
Study Guide, Bible, and something to write with.

WE'RE IN A SPIRITUAL BATTLE
Lesson 1

Finally, my brethren, be strong in the Lord, and in the power of his might. Put on the whole armour of God, that ye may be able to stand against the wiles of the devil. For we wrestle not against flesh and blood, but against principalities, against powers, against the rulers of the darkness of this world, against spiritual wickedness in high places.

Ephesians 6:10-12

God's Word reveals that we are not wrestling against flesh and blood, but demonic powers. Our fight isn't against people but the spiritual forces influencing them. However, most of us simply don't recognise the role the spirit realm plays in our daily lives. We think it's just human – natural – but the devil is busy influencing people every day.

It's useless to debate whether or not an individual is possessed, oppressed, or simply depressed. When the New Testament calls someone "demon possessed," the Greek word there literally means "demonised." They are under the influence and, therefore, control of the devil. This issue people make about whether someone is possessed, oppressed, or just depressed isn't in Scripture. The truth is that people all around the world today are being influenced, controlled, and used – to whatever degree – by the devil.

PROPER PERSPECTIVE

Many Westerners honestly believe that all the demons are over in some third-world country. But anyone who is spiritually perceptive knows that there is an abundance of demonic activity anywhere you go in the world, including the West. We just tend to look at things as being normal and natural. We miss the fact that the origin of many things that happen in our day – things that tick us off and come against us – is spiritual. We fail to recognise the spiritual influence behind it.

However, if you were to adopt the biblical mindset, it would make a huge difference in the way you respond. You'd recognise that it's not that person who sits next to you at work. It's not your neighbour, your spouse, or your circumstances that are really what's coming against you. They can be influenced, inspired, and used by Satan, but they really aren't the source. When you genuinely understand that this isn't a physical battle, it changes the way you respond.

I get a lot of hate mail and criticism because of the things I say. There was a time when I took these things personally and thought, *Why is this individual so upset with me?* I just looked at it and always tried to deal with them on the human level. Since then, I've come to recognise that Satan is the one who's trying to get my attention off of what God has told me to do. I just recognise that the Enemy is using some person to come against me. He's just trying to gain an inroad into my life so he can steal God's Word from me (Mark 4:17). But because I look beyond the individual and don't take it personally, I'm able to put things into proper perspective and deal with it differently.

I've actually had some good friends come against me. Even though they did some pretty mean things, I've been able to look past that and forgive them. I recognised that they had a sensitivity in some area that Satan took advantage of and used them against me. I haven't been angry or bitter toward them, because I understood what the devil was trying to do. Since then, they've turned around and realised what happened. We've been able to completely reestablish our friendship because I recognised that it wasn't just those people, but Satan trying to get at me.

SATAN USES PEOPLE

Jesus exemplified this same perspective. He recognised when the devil was trying to get to Him through a person.

After Peter – under the influence of God – confessed Jesus as **"the Christ, the Son of the living God"** (Matt. 16:16), the Lord started explaining to His disciples about His soon, coming crucifixion, death, and resurrection. Immediately Peter began to rebuke Him, saying:

> *Be it far from thee, Lord: this shall not be unto thee.*
>
> Matthew 16:22

Apparently, Peter had missed Jesus' statement that He would rise again on the third day. Peter didn't even want to consider the thought of his beloved Lord being taken and killed. This was the same man who just moments before had been inspired and controlled by the Holy Spirit. Yet now, Jesus…

> *Turned, and said unto Peter, Get thee behind me, Satan: thou art an offence unto me: for thou savourest not the things that be of God, but those that be of men.*
>
> Matthew 16:23

The Lord recognised that Satan was speaking through Peter. This wasn't something coming from God. Jesus knew it was inconsistent with what the Father had clearly revealed to Him of His will. So even though Peter had just spoken forth a glorious revelation by the Holy Spirit, Christ knew that the inspiration for Peter's rebuke of Him was from hell.

There are times when the devil speaks to you through people. He'll use people to get at you. Of course, they may be unaware of the fact that they're being used by Satan. Peter was probably shocked, hurt, and offended when Jesus turned around and said, "Get behind me, Satan!" However, there are times when you need to rebuke the devil that way too.

WHOSE VOICE IS IT?

Now, don't misunderstand me and go around blasting people. I'm not saying you should rebuke everyone who disagrees with you, declaring, "You're of the devil. Satan is using you in my life." That's not what I'm trying to get across. You just need to recognise that Satan – as well as God – can speak through and use the people in your life. Like Jesus, you need to discern whose voice is coming through.

More than thirty years ago my mother wanted to take my wife, my oldest son (who was one at the time), and I to the Smoky Mountains. This was back during our 'poverty days'. Jamie and I were struggling financially. But since Mother offered to pay for everything on the trip, we decided to go.

At that time, my mother had just started believing God for healing. Since she hadn't seen the manifestation yet in the specific areas she'd been believing for, basically she had suffered a defeat. Due to this, Mother was on the bubble about whether this 'healing stuff' really worked or not. Since then, she's turned around and has received great healing. But this was way back in the beginning of our ministry, when Mother still thought I was somewhere on the fringe of lunacy.

As we began our trip, Mother was nursing a little bit of a cold. She started saying negative things about my son like, "Keep him away from me, or he'll catch this cold."

I'd answer, "No, Mother. He's not going to catch this cold."

Then she'd complain about the money, saying, "I really shouldn't be taking this trip. I don't have the money to do it."

So I just told her, "Hey, Mother. We have zippo, zilch, nada. If you don't have the money to take this trip, we need to go home now because I can't help you."

She'd respond, "Oh, no. I've got plenty of money." Mother was just in a negative mindset, which made it a bad situation.

During the hot summer day, my son sat right in front of the air conditioner. Since I understood that we can have what we say (Mark 11:23), it really bothered me when she said things like, "Don't put him there. He'll catch a cold!"

I'd have to counter that with, "No, he's not going to catch a cold."

"SHUT UP!"

All this griping and complaining was really out of character for my mother. She is a super lady and is usually very positive, but she was just stuck in this negative mindset. She talked doubt and unbelief all day long. It was a constant battle back and forth to counter what was being said. Since this was my mother, I tried to be as polite and kind as I possibly could.

The very first night of the trip, we all stayed in a hotel room together. Our son was sleeping in a little crib. Around eleven o'clock he woke up with this croup in his throat that you could have heard in the next room. It was loud, and he could hardly breathe. So I got up, prayed in tongues, rebuked the croup, and released my faith. He went back to sleep and everything was fine.

Thirty minutes later the same thing happened. I got up, prayed over him, and he went back to sleep. Every thirty minutes, I was up and down like a yo-yo, praying over our son and trying to get him back to sleep. Finally, about three in the morning, on one of my trips back to bed, my mother said, "Admit it, Andy. He's sick!"

I got right down there, stuck my finger in her face, and said, "Satan, in the name of Jesus, I command you to shut up! I will not receive any of your criticism or any of your curses. My son is blessed and not cursed!" Then I started speaking the Word. Mother never said another word, and our son never got up again that night. He was just fine, but Mother didn't say anything for two whole days – and we were together all the time in a car on vacation.

Finally, when she did speak, she cried "Well, I'm sorry you think I'm the devil" and started into this self-pity party.

I said, "Mother, you know enough to know better. I've told you the Word of God. You knew that stuff you were saying was exactly opposite the Word. You'd just given yourself over to Satan. I'm not mad at you. I was just standing against the devil. He was trying to steal my faith for healing."

To this day, Mother continues to be one of my very best friends. She's over ninety-five years old and enjoys the blessing of good health. My approach that night was pretty strong, but I knew Satan was behind it trying to steal my faith.

You can certainly take a stand against what people say with more tact than I displayed back then. I was young in the Lord, and that's just the way I responded. But the principle applies regardless of how you administer it.

STRETCHED TO THE MAX

We are in a spiritual battle! However, most of the time, people don't recognise it. They're just looking at things from a natural, human perspective. They factor God, the devil, and the whole supernatural realm right out of the equation. The average person doesn't realise the spiritual dynamics taking place. God doesn't send bad things our way. It's not just happenstance or fate. There's a real Enemy out there that we must learn to deal with.

The first time I tried to produce a book was about twenty years ago. It was my *Life for Today Study Bible and Commentary*: the Gospels Edition, which is almost six hundred pages long. This was going to be a major expense. At that time, my ministry income was so low that to come up with $50,000 to print a book was two or three months' worth of income for me. This project was really stretching me to the max!

A number of different publishers came and offered to help us with the project. One offered to reduce our cost to $27,000 if we would pay right away. They said, "We're in a bind and need the money. If you pay right away, we'll give you this discount." So I went to my partners, raised the money – more than a month's worth of income at the time – and gave it to them. This was a major deal for us.

However, within a month, I learned that the salesman had run off with our money. In fact, he'd burned several other well-known preachers at the same time!

I remember when I heard this news. My employee said, "This salesman just took our $27,000. We're going to have to come up with an additional $45,000 just in the next week or so to be able to make this project work. All together, we're looking at about $70,000."

SEVENFOLD

My first reaction was one of shock. "Is this really true?" Then came a twinge of wanting to beat the snot out of this salesman. But I recognised who the real culprit was. Satan had come against me and was trying to steal from me.

Immediately Proverbs 6:31 came to mind:

> **But if** [a thief] **be found, he shall restore sevenfold; he shall give all the substance of his house.**
>
> Brackets mine

I recognised that this wasn't just a person trying to steal from me. Obviously, there were demonic entities working behind the scenes. So, within seconds of getting this news, I recognised, "This is the devil stealing from me, and I've caught him. Therefore, according to the Word of God, I demand it back seven times!" Immediately I took a piece of paper and figured out seven times $70,000. Instead of being angry, depressed, and hurt, I started dancing and praising God, saying, "Hallelujah, this is awesome. I'm getting $490,000 back *this* year!" As I continued praising God, that situation never did get me down or discouraged.

When that year was over, we had increased nearly to the penny $490,000 – exactly seven times the amount of money that was taken from us. That was back during a period of time when our entire income was only about $500,000 a year. We nearly doubled our income that year!

What could have been a tragic scenario turned into a positive situation because I recognised that I'm not fighting flesh and blood; I'm fighting a spiritual battle, with spiritual weapons, against spiritual enemies. I realised that Satan was trying to come against me, and then I acted on the Word.

WHO'S INFLUENCING WHOM?

I've actually loaned people money before who have never paid me back. They said they would, but for whatever reason, they didn't. Instead of taking an offense and getting mad at the person, I recognised that this was Satan. Of course, the person cooperated in some measure and allowed him to do it. But I recognise that the devil is trying to get me into unforgiveness. So I just forgave them.

I've actually given money to people who at one time said they'd pay me back. My attitude was, *Hey, just take it as a gift. I'm not going to harbor any animosity over this. It's not worth it.*

You might think, *Man, I'd never do something like that.* But I recognise that there is a spiritual battle raging – and nobody is going to rent space in my mind! Nobody is going to occupy my heart except God. I refuse to harbor unforgiveness toward anyone. I will not allow bitterness, even a toehold, in my life. I'm aware that Satan uses such things as an inroad against me.

Like it or not, there's a spiritual battle raging right now for your heart and mind. What you think in your heart is the way that you'll be (Prov. 23:7). Your thoughts become what you say and do, with your actions being the greatest expression of your authority. Therefore, you'll be influenced, dominated, and ruled by whomever you yield yourself to – God or Satan (Rom. 6:16).

WE'RE IN A SPIRITUAL BATTLE
Lesson 1 – Outline

I. God's Word reveals that we are not wrestling against flesh and blood, but demonic powers:

Finally, my brethren, be strong in the Lord, and in the power of his might. Put on the whole armour of God, that ye may be able to stand against the wiles of the devil. For we wrestle not against flesh and blood, but against principalities, against powers, against the rulers of the darkness of this world, against spiritual wickedness in high places.

Ephesians 6:10-12

  A. Our fight isn't against people, but the spiritual forces influencing them.

  B. However, most of us simply don't recognise the role that the spirit realm plays in our daily lives.

  C. This issue people make about whether someone is possessed, oppressed, or simply depressed isn't in Scripture.

  D. The truth is that people all around the world today are being influenced, controlled, and used – to whatever degree – by the devil.

  E. We just tend to look at things as being normal and natural, so we miss the fact that the origin of many things that happen in our day – things that tick us off and come against us – is spiritual.

II. If you were to adopt the biblical mindset, it would make a huge difference in the way you respond.

  A. You'd recognise that it's not your neighbour, your spouse, or your circumstances that are really what's coming against you.

  B. They can be influenced, inspired, and used of Satan, but they really aren't the source.

  C. When you genuinely understand that this isn't a physical battle, it changes the way you respond.

III. Jesus recognised when the devil was trying to get to Him through a person:

He turned, and said unto Peter, Get thee behind me, Satan: thou art an offence unto me: for thou savourest not the things that be of God, but those that be of men.

Matthew 16:23

  A. The Lord recognised that Satan was speaking through Peter.

- B. So even though Peter had just spoken forth a glorious revelation by the Holy Spirit (Matt. 16:16), Christ knew that the inspiration for Peter's rebuke of Him (Matt. 16:22) was from hell.

- C. You just need to recognise that Satan – as well as God – can speak through and use the people in your life.

- D. Like Jesus, you need to discern whose voice is coming through.

IV. We are in a spiritual battle!

- A. However, most of the time, people don't recognise it.

- B. They're just looking at things from a natural, human perspective.

- C. They factor God, the devil, and the whole supernatural realm right out of the equation.

- D. The average person doesn't realise the spiritual dynamics taking place.

- E. There's a real Enemy out there that we must learn to deal with.

V. Like it or not, there's a spiritual battle raging right now for your heart and mind.

- A. What you think in your heart is the way that you'll be (Prov. 23:7).

- B. Your thoughts become what you say and do, with your actions being the greatest expression of your authority.

- C. Therefore, you'll be influenced, dominated, and ruled by whomever you yield yourself to – God or Satan (Rom. 6:16).

WE'RE IN A SPIRITUAL BATTLE
Lesson 1 – Teacher's Guide

1. God's Word reveals that we are not wrestling against flesh and blood, but demonic powers (Eph. 6:10-12). Our fight isn't against people, but the spiritual forces influencing them. However, most of us simply don't recognise the role that the spirit realm plays in our daily lives. This issue people make about whether someone is possessed, oppressed, or simply depressed isn't in Scripture. The truth is that people all around the world today are being influenced, controlled, and used – to whatever degree – by the devil. We just tend to look at things as being normal and natural, so we miss the fact that the origin of many things that happen in our day – things that tick us off and come against us – is spiritual.

2. If we were to adopt the biblical mindset, it would make a huge difference in the way we respond. We'd recognise that it's not our neighbour, our spouse, or our circumstances that are really what's coming against us. They can be influenced, inspired, and used of Satan, but they really aren't the source. When we genuinely understand that this isn't a physical battle, it changes the way we respond.

3. Jesus recognised when the devil was trying to get to Him through a person (Matt. 16:23). The Lord recognised that Satan was speaking through Peter. So even though Peter had just spoken forth a glorious revelation by the Holy Spirit (Matt. 16:16), Christ knew that the inspiration for Peter's rebuke of Him (Matt. 16:22) was from hell. We just need to recognise that Satan – as well as God – can speak through and use the people in our lives. Like Jesus, we need to discern whose voice is coming through.

4. We are in a spiritual battle! However, most of the time, we don't recognise it. We're just looking at things from a natural, human perspective. We factor God, the devil, and the whole supernatural realm right out of the equation. The average person doesn't realise the spiritual dynamics taking place. There's a real Enemy out there that we must learn to deal with.

1. A. Read Ephesians 6:10-12. What does God's Word reveal that we are not wrestling against? (Flesh and blood)
   B. Most of us simply don't recognise the role that _____ plays in our daily lives. (The spirit realm)
2. A. Is it really our neighbour, spouse, or circumstances that are coming against us? (No)
   B. What happens when we genuinely understand that this isn't a physical battle? (It changes the way we respond)
3. A. Read Matthew 16:16 and 22-23. Who can speak through and use the people in our lives – God, Satan, or both? (Both)
   B. Like Jesus, we need to do what? (Discern whose voice is coming through)
4. A. What are we in? (A spiritual battle)
   B. Who is out there that we must learn to deal with? (A real Enemy)

5. Like it or not, there's a spiritual battle raging right now for our hearts and minds. What we think in our heart is the way that we'll be (Prov. 23:7). Our thoughts become what we say and do, with our actions being the greatest expression of our authority. Therefore, we'll be influenced, dominated, and ruled by whomever we yield ourselves to – God or Satan (Rom. 6:16).

5. A. Read Proverbs 23:7 and Romans 6:16. What becomes what we say and do, with our actions being the greatest expression of our authority? (Our thoughts)
   B. Therefore, who will we be influenced, dominated, and ruled by? (Whomever we yield ourselves to – God or Satan)

WE'RE IN A SPIRITUAL BATTLE
Lesson 1 – Additional Information

The *Life for Today Study Bible and Commentary* is available as a free download at our website. It covers the Gospel of Matthew all the way through 2 Timothy. Print versions are also available to order through our ministry. Please see our different *Life for Today Partnership* options for additional information about how to obtain Andrew's supplemental audio materials for the *Life for Today* commentary series. Through them, Andrew will walk you through the Word one verse at a time.

Another tremendous Bible study and reference resource is the *Andrew Wommack Living Commentary*. This computer software contains Andrew's notes and commentary on scriptures throughout the entire Bible. It's called a "Living Commentary" because each month Andrew adds new notes, which are available as a free download, to those who have purchased this software. If you've ever wondered what Andrew thinks about a particular verse or passage, this is where you'll find it.

WE'RE IN A SPIRITUAL BATTLE
Lesson 1 – Discipleship Questions

1. According to Ephesians 6:10-12, who are we to be strong in?

2. What are we to put on?

3. According to Mark 4:17, what arises for the Word's sake and immediately causes people to be offended?

4. The Word only endured for a time because they had no _____ in themselves.

5. Who was speaking in Matthew 16:16?

6. According to Matthew 16:22-23, whom did Simon Peter begin to rebuke?

7. While speaking to Peter, whom was the Lord really addressing?

8. According to Mark 11:23, what are we to speak to?

9. What shall we have?

10. According to Proverbs 6:31, how much shall a thief who is found be required to restore?

11. According to Proverbs 23:7, we are as we think where?

12. Romans 6:16 reveals that we are _____ to whom we yield.

13. What does yielding to sin manifest in our lives?

14. What does yielding to obedience manifest in our lives?

WE'RE IN A SPIRITUAL BATTLE
Lesson 1 – Answer Key

1. The Lord.
2. The whole armour of God.
3. Affliction or persecution.
4. Root.
5. Simon Peter.
6. The Lord.
7. Satan.
8. The mountain.
9. Whatsoever we say.
10. Sevenfold.
11. In our hearts.
12. Servants.
13. Death.
14. Righteousness.

WE'RE IN A SPIRITUAL BATTLE
Lesson 1 – Scriptures

Finally, my brethren, be strong in the Lord, and in the power of his might. Put on the whole armour of God, that ye may be able to stand against the wiles of the devil. For we wrestle not against flesh and blood, but against principalities, against powers, against the rulers of the darkness of this world, against spiritual wickedness in high places.

Ephesians 6:10-12

And have no root in themselves, and so endure but for a time: afterward, when affliction or persecution ariseth for the word's sake, immediately they are offended.

Mark 4:17

And Simon Peter answered and said, Thou art the Christ, the Son of the living God.

Matthew 16:16

Then Peter took him, and began to rebuke him, saying, Be it far from thee, Lord: this shall not be unto thee. But he turned, and said unto Peter, Get thee behind me, Satan: thou art an offence unto me: for thou savourest not the things that be of God, but those that be of men.

Matthew 16:22-23

For verily I say unto you, That whosoever shall say unto this mountain, Be thou removed, and be thou cast into the sea; and shall not doubt in his heart, but shall believe that those things which he saith shall come to pass; he shall have whatsoever he saith.

Mark 11:23

But if he be found, he shall restore sevenfold; he shall give all the substance of his house.

Proverbs 6:31

For as he thinketh in his heart, so is he: Eat and drink, saith he to thee; but his heart is not with thee.

Proverbs 23:7

Know ye not, that to whom ye yield yourselves servants to obey, his servants ye are to whom ye obey; whether of sin unto death, or of obedience unto righteousness?

Romans 6:16

WHOM HE MAY DEVOUR
Lesson 2

When you yield yourself to sin, you're serving Satan, who is the author of that sin. But when you yield yourself to obedience, you serve God, who is the author of that righteousness.

Know ye not, that to whom ye yield yourselves servants to obey, his servants ye are to whom ye obey; whether of sin unto death, or of obedience unto righteousness?

Romans 6:16

In this spiritual battle, your actions are very important.

Most of you recognise that actions are important in the physical realm. You know there are consequences for what you do. If you're speeding while driving, you could get a ticket or cause a wreck. The ticket could cost money and put points on your license. The wreck could damage cars or even cost someone their life. When we talk negatively about someone, we can hurt their feelings or even loose demonic powers against them.

There's much more to life than just this physical, natural, surface level. There are spiritual dynamics constantly taking place. Whether the person you're speaking evil of ever knows about it or not, you'll be affected. Venting anger, frustration, resentment, or unforgiveness affects you whether it affects anyone else or not. I've actually ridden with people who are very vocal in traffic when someone cuts them off. They've told me, "That person doesn't know what I said. They didn't hear me." It doesn't matter whether they ever hear them or not. If they get angry and bitter, they've just yielded themselves to Satan. Whether they recognise it or not, the devil is the one who influences them to respond in the wrong way (Rom. 6:16).

THE WRATH OF MAN

James 1:20 says,

The wrath of man worketh not the righteousness of God.

Giving place to anger and bitterness doesn't accomplish the righteousness of God. You aren't going to accomplish God's purposes by getting in the flesh, giving in to anger, and losing your temper. That's not the way God's kingdom works. So whether anyone else ever hears you or not, it's having an effect on you.

A fellow I led to the Lord was genuinely converted and had come quite a way in his discipleship. He upholstered cars and was trying to restore a certain old one. One day I went over to his house and knocked on the door, but there was no answer. I knew he was home, so I walked around to the backyard. As I came around the corner of his house, I heard this awful profanity, screaming, and yelling. This brother had a fence post and was beating the fire out of that car!

He was cussing this car up and down as I – his pastor – came around the corner. When he saw me, he stopped for a moment (conviction, I presume) and said, "Well, it's just a car. It's doesn't matter what I say to it. I didn't hurt anybody." I had to explain to him that it didn't matter what it was. When you give place to anger and vent like that, Satan jumps on it like a chicken on a June bug. The Enemy will take full advantage of an open door like that to come and steal, kill, and destroy (John 10:10).

> **Where envying and strife is, there is confusion and every evil work.**
>
> James 3:16

Notice how this didn't say 'some' evil works. It didn't say envying and strife 'could' allow the devil to come against 'certain types of people'. No, when you get into envy and strife, you're flinging the door wide open and saying, "Come on in, Satan, and do your worst in my life." You're drawing a great big target on your back and saying, "Shoot your best shot!" When you give in to envy and strife, you make yourself a target for the devil.

ARE YOU SPIRITUALLY STINKY?

> **We are unto God a sweet savour** [smell] **of Christ, in them that are saved, and in them that perish.**
>
> 2 Corinthians 2:15, brackets mine

What is your spiritual scent? Are you giving off the sweet aroma of Christ, or are you spiritually stinky? Just like flies and rats, demons are attracted to open wounds and garbage in your life. Your rotten attitude – getting mad in traffic, being bitter over whatever, and criticising everything and everyone – is putting out an aroma that's drawing every demon in the county to your house. And you wonder, *Why am I having these problems? Why does nothing go right for me?* That's just ignorance gone to seed. You need to recognise that we're in a spiritual battle. Your thoughts, attitudes, words, and actions are either releasing the power of God in your life, or they're releasing the power of the devil.

You might think, *Fate is against me. I have bad luck.* You may even put it off on the Lord, saying, "God, why have You allowed these things to happen to me?" It's not like that at all. God is good, and He's doing everything He can to save, bless, heal, and prosper you. However, we do have an Enemy who is going around seeking whom he may devour.

> **Be sober, be vigilant; because your adversary the devil, as a roaring lion, walketh about, seeking whom he may devour.**
>
> 1 Peter 5:8

Notice that it's **"whom *may* devour"** (emphasis mine). Satan cannot devour you without your cooperation. One way he gains that cooperation is through ignorance. You may think it doesn't matter if you get mad at the car you're working on or the driver who just cut you off in traffic. You might think that nobody's harmed when you gossip about someone who isn't there, saying, "They won't hear this." But the truth is, once you start venting these things, Satan takes advantage of it.

For some reason or another, we feel like politicians are just fair game. We think we're free to say anything we want about them because the freedom of speech our country enjoys encourages us to voice our disagreement. However, there is a right and wrong way to do it. I've heard Christians rail on a presidential candidate or some other public officer in ways that aren't healthy. We can disagree without putting a person to shame with the words we say. It doesn't matter whether they ever hear us or not. We could be opening up a door to the devil through our words (Rom. 6:16).

SPIRITUAL DYNAMICS

You need to set a watch before your mouth (Ps. 141:3) and take every thought captive to the obedience of Christ (2 Cor. 10:5). You need to control your actions (Gal. 5:22-24) and recognise that the demonic realm is trying to take a shot at you every day of your life. If you allow a door to be opened to them, they'll come in for no other purpose than to steal, kill, and destroy (John 10:10). Satan is looking for whom he may devour (1 Pet. 5:8).

You need to learn to recognise the spiritual dynamics happening in your life. God wants you to yield to Him so that His power and blessings can be released in your life. Satan wants you to yield to him so that destruction and death can be released in your life. In order to gain an inroad, the Enemy is constantly trying to snare you with bitterness, unforgiveness, and ungodliness of all kinds. Therefore, no matter what you do, you're either obeying God or obeying Satan. You're either submitting to God and His influence, or you're submitting to Satan and his influence. Every time you act, you are releasing spiritual power – either God's or the devil's – into your life.

Since most people are ignorant of this truth, they allow all kinds of things in their lives. Yet if they were to recognise the results they're going to reap, they would never do it.

The wife of one of our Bible college students was suffering from severe depression. When I began to tell her how she could be delivered from this, she explained that she had battled depression since she was a little girl. She'd go through a period of one or two months each year when she would be severely depressed and have to treat it with medication.

I told her, "You don't want to live that way anymore. You need to get over this."

She answered, "This is just the way that I am. It's not hurting anything. I get over it. Everything's okay in a month or so." She had totally accepted and embraced this depression, thinking it was only a passing thing that had no lasting impact. But every time we submit to doing things Satan's way, we are having spiritual intercourse with him, which conceives evil. It isn't just benign.

SIN'S CONCEPTION

Every man is tempted, when he is drawn away of his own lust, and enticed. Then when lust hath conceived, it bringeth forth sin: and sin, when it is finished, bringeth forth death.

James 1:14-15

Sin is conceived in your emotions. Every time you have a negative emotion – whether it be sadness, anger, fear, strife, or one of many others – you conceive something. Many people are conceiving things they don't want to give birth to. They don't want depression, strife, suicide, or their marriage to fall apart. Yet they allow these negative emotions to flow through them without recognising they're in a spiritual battle. When you give in to your flesh and start saying and doing these things, you are releasing spiritual forces. There is a battle raging, and the Enemy is looking for an opportunity to come against you.

The devil's will is to devour everyone he can (1 Pet. 5:8). He desires to steal, kill, and destroy every person everywhere (John 10:10). If Satan got what he wanted, then the whole earth would be devastated, and there would be no good anywhere.

However, God has a will too. Jesus said:

I am come that they might have life, and that they might have it more abundantly.

John 10:10

Jesus is trying to release life into you. Satan is trying to steal, kill, and destroy anything good that you have. Both are willing and able to move and manifest those things in your life, but the determining factor is you. You need to recognise this battle that's raging and the fact that everything you say and do is either empowering God or the devil. The Lord wants to release His life into you. Satan wants to steal that life, and kill and destroy you. It's not fate or luck. Your thoughts, choices, and actions make a huge difference in your life.

"GET OUT OF MY LIFE!"

I visited a church once that had previously believed God could heal but that it wasn't His will to heal every single time. However, less than six months before I came, they had changed their minds to come into agreement with the Word, saying, "It's God's will for every person to be well. He heals all the time." This was a brand-new step of faith for them. The congregation was beginning to hear the Word and was starting to believe God for specific manifestations of healing.

Two days before I arrived, that church had a funeral for a seventeen-year-old boy who had died after being in a coma for six weeks. The entire church had fasted and prayed, trying to implement the truths from God's Word that they were being taught. Although they knew it was God's will to heal this boy, he died anyway. Therefore, there was a tremendous amount of conflict, turmoil, and questions in that church.

After the morning meetings, I went out to eat with the parents of the boy every day for three days, trying to figure out exactly what had transpired. Since everyone had given it their best shot – doing everything they knew to do – many people in the church were beginning to back off the Word, saying, "Maybe it's not God's will to heal every time." When I told them that wasn't true, that God had already provided healing and it's His will to heal every single time, they responded, "Well, then, what's the problem?"

As I talked with the boy's parents those three days, I discovered that they had been in so much strife that they were about get a divorce. They'd already made the plans and had talked about it with the children. Therefore, there was much strife, hurt, and negative emotion in that home.

On the morning of the tragedy, the mother had an argument with this boy and told him, "I hate you. Get out of my house and never come back again!" She probably didn't mean what she said. She was just saying it out of the heat of emotion. I know that kids can sometimes get on people's nerves. I've raised some myself. Raising kids is harder than raising the dead – and

I've had to do both in my family. I'm not trying to condemn this lady. However, before this boy left, she said, "Get out of my life and never come back again."

EVERY EVIL WORK

Because the boy had been hurt, he violated school policy, left the school grounds, and went over to this other kid's house to eat lunch. While there, they got out a gun, were playing with it, and he accidentally shot himself in the head. That's the reason he had been in a coma for six weeks.

They just didn't understand how this could have happened. The Word reveals that…

Where envying and strife is, there is confusion and every evil work.
James 3:16, emphasis mine

Many people say, "I agree that strife isn't the best. Nobody likes it, but it's just a normal part of life. Families fight, and then they get over it." Without realising that they're in a spiritual battle, they just tolerate different levels of strife in their lives. The Word says that where envying and strife is, there is confusion.

God is not the author of confusion, but of peace.
1 Corinthians 14:33

If God isn't the author of confusion, guess who is? That's right – Satan. The devil is the one who, wherever envying and strife is, brings confusion and every evil work.

When you fling a door open like that to the devil, don't be surprised if you see different forms of sickness, tragedy, poverty, and death manifest. Satan jumps on opportunities like that and uses them as inroads into your life. As a roaring lion, he's constantly seeking whom he may devour.

WHOM HE MAY DEVOUR
Lesson 2 – Outline

I. In this spiritual battle, your actions are very important.

> **Know ye not, that to whom ye yield yourselves servants to obey, his servants ye are to whom ye obey; whether of sin unto death, or of obedience unto righteousness?**
>
> Romans 6:16

    A. When you yield yourself to sin, you're serving Satan, who is the author of that sin, but when you yield yourself to obedience, you serve God, who is the author of that righteousness.

    B. You aren't going to accomplish God's purposes by getting in the flesh, giving in to anger, and losing your temper (James 1:20).

    C. Whether anyone else ever hears you or not, it's having an effect on you.

II. When you give in to envy and strife, you make yourself a target for the devil.

> **Where envying and strife is, there is confusion and every evil work.**
>
> James 3:16

    A. Are you giving off the sweet aroma of Christ, or are you spiritually stinky?

> **We are unto God a sweet savour [smell] of Christ, in them that are saved, and in them that perish.**
>
> 2 Corinthians 2:15, brackets mine

    B. Your thoughts, attitudes, words, and actions are either releasing the power of God in your life, or they're releasing the power of the devil.

III. God is good, and He's doing everything He can to save, bless, heal, and prosper us, but we do have an Enemy who is going around seeking whom he may devour.

> **Be sober, be vigilant; because your adversary the devil, as a roaring lion, walketh about, seeking whom he may devour.**
>
> 1 Peter 5:8

    A. Satan cannot devour you without your cooperation.

    B. You need to set a watch before your mouth (Ps. 141:3) and take every thought captive to the obedience of Christ (2 Cor. 10:5).

    C. You need to control your actions (Gal. 5:22-24) and recognise that the demonic realm is trying to take a shot at you every day of your life.

IV. You need to learn to recognise the spiritual dynamics happening in your life.

   A. God wants you to yield to Him so that His power and blessings can be released in your life, and Satan wants you to yield to him so that destruction and death can be released in your life.

   B. You're either submitting to God and His influence or Satan and his influence.

   C. Every time you act, you are releasing spiritual power – either God's or the devil's – into your life.

V. Sin is conceived in your emotions.

   Every man is tempted, when he is drawn away of his own lust, and enticed. Then when lust hath conceived, it bringeth forth sin: and sin, when it is finished, bringeth forth death.
   James 1:14-15

   A. Every time you have a negative emotion – whether it be sadness, anger, fear, strife, or one of many others – you conceive something.

   B. Many people are conceiving things that they don't want to give birth to.

   C. When you give in to your flesh and start saying and doing these things, you are releasing spiritual forces.

VI. You need to recognise this battle that's raging and the fact that everything you say and do is either empowering God or the devil.

   The thief cometh not, but for to steal, and to kill, and to destroy: I am come that they might have life, and that they might have it more abundantly.
   John 10:10

   A. The Lord wants to release His life into you.

   B. Satan wants to steal that life, and kill and destroy you.

   C. Your thoughts, choices, and actions make a huge difference in your life.

   D. The devil is the one who, wherever envying and strife is, brings confusion and every evil work (James 3:16 and 1 Cor. 14:33).

   E. As a roaring lion, he's constantly seeking whom he may devour.

WHOM HE MAY DEVOUR
Lesson 2 – Teacher's Guide

1. In this spiritual battle, our actions are very important (Rom. 6:16). When we yield ourselves to sin, we're serving Satan, who is the author of that sin, but when we yield ourselves to obedience, we serve God, who is the author of that righteousness. We aren't going to accomplish God's purposes by getting in the flesh, giving in to anger, and losing our tempers (James 1:20). Whether anyone else ever hears us or not, it's having an effect on us.

2. When we give in to envy and strife, we make ourselves a target for the devil (James 3:16). Are we giving off the sweet aroma of Christ, or are we spiritually stinky (2 Cor. 2:15)? Our thoughts, attitudes, words, and actions are either releasing the power of God in our lives, or they're releasing the power of the devil.

3. God is good, and He's doing everything He can to save, bless, heal, and prosper us, but we do have an Enemy who is going around seeking whom he may devour (1 Pet. 5:8). Satan cannot devour us without our cooperation. We need to set a watch before our mouths (Ps. 141:3) and take every thought captive to the obedience of Christ (2 Cor. 10:5). We need to control our actions (Gal. 5:22-24) and recognise that the demonic realm is trying to take a shot at us every day of our lives.

1. A. Read Romans 6:16 and James 1:20. Who are we serving when we yield ourselves to sin? (Satan – the author of that sin)
   B. We aren't going to accomplish God's purposes by what? (Getting in the flesh, giving in to anger, and losing our temper)
2. A. Read James 3:16 and 2 Corinthians 2:15. When do we make ourselves a target for the devil? (When we give in to envy and strife)
   B. What either releases the power of God in our lives or releases the power of the devil? (Our thoughts, attitudes, words, and actions)
3. A. Read 1 Peter 5:8, Psalm 141:3, 2 Corinthians 10:5, and Galatians 5:22-24. What is God doing? (Everything He can to save, bless, heal, and prosper us)
   B. Satan cannot devour us without what? (Our cooperation)

4. We need to learn to recognise the spiritual dynamics happening in our lives. God wants us to yield to Him so that His power and blessings can be released in our lives, and Satan wants us to yield to him so that destruction and death can be released in our lives. We're either submitting to God and His influence or Satan and his influence. Every time we act, we are releasing spiritual power – either God's or the devil's – into our lives.

5. Sin is conceived in our emotions (James 1:14-15). Every time we have a negative emotion – whether it be sadness, anger, fear, strife, or one of many others – we conceive something. Many people are conceiving things that they don't want to give birth to. When we give in to our flesh and start saying and doing these things, we are releasing spiritual forces.

6. We need to recognise this battle that's raging and the fact that everything we say and do is either empowering God or the devil (John 10:10). The Lord wants to release His life into us. Satan wants to steal that life, and kill and destroy us. Our thoughts, choices, and actions make a huge difference in our lives. The devil is the one who, wherever envying and strife is, brings confusion and every evil work (James 3:16 and 1 Cor. 14:33). As a roaring lion, he's constantly seeking whom he may devour.

4. A. Why does God want us to yield to Him? (So that His power and blessings can be released in our lives)
   B. What are we releasing into our lives every time we act? (Spiritual power – either God's or the devil's)
5. A. Read James 1:14-15. Where is sin conceived? (In our emotions)
   B. What are many people conceiving? (Things that they don't want to give birth to)
6. A. Read John 10:10, James 3:16, and 1 Corinthians 14:33. What makes a huge difference in our lives? (Our thoughts, choices, and actions)
   B. Wherever envying and strife is, the devil brings what? (Confusion and every evil work)

WHOM HE MAY DEVOUR
Lesson 2 – Discipleship Questions

1. According to James 1:20, what doesn't the wrath of man work?

2. John 10:10 reveals that Jesus came for what purpose?

3. James 3:16 says that confusion and every evil work are found where?

4. According to 2 Corinthians 2:15, what are we to God?

5. What does 1 Peter 5:8 command us to be?

6. What does the psalmist ask the Lord to set before his mouth in Psalm 141:3?

7. According to 2 Corinthians 10:5, what are we to do with every imagination and high thing that exalts itself against the knowledge of God?

8. What is listed in Galatians 5:22-24?

9. What have they that are Christ's crucified?

10. According to James 1:14-15, when is every man tempted?

11. When lust has conceived, what does it bring forth?

12. What does sin bring forth when it is finished?

13. According to 1 Corinthians 14:33, is God the author of confusion?

14. What is He the author of?

WHOM HE MAY DEVOUR
Lesson 2 – Answer Key

1. The righteousness of God.
2. That we might have life.
3. Where envying and strife is.
4. A sweet savor of Christ.
5. Sober and vigilant.
6. A watch.
7. Cast them down.
8. The fruit of the Spirit.
9. The flesh.
10. When he is drawn away of his own lust and enticed.
11. Sin.
12. Death.
13. No.
14. Peace.

WHOM HE MAY DEVOUR
Lesson 2 – Scriptures

Know ye not, that to whom ye yield yourselves servants to obey, his servants ye are to whom ye obey; whether of sin unto death, or of obedience unto righteousness?

Romans 6:16

For the wrath of man worketh not the righteousness of God.

James 1:20

The thief cometh not, but for to steal, and to kill, and to destroy: I am come that they might have life, and that they might have it more abundantly.

John 10:10

For where envying and strife is, there is confusion and every evil work.

James 3:16

For we are unto God a sweet savour of Christ, in them that are saved, and in them that perish.

2 Corinthians 2:15

Be sober, be vigilant; because your adversary the devil, as a roaring lion, walketh about, seeking whom he may devour.

1 Peter 5:8

Set a watch, O Lord, before my mouth; keep the door of my lips.

Psalm 141:3

Casting down imaginations, and every high thing that exalteth itself against the knowledge of God, and bringing into captivity every thought to the obedience of Christ.

2 Corinthians 10:5

But the fruit of the Spirit is love, joy, peace, longsuffering, gentleness, goodness, faith, Meekness, temperance: against such there is no law. And they that are Christ's have crucified the flesh with the affections and lusts.

Galatians 5:22-24

But every man is tempted, when he is drawn away of his own lust, and enticed. Then when lust hath conceived, it bringeth forth sin: and sin, when it is finished, bringeth

James 1:14-15

For God is not the author of confusion, but of peace, as in all churches of the saints.

1 Corinthians 14:33

SATAN'S INROADS
Lesson 3

Since you're in a spiritual battle, you can't afford to indulge the "luxury" of strife. If you think a certain amount of strife is just "normal" – the way you're supposed to live – you're wrong. God is a God of peace (Rom. 15:33 and 16:20), and you were created in His image (Gen. 1:27). The fruit of His Spirit working in your life is peace (Gal. 5:22). Therefore, your life should be full of peace, not strife. I'm not saying that you will ever live totally free from all strife from every source, but you should never just accept it, indulge it, or promote it. You ought to actively stand against and fight it, recognising that every time you get into strife, a door is opened for anything the Enemy wants to do in your life. Satan has access to you when you're in strife.

I remember being drafted as a soldier in the army. During basic training, there were many situations where explosions were going off around me all the time. We'd go out on maneuvers, pass through low-crawl pits (with machine guns firing overhead), learn how to use grenades, practice firing our weapons, and many other things. Over a period of six months' time in training, I became accustomed to all the noise. It didn't bother me, because I knew that we were still in our own country, it was training, and nobody was trying to kill me. So I hardened myself to it and got to the point where the explosions just didn't mean anything.

Then I arrived in Long Bien, Vietnam. We got out of our plane at two in the morning, right in the middle of a mortar attack. We literally had to low-crawl from the plane to a bunker and hide in it until the attack was over. After we'd been processed a couple of hours later, I remember lying down in a temporary barracks. My cot was actually bouncing up and down from the explosions. Even though I'd heard many similar noises in basic training, it suddenly dawned on me that this wasn't friendly fire anymore. Somebody out there was shooting rockets at us, and I was close enough to hear the explosions. As I lay there on that bouncing bunk, I realised, "I'm at war! There's an enemy who is trying to kill me." That really sobered me up.

Gone was my half-hearted listening to instructions. They didn't have to do anything to get my full attention. When they started the week of training once we arrived – how to adjust to the country, what would be happening, and things like that – I was all ears. The difference was I realised that this was truly life and death. I recognised that I was now in a battle.

SEEDS ARE BEING PLANTED

Whether you realise it or not, you are now in a battle. Satan is walking about as a roaring lion, seeking whom he may devour. The devil is trying to destroy your life today. You could become overwhelmed with that and be fearful, but God is also going about seeking who will respond to Him. He's trying to get His anointing, power, and blessings into your life. There's no reason to panic and freeze up in fear, because the Lord is infinitely greater than the devil. However, you do need to sober up and realise that you're in a battle. You don't have the luxury of just indulging your negative emotions and getting into the flesh.

I minister to people all the time who desire the results they see in my life but aren't willing to do what I do. They want to sit and watch *As the Stomach Turns* on television. They watch "R-" and "X-" rated movies, indulging negative emotions that I would never indulge. I recognise that there is a spiritual battle going on, and if I ever began to open up and allow such things into my heart and mind, Satan would take advantage of it. So I live a very restricted life, refraining from many things that other people do (Ps. 101:3).

Although many people would like to see blind eyes and deaf ears opened, terminal diseases healed, the dead raised, and financial blessings the way I have (by God's grace), they're not willing to spend the time yielding to and fellowshipping with the Lord in His Word, prayer, and obedience. They'd rather be out in the world, indulging their flesh and thinking, *It's not hurting me to do all of this stuff*. It may not hurt them at that moment, but seeds are being planted.

You can't be tempted with something you don't think (Heb. 11:15). If you would quit opening yourself up to envy, strife, division, and all the other negative things our society uses for 'entertainment', Satan wouldn't have these inroads into your life.

MR. CRITICAL

I led this guy to the Lord who had a pretty rough background. After being born again, he joined our church and began criticising everything. He criticised people for using soap because it wasn't natural. (He could have used a lot of soap too – he needed it!) He criticised people because they peeled their potatoes, saying the skin was the most nutritious part. This guy just had an opinion about everything!

I didn't find out until later, but this fellow had been the first person ever indicted by the California Grand Jury three times before he was a teenager. He had lived in reformatories since the age of five. Because of all this, and growing up around so much strife, there was a tremendous amount of anger and resentment in him.

After a couple of months, he came to me one day and said, "I'm leaving this church. I'm going back out into the desert because there's too much strife here."

I just got bold and told him, "Yes, there is strife in this church, but it's all coming from you. There wasn't any strife among the members until you came in here and started criticising everybody. You're the source of this strife!"

"Really? I didn't realise it."

"You didn't realise that when you criticise people over everything they do that they aren't going to like that?"

This brother just sat down and began to tell me about his background. Then he said, "I guess I just didn't realise it was strife. I just thought it was normal." Then he continued, saying, "If you were to tell me to act healed when I feel sick, I can do that because I've felt healed before. But when you're telling me to walk in love, I guess I don't know how to do that. I've never felt love before."

I just had to take this guy and start teaching him through the life of Jesus what it's like to love people.

Some folks come from a background where screaming, yelling, and throwing things were normal. There are plenty of families like that, but it's not the way God wants us to be (James 3:16).

VIPER IN YOUR HOUSE?

Do you treat strangers better than your own family? Many people wouldn't dare to treat me the way they treat their own children, yet they wonder, *Why am I having these problems with my kids?* Yell at me, "Go make your bed, you lousy kid," scream at me, "Why haven't you done this yet?" and see how our relationship gets along. If that's how you treat your family, you have a double standard.

When you blast your family members – the people you're supposed to love more than anybody else – it's no wonder you're dealing with rebellion, strife, and division. If you want godly relationships, you have to start guarding your tongue. You have to realise that you can't tolerate such strife. Satan comes in through the doors of envy and strife, and works every evil work in your life.

Would you allow a poisonous snake to run loose in your house? If it got into the heating vent, perhaps you wouldn't see it for a week or two. But if you knew it was still lurking there, somewhere, you'd probably say, "I don't care how long it takes, I am not going to live in a house with a dangerous, venomous viper on the loose!" It might not be an immediate threat, but if you never knew just where it was…lurking…

Strife is much more deadly than a poisonous snake! Along with envy, strife opens up an inroad for every evil work in your life. It's time you snap out of complacency and recognise that you're in a spiritual battle. You can't tolerate envy, strife, unforgiveness, or any other negative emotion.

Some people look at pornographic images and think, *Well, I'll never act that out.* Every time you indulge your flesh, you are releasing spiritual powers into your life. As you give more and more of a place to the devil, I guarantee that it will cost you something. Sin will take you further than you want to go, cost you more than you want to pay, and keep you longer than you want to stay.

Every one of us is exposed to the forces of the kingdom of darkness each and every day. We aren't on R & R (rest and relaxation). We aren't in a secured area where our actions don't really count. We're in a spiritual battle, with a real Enemy who wants to take advantage of us any way he can.

RAISED FROM THE DEAD

God's Word says,

> **Neither give place to the devil.**
>
> Ephesians 4:27

You are the one who gives Satan inroads into your life. He takes whatever **"place"** you give him through your thoughts, words, emotions, and actions.

Your emotions can give Satan a place. Perhaps every once in a while you feel like you should just give in and let your guard down. It would just feel good to have a pity party.

I've felt that way before. One night my older son called on the telephone and told me that my younger son had died. Immediately, my wife and I agreed in prayer, spoke our faith, and commanded him to come back to life. As we got dressed and drove the hour into Colorado Springs, I had some negative emotions. I felt like, *How long can you stand? How long can you be strong? Every once in a while, you just need to run up the white flag of surrender and let it out. Why not just gripe and complain?* However, I knew that if I started speaking forth my fears and unbelief, it would have negated my faith. Even though I felt like saying "We lost this one. We're beaten. Let's give it up and quit," I started building myself up and speaking positive words like, "He will not die, but live and declare the works of the Lord" and "You're a good God. I love You!"

All the glory to Jesus, we arrived in Colorado Springs at the hospital to discover that God had raised him from the dead. He had been dead for almost five hours, but about five minutes or so after we received that phone call from my older son, my younger son just sat up and started talking right there on the slab in the hospital morgue. Praise Jesus!

I firmly believe that if I had given in to and vented my negative emotions, we wouldn't have seen the victory. If I had spoken forth my frustration and complained, saying "It's not fair," my son wouldn't have been raised from the dead. Satan will take advantage of whatever we give him. We are often hung by our own tongue.

SATAN'S INROADS
Lesson 3 – Outline

I. Since we're in a spiritual battle, you can't afford to indulge the "luxury" of strife.

    A. If you think that a certain amount of strife is just "normal" – the way you're supposed to live – you're wrong.

    B. God is a God of peace (Rom. 15:33 and 16:20), and we were created in His image (Gen. 1:27).

    C. The fruit of His Spirit working in our lives is peace (Gal. 5:22).

    D. You ought to actively stand against and fight strife, recognising that every time you get into it, a door is opened for anything the Enemy wants to do in your life.

    E. Satan has access to you when you're in strife.

II. The devil is trying to destroy your life today.

    A. You could become overwhelmed with that and be fearful, but God is also going about seeking who will respond to Him.

    B. He's trying to get His anointing, power, and blessings into your life.

    C. There's no reason to panic and freeze up in fear, because the Lord is infinitely greater than the devil.

    D. However, you do need to sober up and realise that you're in a battle.

III. Although many people would like to see blind eyes and deaf ears opened, terminal diseases healed, the dead raised, and financial blessings the way Andrew has (by God's grace), they're not willing to spend the time yielding to and fellowshipping with the Lord in His Word, prayer, and obedience.

    A. They'd rather be out in the world, indulging their flesh.

    B. You can't be tempted with something you don't think (Heb. 11:15).

    C. If you would quit opening yourself up to envy, strife, division, and all the other negative things our society uses for "entertainment," Satan wouldn't have these inroads into your life.

IV. If you want godly relationships, you have to start guarding your tongue.

   A. Strife is much more deadly than a poisonous snake!

   B. You can't tolerate envy, strife, unforgiveness, or any other negative emotion.

   C. As you give more and more of a place to the devil, I guarantee that it will cost you something.

   D. Sin will take you further than you want to go, cost you more than you want to pay, and keep you longer than you want to stay.

V. You are the one who gives Satan inroads into your life.

   Neither give place to the devil.
   Ephesians 4:27

   A. He takes whatever **'place'** you give him through your thoughts, words, emotions, and actions.

   B. Satan will take advantage of whatever we give him.

SATAN'S INROADS
Lesson 3 – Teacher's Guide

1. Since we're in a spiritual battle, we can't afford to indulge the 'luxury' of strife. If we think that a certain amount of strife is just 'normal' – the way we're supposed to live – we're wrong. God is a God of peace (Rom. 15:33 and 16:20), and we were created in His image (Gen. 1:27). The fruit of His Spirit working in our lives is peace (Gal. 5:22). We ought to actively stand against and fight strife, recognising that every time we get into it, a door is opened for anything the Enemy wants to do in our lives. Satan has access to us when we're in strife.

2. The devil is trying to destroy our lives today. We could become overwhelmed with that and be fearful, but God is also going about seeking who will respond to Him. He's trying to get His anointing, power, and blessings into our lives. There's no reason to panic and freeze up in fear, because the Lord is infinitely greater than the devil. However, we do need to sober up and realise that we're in a battle.

3. Although many people would like to see blind eyes and deaf ears opened, terminal diseases healed, the dead raised, and financial blessings the way Andrew has (by God's grace), they're not willing to spend the time yielding to and fellowshipping with the Lord in His Word, prayer, and obedience. They'd rather be out in the world, indulging their flesh.

    We can't be tempted with something we don't think (Heb. 11:15). If we would quit opening ourselves up to envy, strife, division, and all the other negative things our society uses for 'entertainment', Satan wouldn't have these inroads into our lives.

4. If we want godly relationships, we have to start guarding our tongues. Strife is much more deadly than a poisonous snake! We can't tolerate envy, strife, unforgiveness, or any other negative emotion. As we give more and more of a place to the devil, it will cost us something. Sin will take us further than we want to go, cost us more than we want to pay, and keep us longer than we want to stay.

1. A. Read Romans 15:33, 16:20, Genesis 1:27, and Galatians 5:22. Since we're in a spiritual battle, we can't afford to indulge in the 'luxury' of what? (Strife)
   B. Who has access to us when we're in strife? (Satan)
2. A. Whom is God seeking? (Those who will respond to Him)
   B. The Lord is infinitely greater than whom? (The devil)
3. A. Read Hebrews 11:15. In order to be able to see blind eyes and deaf ears opened, terminal diseases healed, the dead raised, and financial blessings manifest, we need to be willing to what? (Spend time yielding to and fellowshipping with the Lord in His Word, prayer, and obedience)
   B. What can't we be tempted with? (Something we don't think)
4. A. Strife is much more deadly than what? (A poisonous snake)
   B. What can't we tolerate? (Envy, strife, unforgiveness, or any other negative emotion)

5. We are the ones who give Satan inroads into our lives (Eph. 4:27). He takes whatever **'place'** we give him through our thoughts, words, emotions, and actions. Satan will take advantage of whatever we give him.

5. A. Read Ephesians 4:27. Who gives Satan inroads into our lives? (We do)
   B. He takes whatever **'place'** we give him through what? (Our thoughts, words, emotions, and actions)

SATAN'S INROADS
Lesson 3 – Discipleship Questions

1. How does Romans 15:33 describe the Lord?

2. According to Romans 16:20, the God of peace shall do what shortly?

3. The grace of whom is with us?

4. According to Genesis 1:27, God created whom in His own image?

5. In the image of God, man was created both what?

6. What fruit of the Spirit are listed in Galatians 5:22?

7. In Psalm 101:3, the psalmist will set what before his eyes?

8. According to Hebrews 11:15, if Abraham and Sarah had been mindful of _____, they might have had opportunity to have returned.

9. James 3:16 reveals that _____ can be found wherever envying and strife are.

10. Ephesians 4:27 instructs us not to give place to whom?

SATAN'S INROADS
Lesson 3 – Answer Key

1. The God of peace.

2. Bruise Satan under our feet.

3. Our Lord Jesus Christ.

4. Man.

5. Male and female.

6. Love, joy, peace, longsuffering, gentleness, goodness, and faith.

7. No wicked thing.

8. That country from whence they came out.

9. Confusion and every evil work.

10. The devil.

SATAN'S INROADS
Lesson 3 – Scriptures

Now the God of peace be with you all. Amen.

Romans 15:33

And the God of peace shall bruise Satan under your feet shortly. The grace of our Lord Jesus Christ be with you. Amen.

Romans 16:20

So God created man in his own image, in the image of God created he him; male and female created he them.

Genesis 1:27

But the fruit of the Spirit is love, joy, peace, longsuffering, gentleness, goodness, faith.

Galatians 5:22

I will set no wicked thing before mine eyes: I hate the work of them that turn aside; it shall not cleave to me.

Psalm 101:3

And truly, if they had been mindful of that country from whence they came out, they might have had opportunity to have returned.

Hebrews 11:15

For where envying and strife is, there is confusion and every evil work.

James 3:16

Neither give place to the devil.

Ephesians 4:27

NO WICKED THING
Lesson 4

There are times in life when we just feel like speaking forth our negative thoughts and emotions. However, in light of the spiritual battle, these are times we must exercise our faith and self-control.

In Matthew 6:31, the Lord reveals to us at what point we take a thought for our own:

Take no thought, saying ...

A thought becomes your own when you begin speaking it out of your mouth.

You can't keep all kinds of thoughts from coming across your mind. When I found out my son was dead, thoughts of grief, fear, and panic crossed my mind. I'm human, just like anybody else. However, you can keep from taking those thoughts as your own.

Kenneth Hagin used to put it this way: "You can't keep a bird from flying over your head, but you can keep it from landing there and building a nest."

Negative thoughts will come at times, but you don't have to receive them. They don't have to become a part of you. If you don't say it, it won't be yours.

HUNG BY THE TONGUE

Satan passes thoughts, feelings, and attitudes across our hearts and minds. How do we prevent these seeds from taking root, beginning to grow, and then producing the negative crop he desires? We...

Take no thought, saying ...

Matthew 6:31

If you don't say it, then it's not yours. However, the moment you start verbalising and speaking forth these negative things, they become yours and begin releasing this negative power in your life. You need to take on this attitude: "I refuse to speak forth anything contrary to what I'm believing for."

Some people are believing for healing. They've asked God to heal them and they're confessing "I believe I'm healed," despite the fact that they haven't seen the physical manifestation yet. But when someone calls them on the phone and asks "How are you doing?" they respond by telling them how bad they feel. Without realising it, they have just released a negative spiritual force.

Death and life are in the power of the tongue.

Proverbs 18:21

We can't only just speak life with your tongue; we can also speak death. Sadly, the truth is that most of us release much more death than life. We counter ourselves with our own words. We're hung by the tongue!

WORDS ARE IMPORTANT

You may be praying for one thing and then speaking against it. You may be praying for restoration in your marriage, yet you constantly criticise, beat down, and speak negatively about it. You are releasing a negative spiritual force – death – that will counter what you're praying. Even though God wants to move on your behalf and bring restoration, you're releasing a contrary spiritual force with those negative words.

You need to be careful how you speak about your children. It's not wrong to state a fact. If somebody asks, don't say, "Everything is perfect," when it isn't. You can say, "There are problems *but*..." and then counter it with what you're believing for. It's okay to say, "Here's the problem, *but* everything will work out." However, if you say, "I'm believing God for a miracle, *but*..." and then you start examining and explaining all of the bad things, you've just destroyed what you're trying to accomplish. It really does matter where you put your *but*.

Sometimes you just have to acknowledge the facts. "Hey, I've got a problem. I'm fighting this sickness ..." But then you counter it with the truth of God's Word. "... But I believe I'm healed, in Jesus' name."

You need to be constantly aware of the truth that your words are either releasing life or releasing death. Don't just allow anything to come out of your mouth. Set a watch over your mouth and speak life (Ps. 141:3) because you will eat the fruit of it.

> ***A man's belly shall be satisfied with the fruit of his mouth; and with the increase of his lips shall he be filled.***
>
> Proverbs 18:20

Every word you say out of your mouth is a seed that produces after its kind. If you are griping, complaining, and speaking forth all this negativity, then that's the kind of fruit you'll wind up eating from those words. If you are bitter in your heart, it started with you speaking forth some things that you shouldn't have said. You can't keep a problem from coming, but you can keep those problems from dominating you by speaking forth the right, positive, Word-oriented things. Your words are important!

BLINDED TO THE TRUTH

In this spiritual battle, Satan takes advantage of the words we say.

> ***For by thy words thou shalt be justified, and by thy words thou shalt be condemned.***
>
> Matthew 12:37

When we don't realise just how important our words are, we speak forth foolishness, doubt, unbelief, and other things that allow Satan to devour us because we let down our guard.

Part of Paul's commission from God, and ours as well, is to ...

> ***Turn them...from the power of Satan unto God.***
>
> Acts 26:18, emphasis mine

Many people don't really recognise that Satan is dominating – exerting power in – their lives. They just think it's circumstances, fate, or luck. This scripture makes it very clear that they have been under the influence of the devil.

> ***And you hath he quickened, who were dead in trespasses and sins; Wherein in time past ye walked according to the course of this world, according to the prince of the power of the air, the spirit that now worketh in the children of disobedience: Among whom also we all had our conversation in times past in the lusts of our flesh, fulfilling the desires of the flesh and of the mind; and were by nature the children of wrath, even as others.***
>
> Ephesians 2:1-3

Before we converted to Christ, we were by nature children of Satan. We lived our lives under his influence and dominion, blinded to the truth.

> ***In whom the god of this world hath blinded the minds of them which believe not, lest the light of the glorious gospel of Christ, who is the image of God, should shine unto them.***
>
> 2 Corinthians 4:4

The devil is actively at work today hardening people and blinding them from the truths of the Gospel. This is not a passive battle. He's aggressively pursuing and trying to destroy people. One of the reasons why the Enemy has such a strong hold on so many people is because the church hasn't really recognised the spiritual battle it's in.

CORRUPTING GOOD MANNERS

As a minister of the Gospel, I use daily programs on both television and radio to share the truth of God's Word all around the world. However, most of the other programs people watch and listen to on television and radio are used of the devil to strengthen his influence and control. Both non-believers and Christians alike are plugged into it and, to one degree or another, are fed a steady diet of ungodliness – sexual immorality, violence, strife, hatred, and sarcasm. We allow this sewage to pour into our homes, and Satan uses it in our lives. It's not that television or radio are evil in and of themselves. God is using both of them mightily to advance His kingdom. However, Satan is also using the vast majority of its programming to destroy people's lives.

Some folks think, *Oh, I can watch this stuff, and it doesn't affect me.* God's Word says they're deceived.

> ***Be not deceived: evil communications corrupt good manners.***
>
> 1 Corinthians 15:33

You may convince yourself that you're not being influenced or corrupted, but the Word reveals otherwise. You simply cannot maintain your spiritual equilibrium while indulging your eyes on ungodliness.

David – the man after God's own heart – understood this. He said,

> ***I will set no wicked thing before mine eyes.***
>
> Psalm 101:3

As a follower of the Lord Jesus Christ, you need to make the same commitment, saying, "I will not watch anything wicked. I refuse to paint a picture on the inside of me of lust, anger, immorality, hatred, strife, or murder. I recognise that every time I open myself up to such things, there is a negative spiritual power there waiting to gain an inroad into my life. By God's grace, I will not give the devil any access into my life!"

PAINTING PICTURES

One of the reasons we have so much violence and immorality in our society is because there's so much violence and immorality on television. These images are painting pictures in the hearts and minds of people, who are then going out and acting on them. We can't be tempted by what we don't think (Heb. 11:15). However, what we constantly think about will become what we talk about and do.

Everything you say and/or do is releasing either God's or Satan's power in your life. Your Enemy is an active force at work in the world seeking whom he may devour (1 Pet. 5:8). He blinds the minds of those who don't believe, in order to steal, kill, and destroy them (2 Cor. 4:4). Just putting your head in the sand and saying "I don't believe we're in a battle. I'm just going to continue on the way I've been" isn't going to change the situation. It just means that you'll be one of the casualties. It's to your advantage to recognise the reality of the fight and make the necessary adjustments in your thinking and lifestyle.

We are responsible to submit to God and resist the devil (James 4:7). Our thoughts, emotions, words, and actions are either giving place to God or giving place to the devil (Eph. 4:27). We need to recognise the spiritual dynamics happening all around us.

I'm amazed how many people don't associate their actions with the results they're experiencing. They totally miss the correlation and don't have a clue how Satan is destroying them. While living a life in opposition to God, they come up to me and say, "I just don't understand why the devil is after me."

"ARE YOU MARRIED?"

One time I had a man in our church come out to shoe my horse. While he was doing that, we began talking and he kept referring to his "girlfriend." I'd seen him at church with this woman and thought she was his wife. However, the way he kept talking about his girlfriend led me to believe they weren't married. So finally, I just asked him, "Are you married?"

He answered, "Oh, no. We're just living together. We've had so many friends that have married and divorced that we think it's wisdom to live together for a while and see if we should get married or not. It's been about six months now."

Immediately, I asked, "I thought you said you were a Christian?"

"Well, I am. I was born again four months ago."

"Don't you realise that living together is contrary to God's Word?"

This guy was a brand-new believer and totally ignorant. "You mean God says something about just living with a person before you get married?"

So I started sharing the Word with him. After a little while, he said, "Well, we love each other, and we're going to get married. So it'll be okay."

I had to explain to him, "It doesn't matter what's going to happen in the future. Right now you are living in a way that exempts you from God's power. You have yielded yourself to Satan and have violated God's Word. By doing so, you have released demonic power in your life. The devil is just having a heyday with you!"

FOLLOW GOD'S INSTRUCTIONS

As we continued talking, he began to open up his heart. Usually it takes thirty minutes to shoe a horse, but this one took three hours. He was just soaking it up. This brother changed his mind, moved out, and they straightened up their act.

When you disobey God, you open up a door to the devil. Contrary to what religion says, God still loves you. He's not mad at you, but He wants better for you. By violating God's instructions in His Word and obeying the lust of your flesh, you've thrown open a door to the devil. Satan will come in, eat your lunch, and pop the bag!

You don't want that. You need to change your mind and adjust your actions. We're in a spiritual battle, and you can't afford the luxury of just ignoring the instructions God has given you.

NO WICKED THING
Lesson 4 – Outline

I. A thought becomes your own when you begin speaking it out of your mouth.

> ***Take no thought, saying…***
> Matthew 6:31

    A. Satan passes thoughts, feelings, and attitudes across our hearts and minds.

    B. If you don't say it, then it's not yours.

    C. You need to take on this attitude: "I refuse to speak forth anything contrary to what I'm believing for."

II. You need to be constantly aware of the truth that your words are either releasing life or releasing death.

    A. Set a watch over your mouth and speak life (Ps. 141:3) because you will eat the fruit of it.

> ***A man's belly shall be satisfied with the fruit of his mouth; and with the increase of his lips shall he be filled. Death and life are in the power of the tongue: and they that love it shall eat the fruit thereof.***
> Proverbs 18:20-21

    B. Every word you say out of your mouth is a seed that produces after its kind.

    C. You can't keep a problem from coming, but you can keep those problems from dominating you by speaking forth the right, positive, Word-oriented things.

III. In this spiritual battle, Satan takes advantage of the words we say.

> ***For by thy words thou shalt be justified, and by thy words thou shalt be condemned.***
> Matthew 12:37

    A. When we don't realise just how important our words are, we speak forth foolishness, doubt, unbelief, and other things that allow Satan to devour us because we let down our guard.

    B. Many people don't really recognise that Satan is dominating – exerting influence and power in – their lives (Eph. 2:1-3).

    C. Before we converted to Christ, we were by nature children of Satan – living our lives under his influence and dominion, blinded to the truth.

> ***In whom the god of this world hath blinded the minds of them which believe not, lest the light of the glorious gospel of Christ, who is the image of God, should shine unto them.***
>
> 2 Corinthians 4:4

    D. The devil is actively at work today hardening people and blinding them from the truths of the Gospel.

IV. Although God is using both radio and television mightily to advance His kingdom, Satan is also using the vast majority of its programming to destroy people's lives.

    A. You may convince yourself that you're not being influenced or corrupted, but the Word reveals otherwise (1 Cor. 15:33).

    B. You simply cannot maintain your spiritual equilibrium while indulging your eyes on ungodliness (Ps. 101:3).

    C. What we constantly think about will become what we talk about and do.

V. Everything you say and/or do is releasing either God's or Satan's power in your life.

    A. Your Enemy is an active force at work in the world seeking whom he may devour (1 Pet. 5:8).

    B. He blinds the minds of those who don't believe, in order to steal, kill, and destroy them (2 Cor. 4:4).

    C. It's to your advantage to recognise the reality of the fight and make the necessary adjustments in your thinking and lifestyle (Eph. 4:27).

    D. We are responsible to submit to God and resist the devil (James 4:7).

VI. When you disobey God, you open up a door to the devil.

    A. Contrary to what religion says, God still loves you.

    B. He's not mad at you, but He wants better for you.

    C. By violating God's instructions in His Word and obeying the lust of your flesh, you've thrown open a door to the devil.

    D. You need to change your mind and adjust your actions.

NO WICKED THING
Lesson 4 – Teacher's Guide

1. A thought becomes our own when we begin speaking it out of our mouths (Matt. 6:31). Satan passes thoughts, feelings, and attitudes across our hearts and minds. If we don't say it, then it's not ours. We need to take on this attitude: "I refuse to speak forth anything contrary to what I'm believing for."

2. We need to be constantly aware of the truth that our words are either releasing life or releasing death. Let's set a watch over our mouths and speak life (Ps. 141:3) because we will eat the fruit of it (Prov. 18:20-21). Every word we say out of our mouths is a seed that produces after its kind. We can't keep a problem from coming, but we can keep those problems from dominating us by speaking forth the right, positive, Word-oriented things.

3. In this spiritual battle, Satan takes advantage of the words we say (Matt. 12:37). When we don't realise just how important our words are, we speak forth foolishness, doubt, unbelief, and other things that allow Satan to devour us because we let down our guard. Many people don't really recognise that Satan is dominating – exerting influence and power in – their lives (Eph. 2:1-3). Before we converted to Christ, we were by nature children of Satan – living our lives under his influence and dominion, blinded to the truth (2 Cor. 4:4). The devil is actively at work today hardening people and blinding them from the truths of the Gospel.

4. Although God is using both radio and television mightily to advance His kingdom, Satan is also using the vast majority of its programming to destroy people's lives. We may convince ourselves that we're not being influenced or corrupted, but the Word reveals otherwise (1 Cor. 15:33). We simply cannot maintain our spiritual equilibrium while indulging our eyes on ungodliness (Ps. 101:3). What we constantly think about will become what we talk about and do.

1. A. Read Matthew 6:31. When does a thought become our own? (When we begin speaking it out of our mouths)
   B. What attitude do we need to take on? (I refuse to speak forth anything contrary to what I'm believing for)
2. A. Read Psalm 141:3 and Proverbs 18:20-21. What is every word we say out of our mouths? (A seed that produces after its kind)
   B. How do we keep problems from dominating us? (By speaking forth the right, positive, Word-oriented things)
3. A. Read Matthew 12:37, Ephesians 2:1-3, and 2 Corinthians 4:4. In this spiritual battle, who takes advantage of the words we say? (Satan)
   B. What is the devil actively at work today doing? (Hardening people and blinding them from the truths of the Gospel)
4. A. Read 1 Corinthians 15:33 and Psalm 101:3. We simply cannot maintain our spiritual equilibrium while doing what? (Indulging our eyes on ungodliness)
   B. What will become what we talk about and do? (What we think about constantly)

5. Everything we say and/or do is releasing either God's or Satan's power in our lives. Our Enemy is an active force at work in the world seeking whom he may devour (1 Pet. 5:8). He blinds the minds of those who don't believe in order to steal, kill, and destroy them (2 Cor. 4:4). It's to our advantage to recognise the reality of the fight and make the necessary adjustments in our thinking and lifestyle (Eph. 4:27). We are responsible to submit to God and resist the devil (James 4:7).

6. When we disobey God, we open up a door to the devil. Contrary to what religion says, God still loves us. He's not mad at us, but He wants better for us. By violating God's instructions in His Word and obeying the lust of our flesh, we've thrown open a door to the devil. We need to change our minds and adjust our actions.

---

5. A. Read 1 Peter 5:8, 2 Corinthians 4:4, Ephesians 4:27, and James 4:7. Everything we say and/or do is releasing what? (Either God's or Satan's power in our lives)
   B. Who is responsible to submit to God and resist the devil? (We are)
6. A. How do we open up a door for the devil? (When we disobey God)
   B. What do we need to do? (Change our minds and adjust our actions)

NO WICKED THING
Lesson 4 – Discipleship Questions

1. According to Matthew 6:31, Jesus told us to take no thought by doing what?

2. Proverbs 18:20-21 reveals that a man's belly shall be satisfied by what?

3. What shall he be filled with?

4. In Psalm 141:3, the psalmist asks the Lord to keep what?

5. According to Matthew 12:37, by what shall we be justified and/or condemned?

6. Acts 26:18 shows that when we turn from darkness to light, we are turning from the power of Satan unto whom?

7. When we do so, what do we receive in addition to forgiveness of sins?

8. Before we were born again, Ephesians 2:1-3 reveals that we were dead in what?

9. What were we by nature?

10. According to 2 Corinthians 4:4, the minds of them that don't believe are what?

11. By whom?

12. What does 1 Corinthians 15:33 say that evil communications corrupts?

13. In Psalm 101:3, what does the psalmist hate?

14. According to 1 Peter 5:8, who is our adversary?

15. James 4:7 tells us to submit ourselves to whom?

NO WICKED THING
Lesson 4 – Answer Key

1. Saying.

2. The fruit of his mouth.

3. The increase of his lips.

4. The door of his lips.

5. Our words.

6. God.

7. An inheritance among them that are sanctified by faith.

8. Trespasses and sins.

9. The children of wrath.

10. Blinded.

11. The god of this world.

12. Good manners.

13. The work of them that turn aside.

14. The devil.

15. God.

NO WICKED THING
Lesson 4 – Scriptures

Therefore take no thought, saying, What shall we eat? or, What shall we drink? or, Wherewithal shall we be clothed?

Matthew 6:31

A man's belly shall be satisfied with the fruit of his mouth; and with the increase of his lips shall he be filled. Death and life are in the power of the tongue: and they that love it shall eat the fruit thereof.

Proverbs 18:20-21

Set a watch, O LORD, before my mouth; keep the door of my lips.

Psalm 141:3

For by thy words thou shalt be justified, and by thy words thou shalt be condemned.

Matthew 12:37

To open their eyes, and to turn them from darkness to light, and from the power of Satan unto God, that they may receive forgiveness of sins, and inheritance among them which are sanctified by faith that is in me.

Acts 26:18

And you hath he quickened, who were dead in trespasses and sins; Wherein in time past ye walked according to the course of this world, according to the prince of the power of the air, the spirit that now worketh in the children of disobedience: Among whom also we all had our conversation in times past in the lusts of our flesh, fulfilling the desires of the flesh and of the mind; and were by nature the children of wrath, even as others.

Ephesians 2:1-3

In whom the god of this world hath blinded the minds of them which believe not, lest the light of the glorious gospel of Christ, who is the image of God, should shine unto them.

2 Corinthians 4:4

Be not deceived: evil communications corrupt good manners.

1 Corinthians 15:33

I will set no wicked thing before mine eyes: I hate the work of them that turn aside; it shall not cleave to me.

Psalm 101:3

And truly, if they had been mindful of that country from whence they came out, they might have had opportunity to have returned.

Hebrews 11:15

Be sober, be vigilant; because your adversary the devil, as a roaring lion, walketh about, seeking whom he may devour.

1 Peter 5:8

Submit yourselves therefore to God. Resist the devil, and he will flee from you.

James 4:7

Neither give place to the devil.

Ephesians 4:27

UNCONDITIONAL AUTHORITY
Lesson 5

In the previous chapters, I've established that we are in a battle. This isn't something that just some people experience or that will come to us in the future; we are facing a spiritual battle every day. So we need to define who our Enemy is and reveal what power he has.

In almost forty years of being a Christian and actively studying God's Word, I've come across several different opinions about where Satan came from and how he got his power. I've heard all kinds of messages on this subject, and in my personal study, I've read many different commentaries, study Bibles, and books. However, in the midst of these different variations, a dominant doctrine has emerged in popular theology.

This widely-held understanding says God created a powerful, beautiful, godly angel named 'Lucifer' (Is. 14:12). This Lucifer was the anointed cherub that covered on God's holy mountain (Ezek. 28:14). Many people believe that he had musical instruments – pipes and tambourines – built into his body (Ezek. 28:13). Lucifer was perfect in all his ways (Ezek. 28:15). However, this Lucifer became prideful, turned into Satan, and rebelled against God.

At this point, popular theology also says Satan convinced one-third of the angels to follow him in rebellion. Together, they attempted to overthrow God, were defeated, and were then all cast down to the earth. They base this premise upon Revelation 12:4, which is the only scripture in the entire Bible that even makes reference to this. Basing a major doctrine on a single passage of Scripture, especially one so full of symbolism, is not good Bible interpretation.

CHILD ABUSE?

Some people take this even further, saying that Satan ruled over a pre-Adamic civilisation once he was thrown down from heaven to earth. They argue that God brought a cataclysmic judgement upon the devil and his kingdom and that the earth was completely destroyed between Genesis 1:1 (**"God created the heaven and the earth"**) and 1:2 (**"The earth was without form, and void"**). They propose that Genesis 1:2 is actually the re-creation.

Finis Dake, through the extensive notes in his study Bible and commentary, really popularised this theory. This is where most people who teach this point of view today – either directly or indirectly – received their information.

They also say Satan and his demons came from this pre-Adamic civilisation. Once Adam and Eve were created, God allowed Satan – with all of his evilness and corruption – into the Garden of Eden so that man would have a choice between good and evil. That's like saying, "God took His man and put him in the Garden with this evil, wild beast just to tempt him and see how he would do."

Most people don't really give serious thought to why things are the way they are. Like life, they just deal with the Bible on a surface level. Have you ever pondered the question, "If God is a good and loving God, then why did He allow Satan to come into the Garden and tempt Adam and Eve?" That's comparable to letting your two-year-old child go out in the backyard to play, knowing full well that a hungry lion or bear – something that could literally destroy them – is lurking in the bushes. We'd consider that irresponsible.

In the natural realm, we'd take kids away from a parent who didn't take care of and protect their children any better than that. A parent who would knowingly and willingly expose their children to such a dangerous predator would be arrested, convicted, and thrown in jail on charges of child abuse. Yet this popular theology insinuates that our heavenly Father turned Satan loose in the Garden of Eden to tempt Adam and Eve.

I don't believe that's the way it happened at all. Now, the Bible doesn't totally explain why God did what He did with man and Satan, but I believe there are clues. And it's these clues that have led me to some totally different conclusions than what are popularly believed.

MINISTERING SPIRITS

God sent Lucifer – His top angel – down to earth to minister to Adam and Eve. Lucifer hadn't transgressed against God – and become Satan – yet. He was a godly angel in the Garden of Eden on special assignment from the Lord Himself.

> **Are they** [angels] **not all ministering spirits, sent forth to minister for them who shall be heirs of salvation?**
>
> Hebrews 1:14, brackets mine

Angels are all sent to minister to us. God didn't send Lucifer to the earth to tempt Adam and Eve, but to serve them and minister to them. He came to the Garden on a divine mission. However, once there, he transgressed.

Isaiah 14 and Ezekiel 28 provide us with the vast majority of the Old Testament information that we have about this angel called Lucifer who became Satan. In both passages, the prophet began by addressing a physical person (the king of Babylon – Is. 14:4 and the king of Tyrus – Ezek. 28:12). However, it becomes obvious through the prophet's words (Is. 14:12 and Ezek. 28:13) that the demonic power behind that physical person was really who's being addressed.

SUBTLE SWITCH

In the New Testament, Jesus did the same thing when He turned to Peter and said,

> **Get thee behind me, Satan: thou art an offence unto me: for thou savourest not the things that be of God, but those that be of men.**
>
> Matthew 16:23

He was addressing the demonic power operating through the physical human being.

Keep this in mind, and watch for the subtle switch as we begin looking at this passage of Scripture.

*Moreover the word of the L*ORD *came unto me, saying, Son of man, take up a lamentation upon the king of Tyrus* [a physical human being], *and say unto him.*

Ezekiel 28:11-12, brackets mine

LUCIFER'S TRANSGRESSION

Now this next section is clearly speaking to the demonic personality – Satan himself – who was operating through this physical human being. It's obvious because of what the next few verses say.

Thou hast been in Eden the garden of God; every precious stone was thy covering, the sardius, topaz, and the diamond, the beryl, the onyx, and the jasper, the sapphire, the emerald, and the carbuncle, and gold: the workmanship of thy tabrets and of thy pipes was prepared in thee in the day that thou wast created. Thou art the anointed cherub that covereth; and I have set thee so: thou wast upon the holy mountain of God; thou hast walked up and down in the midst of the stones of fire. Thou wast perfect in thy ways from the day that thou wast created, till iniquity was found in thee.

Ezekiel 28:13-15

This is describing Lucifer, specifically in the Garden of Eden. Notice how it's describing him still in a sinless state. God sent Lucifer – the most honoured and respected angel He created – down to the Garden of Eden to be a servant to mankind.

Lucifer's transgression against God came in the Garden of Eden. It's described in Genesis 3, when he entered into the snake and used this serpent to speak to Eve and tempt her. Then he persuaded both Eve and Adam to eat of the forbidden fruit. That's when Lucifer transgressed against God.

Revelation 12:3-4, where the dragon took one-third of the stars and threw them to the earth, is a flimsy basis for saying that Satan took one-third of the angels and rebelled against God. The devil wouldn't have won if he had 100 percent of the angels, much less only one-third. There's no way Satan could even come close to winning a direct confrontation with God.

NO RESTRICTIONS

Lucifer came to the earth as an anointed angel on a divine assignment to minister to Adam and Eve. However, he saw something in them that he didn't have. As an angel, his power and authority was conditional (my supposition). But Adam and Eve had been given unconditional power and authority over this earth.

We see this where God created Adam and Eve in the creation story of Genesis 1.

God said, Let us make man in our image, after our likeness: and let them have dominion [power and authority] **over the fish of the sea, and over the fowl of the air, and over the cattle, and** over all the earth, and over every creeping thing that creepeth upon the earth. **So God created man in his own image, in the image of God created he him; male and female created he them. And God blessed them, and** God said unto them, **Be fruitful, and multiply,**

and replenish the earth, and subdue it: and have dominion **over the fish of the sea, and over the fowl of the air, and** over every living thing that moveth upon the earth.

Genesis 1:26-28, brackets and emphasis mine

When God created man, He spoke and gave them dominion – power and authority – over all the earth. Notice that there were no restrictions placed on this. God didn't say to them, "Now, as long as you follow My leading and do what I want you to do, I'll let you have dominion over the earth." No, God placed zero qualifications on this dominion that He gave mankind.

GOD'S INTEGRITY

Once God speaks, it's done. He never goes back on His Word.

My covenant will I not break, nor alter the thing that is gone out of my lips.

Psalm 89:34

According to Hebrews 6:18, it is …

Impossible for God to lie.

Because …

God is not a man, that he should lie; neither the son of man, that he should repent: hath he said, and shall he not do it? or hath he spoken, and shall he not make it good?

Numbers 23:19

The integrity of God's Word is what makes the universe consist and hold together. God upholds …

All things by the word of his power.

Hebrews 1:3

God will not violate what He has said. So when He told Adam and Eve "You have dominion. You have power and authority over this earth. You rule it and subdue it. It's under your control," He meant it. God gave them dominion over this earth.

BOUND BY HIS WORD

Of course, the Lord never meant for man to use that power and authority in the way he did. He didn't mean for us to just turn it over to Satan. However, because of God's own integrity, once we did yield that dominion over to the devil, He couldn't just say, "Time out. King's X. This isn't what I intended. Stop. We're going to do this all over again. I take back this authority. You can't run the earth anymore." That's what we would tend to do if someone abused the privilege we gave them. But that's not how He is. God was bound by His own Word.

Think about it: God has magnified His Word above His name.

Thou hast magnified thy word above all thy name.

Psalm 138:2

At the name of Jesus – the name which is above all names – every knee will bow and every tongue will confess that He is Lord (Phil. 2:9-11). The name of the Lord is a strong tower (Prov. 18:10), yet the Word of God is magnified even above the name of Jesus.

Knowing God as he did, Lucifer's antennae went up when he heard the Lord say to Adam and Eve "You have dominion" without any restrictions or qualifications. That got the top angel's attention because he knew that the God-given authority he operated in was conditional (again, my supposition). If Lucifer were to disobey God, this divine power that had been delegated to him would have instantly been taken away. He had no ability to use the power God had given him to fight against Him. There was no chance of Lucifer directly rebelling at God. But perhaps he could rebel if somehow he could get a hold of that unconditional power and authority that had been given to man.

I admit that some of these things aren't clearly spelled out in Scripture. We may indeed be bumping up against some things that are beyond our ability to know.

> **The secret things belong unto the Lord our God: but those things which are revealed belong unto us and to our children for ever.**
>
> Deuteronomy 29:29

God hasn't revealed every single thing to us. However, from what I do know of God's nature, character, and Word, the evidence points strongly in this direction.

AN OPPORTUNITY

The Bible reveals that angels also have a free will.

> **God spared not the angels that sinned, but cast them down to hell, and delivered them into chains of darkness, to be reserved unto judgement.**
>
> 2 Peter 2:4

Although angels have a free will, there's no reason to believe that their power and authority is unconditional like Adam and Eve's. Therefore, if an angel got out of line, God could, in a sense, just fire them. He could cancel and recall the power and authority He had given them, and they'd be absolutely defeated.

In light of this, there's no way Satan and one-third of the angels could charge God on His throne, who still retained two-thirds of the angels. However, Lucifer saw an opportunity with the unconditional authority over the earth that God had given to mankind.

UNCONDITIONAL AUTHORITY
Lesson 5 – Outline

I. In almost forty years of being a Christian and actively studying God's Word, Andrew has come across several different opinions about where Satan came from and how he got his power.

    A. In the midst of these different variations, a dominant doctrine has emerged in popular theology.

    B. This widely-held understanding says God created a powerful, beautiful, godly angel named "Lucifer" (Is. 14:12 and Ezek. 28:13-15).

    C. This Lucifer became prideful, turned into Satan, and rebelled against God.

    D. At this point, popular theology also says Satan convinced one-third of the angels to follow him in rebellion.

    E. This popular theology insinuates that our heavenly Father turned Satan loose in the Garden of Eden to tempt Adam and Eve.

II. God sent Lucifer – His top angel – down to earth to minister to Adam and Eve.

> ***Are they** [angels] **not all ministering spirits, sent forth to minister for them who shall be heirs of salvation?***
>
> Hebrews 1:14, brackets mine

    A. Lucifer hadn't transgressed against God – and become Satan – yet.

    B. He came to the Garden on a divine mission – to serve and to minister to Adam and Eve.

> ***Thou hast been in Eden the garden of God; every precious stone was thy covering, the sardius, topaz, and the diamond, the beryl, the onyx, and the jasper, the sapphire, the emerald, and the carbuncle, and gold: the workmanship of thy tabrets and of thy pipes was prepared in thee in the day that thou wast created. Thou art the anointed cherub that covereth; and I have set thee so: thou wast upon the holy mountain of God; thou hast walked up and down in the midst of the stones of fire. Thou wast perfect in thy ways from the day that thou wast created, till iniquity was found in thee.***
>
> Ezekiel 28:13-15

    C. Lucifer's transgression against God came in the Garden of Eden.

    D. It's described in Genesis 3, when he entered into the snake and used this serpent to speak to Eve and tempt her.

E. Then he persuaded both Eve and Adam to eat of the forbidden fruit.

III. Lucifer came to the earth as an anointed angel on a divine assignment to minister to Adam and Eve.

A. However, he saw something in them that he didn't have.

B. As an angel, his power and authority was conditional (Andrew's supposition) – but Adam and Eve had been given unconditional power and authority over this earth.

> **God said, Let us make man in our image, after our likeness: and** let them have dominion [power and authority] **over the fish of the sea, and over the fowl of the air, and over the cattle, and** over all the earth, and over every creeping thing that creepeth upon the earth. **So God created man in his own image, in the image of God created he him; male and female created he them. And God blessed them, and** God said unto them, **Be fruitful, and multiply, and replenish the earth, and subdue it: and** have dominion **over the fish of the sea, and over the fowl of the air, and** over every living thing that moveth upon the earth.
> Genesis 1:26-28, brackets and emphasis mine

C. When God created man, He spoke and gave them dominion – power and authority – over all the earth (Ps. 89:34; Heb. 1:3, 6:18; and Num. 23:19).

D. Knowing God as he did, Lucifer's antennae went up when he heard the Lord say to Adam and Eve "You have dominion" without any restrictions or qualifications.

E. There was no chance of Lucifer directly rebelling at God, but perhaps he could rebel if somehow he could get a hold of that unconditional power and authority that had been given to man.

IV. Although angels have a free will, there's no reason to believe that their power and authority is unconditional like Adam and Eve's.

A. Therefore, if an angel got out of line, God could cancel and recall the power and authority He had given them, and they'd be absolutely defeated.

B. In light of this, there's no way Satan and one-third of the angels could charge God on His throne, who still retained two-thirds of the angels.

C. However, Lucifer saw an opportunity with the unconditional authority over the earth that God had given to mankind.

UNCONDITIONAL AUTHORITY

Lesson 5 – Teacher's Guide

1. In almost forty years of being a Christian and actively studying God's Word, Andrew has come across several different opinions about where Satan came from and how he got his power. In the midst of these different variations, a dominant doctrine has emerged in popular theology. This widely-held understanding says God created a powerful, beautiful, godly angel named "Lucifer" (Is. 14:12 and Ezek. 28:13-15). This Lucifer became prideful, turned into Satan, and rebelled against God. At this point, popular theology also says that Satan convinced one-third of the angels to follow him in rebellion. This popular theology insinuates that our heavenly Father turned Satan loose in the Garden of Eden to tempt Adam and Eve.

2. God sent Lucifer – His top angel – down to earth to minister to Adam and Eve (Heb. 1:14). Lucifer hadn't transgressed against God – and become Satan – yet. He came to the Garden on a divine mission – to serve them and to minister to Adam and Eve (Ezek. 28:13-15). Lucifer's transgression against God came in the Garden of Eden. It's described in Genesis 3, when he entered into the snake and used this serpent to speak to Eve and tempt her. Then he persuaded both Eve and Adam to eat of the forbidden fruit.

3. Lucifer came to the earth as an anointed angel on a divine assignment to minister to Adam and Eve. However, he saw something in them that he didn't have. As an angel, his power and authority was conditional (Andrew's supposition), but Adam and Eve had been given unconditional power and authority over this earth (Gen. 1:26-28). When God created man, He spoke and gave them dominion – power and authority – over all the earth (Ps. 89:34; Heb. 1:3, 6:18; and Num. 23:19). Knowing God as he did, Lucifer's antennae went up when he heard the Lord say to Adam and Eve "You have dominion" without any restrictions or qualifications. There was no chance of Lucifer directly rebelling at God, but perhaps he could rebel if somehow he could get a hold of that unconditional power and authority that had been given to man.

1. A. Read Isaiah 14:12 and Ezekiel 28:13-15. What was the name of the powerful, beautiful, godly angel that God created? (Lucifer)
   B. What happened to him when he became prideful and rebelled against God? (He turned into Satan)
2. A. Read Hebrews 1:14, Genesis 3, and review Ezekiel 28:13-15. Why did God send Lucifer – His top angel – down to earth to the Garden? (To serve and to minister to Adam and Eve)
   B. Where and when did Lucifer's transgression against God come? (In the Garden of Eden)
3. A. Read Genesis 1:26-28; Psalm 89:34; Hebrews 1:3, 6:18; and Numbers 23:19. What did Lucifer see in Adam and Eve? (Something that he didn't have)
   B. When God created man, what did He speak and give them? (Dominion – unconditional power and authority – over all the earth)

4. Although angels have a free will, there's no reason to believe that their power and authority is unconditional like Adam and Eve's. Therefore, if an angel got out of line, God could cancel and recall the power and authority He had given them, and they'd be absolutely defeated. In light of this, there's no way Satan and one-third of the angels could charge God on His throne, who still retained two-thirds of the angels. However, Lucifer saw an opportunity with the unconditional authority over the earth that God had given to mankind.

4. A. What could God do if an angel got out of line? (Cancel and recall the power and authority He had given them)
   B. What did Lucifer see with the unconditional authority over the earth that God had given to mankind? (An opportunity)

UNCONDITIONAL AUTHORITY
Lesson 5 – Discipleship Questions

1. Who is Isaiah 14:12 talking about?

2. Who did Ezekiel 28:11-15 start out addressing?

3. Revelation 12:3-4 speaks of a great red what?

4. In Genesis 1:1-2, who moved upon the face of the waters?

5. Hebrews 1:14 reveals that angels are sent forth to minister for whom?

6. According to Genesis 1:26-28, God said "Let them have dominion" to whom?

7. Psalm 89:34 shows us that God will not break what?

8. Hebrews 6:18 and Numbers 23:19 say that it's impossible for God to what?

9. According to Hebrews 1:3, what is held up by the word of His power?

10. Psalm 138:2 tells us that God has magnified _____ above His name.

11. At whose name shall every knee bow, according to Philippians 2:9-11?

12. In Proverbs 18:10, what is the name of the Lord?

13. What does Deuteronomy 29:29 say belongs to the Lord?

14. What belongs to us and to our children forever?

15. Second Peter 2:4 reveals that God spared not whom?

UNCONDITIONAL AUTHORITY
Lesson 5 – Answer Key

1. Lucifer.
2. The king of Tyrus.
3. Dragon.
4. The Spirit of God.
5. Those who shall be heirs of salvation.
6. Man.
7. His covenant.
8. Lie.
9. All things.
10. His Word.
11. The name of Jesus.
12. A strong tower.
13. The secret things.
14. Those things which are revealed.
15. The angels that sinned.

UNCONDITIONAL AUTHORITY
Lesson 5 – Scriptures

How art thou fallen from heaven, O Lucifer, son of the morning! how art thou cut down to the ground, which didst weaken the nations!

Isaiah 14:12

Moreover the word of the LORD came unto me, saying, Son of man, take up a lamentation upon the king of Tyrus, and say unto him, Thus saith the Lord God; Thou sealest up the sum, full of wisdom, and perfect in beauty. Thou hast been in Eden the garden of God; every precious stone was thy covering, the sardius, topaz, and the diamond, the beryl, the onyx, and the jasper, the sapphire, the emerald, and the carbuncle, and gold: the workmanship of thy tabrets and of thy pipes was prepared in thee in the day that thou wast created. Thou art the anointed cherub that covereth; and I have set thee so: thou wast upon the holy mountain of God; thou hast walked up and down in the midst of the stones of fire. Thou wast perfect in thy ways from the day that thou wast created, till iniquity was found in thee.

Ezekiel 28:11-15

And there appeared another wonder in heaven; and behold a great red dragon, having seven heads and ten horns, and seven crowns upon his heads. And his tail drew the third part of the stars of heaven, and did cast them to the earth: and the dragon stood before the woman which was ready to be delivered, for to devour her child as soon as it was born.

Revelation 12:3-4

In the beginning God created the heaven and the earth. And the earth was without form, and void; and darkness was upon the face of the deep. And the Spirit of God moved upon the face of the waters.

Genesis 1:1-2

Are they not all ministering spirits, sent forth to minister for them who shall be heirs of salvation?

Hebrews 1:14

That thou shalt take up this proverb against the king of Babylon, and say, How hath the oppressor ceased! the golden city ceased!

Isaiah 14:4

But he turned, and said unto Peter, Get thee behind me, Satan: thou art an offence unto me: for thou savourest not the things that be of God, but those that be of men.

Matthew 16:23

And God said, Let us make man in our image, after our likeness: and let them have dominion over the fish of the sea, and over the fowl of the air, and over the cattle, and over all the earth, and over every creeping thing that creepeth upon the earth. So God created man in his own image, in the image of God created he him; male and female created he them.

And God blessed them, and God said unto them, Be fruitful, and multiply, and replenish the earth, and subdue it: and have dominion over the fish of the sea, and over the fowl of the air, and over every living thing that moveth upon the earth.

Genesis 1:26-28

My covenant will I not break, nor alter the thing that is gone out of my lips.

Psalm 89:34

That by two immutable things, in which it was impossible for God to lie, we might have a strong consolation, who have fled for refuge to lay hold upon the hope set before us.

Hebrews 6:18

God is not a man, that he should lie; neither the son of man, that he should repent: hath he said, and shall he not do it? or hath he spoken, and shall he not make it good?

Numbers 23:19

Who being the brightness of his glory, and the express image of his person, and upholding all things by the word of his power, when he had by himself purged our sins, sat down on the right hand of the Majesty on high.

Hebrews 1:3

I will worship toward thy holy temple, and praise thy name for thy lovingkindness and for thy truth: for thou hast magnified thy word above all thy name.

Psalm 138:2

Wherefore God also hath highly exalted him, and given him a name which is above every name: That at the name of Jesus every knee should bow, of things in heaven, and things in earth, and things under the earth; And that every tongue should confess that Jesus Christ is Lord, to the glory of God the Father.

Philippians 2:9-11

The name of the LORD is a strong tower: the righteous runneth into it, and is safe.

Proverbs 18:10

The secret things belong unto the LORD our God: but those things which are revealed belong unto us and to our children for ever, that we may do all the words of this law.

Deuteronomy 29:29

For if God spared not the angels that sinned, but cast them down to hell, and delivered them into chains of darkness, to be reserved unto judgement.

2 Peter 2:4

GOD OF THIS WORLD

Lesson 6

The Lord made Adam and Eve the gods of this world.

> ***I have said, Ye are gods; and all of you are children of the most High.***
>
> Psalm 82:6

In context, this was God creating man and saying to him, "You are gods." This isn't 'Gods' in the sense of divinity, but 'gods' in the sense of rulership. We were given dominion – power and authority – over the earth. Since it was ours to rule and reign, we were gods over this earth.

> ***The heaven, even the heavens, are the LORD'S: but the earth hath he given to the children of men.***
>
> Psalm 115:16

God literally gave the earth to mankind. The Creator gave us the power and authority to rule over this earth as if we were the creator. We weren't the Creator, but that's how much dominion He gave us.

"I WILL..."

When Lucifer – still the sinless, perfect angel of God in the Garden sent to minister to Adam and Eve – saw the unconditional authority over the earth that God had given to man, he recognised an opportunity. Isaiah 14 reveals his thought process.

> ***O Lucifer, son of the morning ... thou hast said in thine heart,*** I will ***ascend into heaven,*** I will ***exalt my throne above the stars of God:*** I will ***sit also upon the mount of the congregation, in the sides of the north:*** I will ***ascend above the heights of the clouds:*** I will ***be like the most High.***
>
> Isaiah 14:12-14, emphasis mine

Lucifer envied God. He wasn't content with being the top angel. He was jealous and wanted God's position. But he couldn't just take that place with the delegated power he had been created with. If he would have rebelled, that power would have instantly been taken away, and he would have been destroyed. However, he saw an opportunity with man because God had given Adam and Eve something that He'd never given to the angels – an unconditional, no reservations or qualifications, no-strings-attached authority over the earth. Lucifer saw that if he could get Adam and Eve to yield to him and rebel against God, then he could become the new 'god' of this world (2 Cor. 4:4).

Even though the Bible hadn't been written down yet, Lucifer knew that the Word of God was settled from the beginning (Ps. 119:89) and that the Lord never changes (Mal. 3:6).

Therefore, His creation has always operated under His unchangeable, spiritual laws, which include:

> ***Know ye not, that to whom ye yield yourselves servants to obey, his servants ye are to whom ye obey; whether of sin unto death, or of obedience unto righteousness?***
>
> Romans 6:16

Understanding how God's kingdom works, Lucifer knew that if he could trick Adam and Eve into yielding to and obeying him, then he could become their master. Then he could take the power and authority that had been given to mankind and use it to begin thwarting the kingdom of God and start receiving this praise, adoration, and glory that he felt he desired. That's how it happened.

TAKEN HOSTAGE

When someone robs a bank, they often take a hostage. A bank usually has all kinds of powerful security – locks, alarms, vaults, cameras, and armed guards. One person with a gun isn't really sufficient to go in and overpower all of that security. However, if the thief grabs a hostage and puts a gun to their head, they know their demands will be met. The people who run the bank aren't willing to see a hostage killed just to protect some money. Therefore, one person with a gun and six bullets can challenge the far greater force of multiple guards with automatic weapons and several cartridges each. Technically, the thief shouldn't be able to overpower the security. But with a hostage, they're able to get away with the robbery.

Satan knew he couldn't overpower God in a direct confrontation. However, he saw how God gave Adam and Eve unconditional authority. If they of their own free will yielded to him, they would transfer that authority over to him as well.

As Creator and owner, God could have come down and wiped out the world. He could have destroyed Adam and Eve, the devil, and all of the angels that rebelled. As Creator, He had the right to do that and start over. However, to intervene in the affairs of this world like that would have violated His Word. He had given the dominion over this earth to Adam and Eve. He had given the power and authority to rule over this world to physical human beings. If God would have intervened, He would have violated His Word, and the entire universe would have self-destructed because it's held together by the integrity of His Word (Heb. 1:3).

For God to maintain His integrity and stand by what He had previously said – "You have dominion" – He had to give Adam and Eve their freedom. If they wanted to yield their authority and power over earth to Satan, then technically it was their right to do so. God would have been unjust to come down here, destroy Satan, say "Adam and Eve, don't do this again" and then redeem them. He couldn't do that and still be faithful to the Word He had spoken over them. They had a choice.

Lucifer saw how much God loved them. God met with them every day in the cool of the evening. After creating the whole universe – billions and billions of galaxies, stars, and planets – God was bound to have other things to do. Yet He spent time with Adam and Eve every single day. So Satan gambled that God wouldn't come down and wipe out this creation He'd made.

SATAN NEEDS SUBMISSION

Satan was using Adam and Eve as hostages to hide behind, saying, "God, they gave me this authority. It was their choice. I didn't force them." Satan didn't come with a mammoth and put his foot on Eve's head. He didn't come and overpower them. The devil came with deception, and they willingly yielded to him. This is where his transgression took place – in the Garden of Eden. He used them like a hostage, saying, "God, if You want to do anything to me, You'll have to destroy Adam and Eve too. They did this of their own free will."

Due to God's great love for mankind, Satan was allowed to become god of this world. Instead of wiping us out and starting this whole thing over, God allowed what we did to stand. ***We are the ones who made Satan.*** We are the ones who enabled Lucifer to leave his position in heaven, come into a fallen state, and rule the earth as Satan – the god of this world.

We were originally intended to be gods – absolute rulers – over this world. But mankind gave their dominion – authority and power – to Lucifer. So God created Lucifer, but Adam and Eve made Satan. They didn't create Satan, in the sense that God had already created Lucifer as an angelic being. However, Adam and Eve *made* Satan who he was by giving him their power and authority.

Most people believe that Satan is using a superior power and authority to oppress mankind. They see him as this huge, powerful being who is so much superior to any of us. This is reflected in television shows and horror movies. Satan and his demons are portrayed as these strong, powerful beings. Most people see the devil as a superior being in power and authority.

However, Lucifer lost his divinely delegated – God-given – power the very instant he transgressed and became Satan. The devil is not using a superior power and authority against us. He's actually using the same power and authority that God gave mankind to rule and reign with over this earth. It's our own power and authority that he uses against us.

On his own, Satan is powerless. He depends completely on physical human beings yielding to and empowering him. Even under the Old Covenant, Satan didn't have the power to control and dominate people. He has to use our own power and authority against us. It's only as we submit to him that Satan is able to do anything.

A DEMON NEEDS A BODY

The devil and his demons – as spirit beings – have no power or authority on this earth apart from physical human beings yielding it to them.

Consider the example of Jesus casting out the demons in Luke 8. When the Lord commanded the unclean spirit out of a man, the demons identified themselves as 'Legion' because they were many (Luke 8:30). They begged Jesus, "Don't cast us out into the deep, but send us into that nearby herd of swine." When the demons entered these 2,000 pigs, they immediately took off running, jumped off a steep cliff, and drowned themselves in a lake.

Demons are looking for a physical body, a willing vessel. They need somebody who will submit to them.

The power that the devil, or any other demon, uses against us is our own. Satan has zero angelic, spiritual power. All his authority comes from man. The only reason Satan exists and functions is because people cooperate with and empower him. That's why he always seeks to inhabit a body.

Even a pig has more authority on earth than a demon. An ant, a fly, or a snail has more power on this earth than Satan because they have physical bodies. He is absolutely powerless to do anything unless he can get a physical body to cooperate with him.

THE RIGHT TO USE POWER

God is the author of all power and authority. When He created mankind, He gave Adam and Eve dominion over the earth (Gen. 1:26-28). God gave us – physical human beings – power and authority to rule this world. Authority is simply the right to use power. God gave that right to use power to Adam and Eve.

Basically, God said, "Here's My power. Now I give you the right to use My power. Everything I have created will respond to you."

God is a Spirit (John 4:24). Satan is a spirit too (Eph. 2:2). He doesn't have a physical body. Therefore, Satan can't come and make anyone do anything. First, he must gain their cooperation.

Many Christians see Satan as an angelic being with godlike supernatural power and authority over man. They see him coming and overpowering them, when the truth is that the devil can't force them to do anything. He lost his power when he rebelled at God. The only power and authority Satan is functioning under now is human power and authority.

It takes your cooperation for the devil to do anything in your life. That's why he seeks whom he *may* devour. Satan doesn't have the authority and power to devour you unless you quit obeying God and yield yourself to sin. Romans 6:16 says that when you yield yourself to sin, you're actually yielding yourself to the author of that sin, which is Satan. Satan can't just destroy you without your cooperation. But when you sin, you are empowering the devil.

EARTHSUITS

Most people don't see it this way. They understand that according to Scripture, Satan was originally created as an angel. Angels have a higher power than what we do, but they don't have the authority, or right, to exercise that power in the earth. However, most people assume that Satan has a higher power and authority than we have, and they are intimidated by it. They don't realise that he lost all of his angelic power when he rebelled, and now his authority is totally tied to us. Since God gave the authority over this earth, and everything going on in it, to physical human beings, Satan – who is without a physical body – is absolutely powerless unless we empower him by yielding to and indulging his lust, lies, anger, bitterness, unforgiveness, or some other sin.

This is why our actions are so important. Your physical body is what gives you authority here on the earth. The Apostle Paul doesn't have any power or influence over you today. He's still alive, but he's no longer in a physical body. The only influence he has on anyone today is through the physical writings he left behind. People can read them and be influenced. However, Paul doesn't have the authority to function and operate any longer on this earth, because he no longer has a physical body.

I have a physical body. I have more authority and power on this earth than the Apostle Paul right now because he has lost his earthsuit. This earthsuit – my physical body – is what empowers me and gives me authority.

Satan can't do anything without somebody in an earthsuit yielding to him. This is why he's constantly vying for your heart, trying to get you to yield to him through anger, fear, hurt, pain, and depression. Every time you move away from what God's Word says and act in union with what the devil is trying to do, you yield authority to him. Every time you quit believing and receiving God's supernatural power and ability, and sin instead, you empower the Enemy. Satan can only function as he keeps people submitted to himself through lies and deception.

It's sad to say, but one of his greatest weapons of deception has been the church. The church has taught that Satan is a superior power. He isn't. He's actually using nothing but human power and human authority that requires our cooperation for him to work.

MY OWN HUMAN AUTHORITY

Does that mean Satan isn't a factor? No, he is a factor. There are millions of people on the face of the earth who are yielded to the devil today. They are operating in sexual immorality, lies, deception, hurt, fear, hatred, idolatry, and more. Every time we yield to something negative, we empower the devil. So, yes, Satan is a factor, and he has to be dealt with.

But as far as my individual life goes, Satan can't do anything without my consent and cooperation. Understanding that the power and authority Satan uses is human power – the power God has given to me, a physical human being, to rule and reign over this earth – has put everything in a brand-new light. Now, instead of being intimidated by the Enemy, I have boldness toward the devil. I understand that if I were to start doing the wrong things in my actions, saying the wrong things with my words, and indulging negative emotions, Satan would take advantage of it. He'd come in, eat my lunch, and pop the bag. I'm not ignorant of his devices, but I'm also not afraid of him. I'm not being passive toward him, but I'm actively and intentionally resisting him. I realise that all he's doing is coming against me with my own human authority and power.

I received a testimony from a woman who had been a Satanist before converting to Christ. Even after being born again, she suffered many problems because she was afraid that Satan was mad at her and was trying to punish her for turning away from him. When she heard this teaching on the believer's authority, it set her free. All her fears left as she realised that the devil couldn't do anything to her without her consent and cooperation. These truths liberated this precious sister, and they'll liberate you too!

GOD OF THIS WORLD
Lesson 6 – Outline

I. We were given dominion – power and authority – over the earth.

> *I have said, Ye are gods; and all of you are children of the most High.*
>
> Psalm 82:6

    A.   Since it was ours to rule and reign, we were gods over this earth.

> *The heaven, even the heavens, are the LORD'S: but the earth hath he given to the children of men.*
>
> Psalm 115:16

    B.   The Creator gave us the power and authority to rule over this earth as if we were the creator.

II. When Lucifer – still the sinless, perfect angel of God in the Garden sent to minister to Adam and Eve – saw the unconditional authority over the earth that God had given to man, he recognised an opportunity.

> *O Lucifer, son of the morning … thou hast said in thine heart,* I will *ascend into heaven,* I will *exalt my throne above the stars of God:* I will *sit also upon the mount of the congregation, in the sides of the north:* I will *ascend above the heights of the clouds:* I will *be like the most High.*
>
> Isaiah 14:12-14, emphasis mine

    A.   Lucifer saw that if he could get Adam and Eve to yield to him and rebel against God, then he could become the new 'god' of this world (2 Cor. 4:4).

    B.   Understanding how God's kingdom works, Lucifer knew that if he could trick Adam and Eve into yielding to and obeying him, then he could become their master.

    C.   Then he could take the power and authority that had been given to mankind and use it to begin thwarting the kingdom of God and start receiving this praise, adoration, and glory that he felt he desired.

    D.   For God to maintain His integrity and stand by what He had previously said – "You have dominion" – He had to give Adam and Eve their freedom.

    E.   If they wanted to yield their authority and power over earth to Satan, then technically it was their right to do so.

III. Due to God's great love for mankind, Satan was allowed to become god of this world.

    A. Instead of wiping us out and starting this whole thing over, God allowed what we did to stand.

    B. We are the ones who enabled Lucifer to leave his position in heaven, come into a fallen state, and rule the earth as Satan – the god of this world.

    C. Adam and Eve *made* Satan who he was by giving him their power and authority.

IV. The devil is not using a superior power and authority against us.

    A. It's our own power and authority that he uses against us.

    B. On his own, Satan is powerless – he depends completely on physical human beings yielding to and empowering him.

    C. It's only as we submit to him that Satan is able to do anything.

V. The devil and his demons – as spirit beings – have no power or authority on this earth apart from physical human beings yielding it to them.

    A. The only reason Satan exists and functions is because people cooperate with and empower him.

    B. That's why he always seeks to inhabit a body.

    C. Satan is a spirit (Eph. 2:2) – he doesn't have a physical body.

VI. It takes your cooperation for the devil to do anything in your life, which is why your actions are so important.

    A. Your physical body is what gives you authority here on the earth.

    B. Satan can't do anything without someone in an earthsuit yielding to him.

    C. Every time you move away from what God's Word says and act in union with what the devil is trying to do, you yield authority to him.

    D. Every time you quit believing and receiving God's supernatural power and ability, and sin instead, you empower the Enemy.

    E. Satan can only function as he keeps people submitted to himself through lies and deception.

GOD OF THIS WORLD
Lesson 6 – Teacher's Guide

1. We were given dominion – power and authority – over the earth (Ps. 82:6). Since it was ours to rule and reign, we were gods over this earth (Ps. 115:16). The Creator gave us the power and authority to rule over this earth as if we were the creator.

2. When Lucifer – still the sinless, perfect angel of God in the Garden sent to minister to Adam and Eve – saw the unconditional authority over the earth that God had given to man, he recognised an opportunity (Is. 14:12-14). Lucifer saw that if he could get Adam and Eve to yield to him and rebel against God, then he could become the new 'god' of this world (2 Cor. 4:4). Understanding how God's kingdom works, Lucifer knew that if he could trick Adam and Eve into yielding to and obeying him, then he could become their master. Then he could take the power and authority that had been given to mankind and use it to begin thwarting the kingdom of God and start receiving this praise, adoration, and glory that he felt he desired. For God to maintain His integrity and stand by what He had previously said – "You have dominion" – He had to give Adam and Eve their freedom. If they wanted to yield their authority and power over earth to Satan, then technically it was their right to do so.

3. Due to God's great love for mankind, Satan was allowed to become god of this world. Instead of wiping us out and starting this whole thing over, God allowed what we did to stand. We are the ones who enabled Lucifer to leave his position in heaven, come into a fallen state, and rule the earth as Satan – the god of this world. Adam and Eve *made* Satan who he was by giving him their power and authority.

1. A. Read Psalms 82:6 and 115:16. What were we given dominion – power and authority – over? (The earth)
   B. Since it was ours to rule and reign, we were what? (We were gods over this earth)
2. A. Read Isaiah 14:12-14 and 2 Corinthians 4:4. What would happen if Lucifer could get Adam and Eve to yield to him and rebel against God? (He could become the new 'god' of this world)
   B. Why did God have to give Adam and Eve their freedom? (To maintain His integrity and stand by what He had previously said – "You have dominion")
3. A. Satan was allowed to become god of this world due to what? (God's great love for mankind)
   B. Who enabled Lucifer to leave his position in heaven, come into a fallen state, and rule the earth as Satan – the god of this world? (We did)
   C. How did Adam and Eve *make* Satan who he was? (By giving him their power and authority)

4. The devil is not using a superior power and authority against us. It's our own power and authority that he uses against us. On his own, Satan is powerless – he depends completely on physical human beings yielding to and empowering him. It's only as we submit to him that Satan is able to do anything.

5. The devil and his demons – as spirit beings – have no power or authority on this earth apart from physical human beings yielding it to them. The only reason Satan exists and functions is because people cooperate with and empower him. That's why he always seeks to inhabit a body. Satan is a spirit (Eph. 2:2) – he doesn't have a physical body.

6. It takes our cooperation for the devil to do anything in our lives, which is why our actions are so important. Our physical bodies are what give us authority here on the earth. Satan can't do anything without someone in an earthsuit yielding to him. Every time we move away from what God's Word says and act in union with what the devil is trying to do, we yield authority to him. Every time we quit believing and receiving God's supernatural power and ability, and sin instead, we empower the Enemy. Satan can only function as he keeps people submitted to himself through lies and deception.

4. A. Is the devil using a superior power and authority against us? (No)
   B. Whose power and authority does he use against us? (Our own)
5. A. Read Ephesians 2:2. As spirit beings, the devil and his demons have no power or authority on this earth apart from whom yielding it to them? (Physical human beings)
   B. This is why he always seeks to inhabit what? (A body)
6. A. What is it that gives us authority here on the earth? (Our physical bodies)
   B. Satan can only function as he keeps people submitted to himself how? (Through lies and deception)

GOD OF THIS WORLD
Lesson 6 – Discipleship Questions

1. Psalm 115:16 reveals that God has given the earth to whom?

2. How is Lucifer described in Isaiah 14:12-14?

3. According to 2 Corinthians 4:4, who has blinded the minds of unbelievers?

4. What has he blinded them from?

5. Who is the image of God?

6. According to Psalm 119:89, what is settled in heaven?

7. According to Malachi 3:6, does the Lord change?

8. Hebrews 1:3 says that Jesus is the brightness of His Father's glory and the _____ of His person?

9. What question did Jesus ask in Luke 8:30?

10. According to Genesis 1:26-28, God blessed man and woman and told them to be fruitful, to multiply, to replenish the earth, and to do what?

11. According to John 4:24, what is God?

12. How must we worship Him?

13. Ephesians 2:2 says that in time past (before we were born again) we walked how?

14. Who is the spirit that now works in the children of disobedience?

GOD OF THIS WORLD
Lesson 6 – Answer Key

1. The children of men.

2. Fallen from heaven and cut down to the ground.

3. The god of this world.

4. The light of the glorious Gospel of Christ.

5. Christ.

6. God's Word.

7. No.

8. Express image.

9. What is thy name?

10. Subdue it.

11. A Spirit.

12. In spirit and in truth.

13. According to the course of this world.

14. The prince of the power of the air.

GOD OF THIS WORLD
Lesson 6 – Scriptures

I have said, Ye are gods; and all of you are children of the most High.

Psalm 82:6

The heaven, even the heavens, are the LORD'S: but the earth hath he given to the children of men.

Psalm 115:16

How art thou fallen from heaven, O Lucifer, son of the morning! how art thou cut down to the ground, which didst weaken the nations! For thou hast said in thine heart, I will ascend into heaven, I will exalt my throne above the stars of God: I will sit also upon the mount of the congregation, in the sides of the north: I will ascend above the heights of the clouds; I will be like the most High.

Isaiah 14:12-14

In whom the god of this world hath blinded the minds of them which believe not, lest the light of the glorious gospel of Christ, who is the image of God, should shine unto them.

2 Corinthians 4:4

For ever, O LORD, thy word is settled in heaven.

Psalm 119:89

For I am the LORD, I change not; therefore ye sons of Jacob are not consumed.

Malachi 3:6

Know ye not, that to whom ye yield yourselves servants to obey, his servants ye are to whom ye obey; whether of sin unto death, or of obedience unto righteousness?

Romans 6:16

Who being the brightness of his glory, and the express image of his person, and upholding all things by the word of his power, when he had by himself purged our sins, sat down on the right hand of the Majesty on high.

Hebrews 1:3

And Jesus asked him, saying, What is thy name? And he said, Legion: because many devils were entered into him.

Luke 8:30

And God said, Let us make man in our image, after our likeness: and let them have dominion over the fish of the sea, and over the fowl of the air, and over the cattle, and over all the earth, and over every creeping thing that creepeth upon the earth. So God created man in his own image, in the image of God created he him; male and female created he them. And God blessed them, and God said unto them, Be fruitful, and multiply, and replenish the earth, and subdue it: and have dominion over the fish of the sea, and over the fowl of the air, and over every living thing that moveth upon the earth.

Genesis 1:26-28

God is a Spirit: and they that worship him must worship him in spirit and in truth.

John 4:24

Wherein in time past ye walked according to the course of this world, according to the prince of the power of the air, the spirit that now worketh in the children of disobedience.

Ephesians 2:2

UNDER THE UMBRELLA
Lesson 7

In light of what we've seen thus far, Ephesians 6:10-11 ought to make a lot more sense.

Finally, my brethren, be strong in the Lord, and in the power of his might. Put on the whole armour of God, that ye may be able to stand against the wiles of the devil.

Wiles literally means 'cunningness, craftiness, and deception'. Satan's only power is deception. He can't force you to do anything. He can't make you sin. People tell me, "I don't want to commit sexual sin, but I just don't have the power. Satan is stronger than I am." Not true. Satan doesn't have the power or authority to force you to do anything. The problem is that he's a master liar, intimidator, and deceiver. It's all deception. When we don't know the truth about who we are in Christ and the power we've been given, then – in a very real sense – we are the ones who are giving Satan the power and authority to rule and dominate us. You can break that.

Just this week, I was speaking to one of our Bible college students. When I asked them about a certain area in their life, they admitted, "I know I'm wrong in this area. It's rebellion and I want to break it, but there's just something in me that I have trouble doing the right thing. I just can't seem to overcome it."

I told them, "Here's how you can overcome it. Do every day what you know you're supposed to do, but don't feel like doing. It doesn't matter that you don't feel like doing it. Do it every day. If you'll start obeying and yielding your actions to the Lord, then He'll be strengthened in your life. As you quit obeying and yielding your body to the devil, it'll weaken him in your life." That's why the Bible says you have to stand against the wiles, deception, lies, and deceit of the devil.

Satan is out to deceive you, and he's coming at you every which way through all of the help and support he gets from people. Our airwaves are full of lust and lies. Every time you yield to them, you are the one who empowers the devil to come in and destroy your life.

WHY JESUS CAME

Since God is a Spirit (John 4:24) and He gave the power and authority over the earth to physical human beings, He would have been unjust to come down here and intervene in the affairs of man. Since God had given dominion over the earth to man, He couldn't just step in and straighten out the mess (Gen. 1:28). He had the power to do so, and as Judge He could have said, "All right, I'm tired of this whole mess. I'm going to wipe out the entire human race." He came close to doing that with Noah and the Flood. As Creator and owner, He's always had the right and privilege. But outside of total judgement, He didn't have the authority to just come into the affairs of man and change things. He didn't have it, because He had given that authority to rule and reign over the earth to mankind (Ps. 115:16). Even though they used it in a way contrary to what He desired, God would have been unjust and untrue to His own statements to come down here and do that.

This is why God had to become a man. This is the reason that God had to send His Son, the Lord Jesus Christ, to this earth. It all comes back to this issue of authority being given to physical human beings. God didn't have a physical human body (John 4:24). Therefore, He wasn't free to operate unrestricted on this earth. He had to become a man. Jesus – the Word made flesh, the God-Man – had to become a physical person so He could have authority on this earth.

God couldn't have saved mankind any other way. Until He obtained a physical human body, He was limited in what He could do. He tried to work through people, but they were all corrupted, deceived, and under the devil's control.

> *I sought for a man among them, that should make up the hedge, and stand in the gap before me for the land, that I should not destroy it: but I found none ... he saw that there was no man, and wondered that there was no intercessor: therefore his arm brought salvation unto him; and his righteousness, it sustained him.*
>
> Ezekiel 22:30 and Isaiah 59:16

Since there was no person sinless, pure, and able to bring God's righteousness into the earth, He had to come and save us Himself. He had given the dominion of this world to physical human beings, so He had to become one. God Himself took upon Himself flesh and limited Himself to a physical body.

4,000 YEARS

God spoke Adam's body into existence when He had absolute authority over the earth.

> ***God said, Let us make man.***
>
> Genesis 1:26

God created them by speaking words. After He created them, He spoke words, giving them dominion – authority and power – over the earth. In doing so, He limited His own authority. Man corrupted himself by selling out to the devil and making him the god of this world. God wasn't in control. He didn't have dominion over the earth, because He had given it to man.

That's why God wasn't able to just speak the physical body of Jesus into existence on His own. He had to speak to the spirits of men – the corrupted spirit within them – and then they had to take those words and speak them out of their mouths. It literally took God four thousand years to find enough people who would operate in enough faith to speak forth and prophesy the things that needed to be spoken for Jesus' body to be created.

There's no telling how many people God inspired to say **"A virgin shall conceive, and bear a son"** before Isaiah actually spoke it (Is. 7:14). Not many prophets would like to stand up and go on record declaring such a thing. It took a lot of faith for Isaiah to say that.

> ***After all of these prophecies had been spoken over four thousand years, the angel approached Mary and told her what would happen. She humbled herself and said:***
>
> Luke 1:38

The angel took all of those prophecies – the spoken words of God – and the Word entered into Mary's womb.

The Word was made flesh, and dwelt among us.

John 1:14

God created the physical body for Jesus to inhabit by speaking words over a four- thousand-year period of time through anointed men. Then those words entered into the womb of Mary, and that's how Jesus was conceived. That's why He had authority on earth to do what He did.

SHIELDED FROM THE RAIN

Satan was in trouble now. God always had the power to intervene, but He had given the authority over the earth to mankind. His ability to intervene in the affairs of man was limited because He didn't have a physical body. When man turned from God and gave this authority and power to the devil, the devil began to oppress the human race. God wanted to redeem us, but He had to have a physical human being – a person with a physical body – here on the earth so He could have power to do battle with the devil.

When you're under an umbrella, it shields you from the rain. The rain may be falling, but it isn't touching you. When Satan rebelled against God, he came under the protective 'umbrella' of the authority God had given to mankind. Therefore, this human authority shielded the devil from God getting to him and stripping him of all this power. God couldn't get to Satan directly without violating His Word because He had given this authority over the earth to people with physical human bodies. This is why Jesus had to become a Man.

Christ said it this way:

For as the Father hath life in himself; so hath he given to the Son to have life in himself; And hath given him authority to execute judgement also, because he is the Son of man.

John 5:26-27

Jesus said the reason He had authority to execute judgement was because He was the Son of Man.

THE GOD-MAN

Both of the terms 'Son of God' and 'Son of Man' refer to Jesus. Son of Man emphasises His humanity and physical side. Son of God emphasises His divinity and the presence of Almighty God that indwelt Christ's body. Jesus existed before the worlds began, and He created all things (Col. 1:16-17). Jesus was God manifest in the flesh (1 Tim. 3:16). He was fully God and fully man simultaneously. Therefore, Jesus was the God-Man.

So when Jesus said that the Father had given Him authority to execute judgement because He was the Son of Man, He was making a direct reference to the fact that He had a physical body. He always had power as Creator, but He didn't have the authority to use that power until He took on flesh.

All this is because of the integrity of God's Word. Once He spoke "You have dominion" to mankind, it was theirs. He limited His own authority and power by giving it to us, and God never breaks His Word.

One of my employees was believing God for a car. When the Lord blessed me with a better vehicle, I gave my previous car to him. It was a very nice car. It was brand-new when I got it, and we'd only used it for two or three years. I gave this car to him as a gift, and I signed the title over to him.

A year or so later, this brother came up to me and asked if it would be okay with me if he used that car as a trade-in toward a better one. I told him, "You can do anything you want with that car. It's not mine – it's yours." He felt he needed to get my permission, but it wasn't necessary. In every way I had given him that car. It was legally his. If he wanted to park it on the curb and charge ten dollars each for people to take a swing at it with a sledgehammer in order to raise money for another car, he could have done so. He could have done anything with it that he wanted.

That's integrity. If I gave someone a car and signed it over to them – it's theirs. If a couple of years later I find them selling swings with a sledgehammer for ten bucks each – and that's not what I intended – it would be wrong for me to come up to them and say something. If I truly gave it to them – no strings attached – then it's their business, not mine. They now have the authority over it.

A PHYSICAL BODY

That's how God gave authority over this earth to us. God Himself was limited until He became a physical human being. Jesus wasn't only physical, but He – God Himself – inhabited a physical body on the earth. Now the devil was in trouble. He'd been using Adam and Eve like a hostage, saying, "God, if You do anything to me, You'll have to destroy these people You have made too." But now Jesus became one of the hostages – a physical human being.

Jesus entered into the devil's kingdom and destroyed it. He took away all authority and power from Satan and reduced him to a zero with the rim knocked off. The Enemy has zippo, zilch, nada power and authority against us. All Satan can do is tempt us. If we yield to him, we're doing the same thing Adam and Eve did – *we* are yielding *our* human power and authority. Satan can't do anything to you without your consent and cooperation.

This is completely opposite of so much of what the church has taught. Most people think that Satan is a major force to be reckoned with. He does exist, and you can't just be ignorant of his devices (2 Cor. 2:11). You need to know what's going on. But the devil is not someone to be feared. He's someone you need to recognise and resist, but Satan can't do anything to you without your consent and cooperation.

Understanding this truth has transformed my life and given me a tremendous advantage over the devil. Now I recognise that if I'm having a feeling, a desire, a drawing, or a lust in some direction, all I have to do is quit yielding to those things that are allowing Satan to draw me in that way. I just use my physical body to go in the exact opposite direction. What I do with my physical body releases either the power of God or the power of the devil.

UNDER THE UMBRELLA
Lesson 7 – Outline

I. Satan's only power is deception.

> *Finally, my brethren, be strong in the Lord, and in the power of his might. Put on the whole armour of God, that ye may be able to stand against the wiles of the devil.*
>
> Ephesians 6:10-11

    A. *Wiles* literally means 'cunningness, craftiness, and deception'.

    B. Satan doesn't have the power or authority to force you to do anything.

    C. The problem is that he's a master liar, intimidator, and deceiver.

    D. When we don't know the truth about who we are in Christ and the power we've been given, then – in a very real sense – we are the ones who are giving Satan the power and authority to rule and dominate us.

    E. That's why the Bible says you have to stand against the wiles, deception, lies, and deceit of the devil.

II. Since God had given dominion over the earth to man, He couldn't just step in and straighten out the mess (Gen. 1:28).

    A. As Creator and owner, He's always had the right and privilege, but outside of total judgement, He didn't have the authority to just come into the affairs of man and change things (Ps. 115:16).

    B. Even though mankind used that authority in a way contrary to what God desired, He would have been unjust and untrue to His own statements to come down here and do that.

    C. This is why God had to become a man.

    D. Jesus – the Word made flesh, the God-Man – had to become a physical person so that He could have authority on this earth.

III. Since there was no person sinless, pure, and able to bring God's righteousness into the earth, He had to come and save us Himself.

> *I sought for a man among them, that should make up the hedge, and stand in the gap before me for the land, that I should not destroy it: but I found none ... he saw that there was no man, and wondered that there was no intercessor: therefore his arm brought salvation unto him; and his righteousness, it sustained him.*
>
> Ezekiel 22:30 and Isaiah 59:16

- A. God created the physical body for Jesus to inhabit by speaking words over a four-thousand-year period of time through anointed men.

- B. Then those words entered into the womb of Mary, and that's how Jesus was conceived (Luke 1:38 and John 1:14).

- C. That's why He had authority on earth to do what He did.

IV. God couldn't get to Satan directly without violating His Word because He had given authority over the earth to people with physical human bodies.

- A. Jesus said the reason He had authority to execute judgement was because He was the Son of Man.

    For as the Father hath life in himself; so hath he given to the Son to have life in himself; And hath given him authority to execute judgement also, because he is the Son of man.
    John 5:26-27

- B. When Jesus said that the Father had given Him authority to execute judgement because He was the Son of Man, He was making a direct reference to the fact that He had a physical body.

- C. He always had power as Creator, but He didn't have the authority to use that power until He took on flesh.

- D. He limited His own authority and power by giving it to us, and God never breaks His Word.

V. Jesus entered into the devil's kingdom and destroyed it.

- A. He took away all authority and power from Satan and reduced him to a zero with the rim knocked off.

- B. If we yield to the devil, we're doing the same thing Adam and Eve did – *we* are yielding *our* human power and authority.

- C. Satan can't do anything to you without your consent and cooperation.

UNDER THE UMBRELLA
Lesson 7 – Teacher's Guide

1. Satan's only power is deception (Eph. 6:10-11). *Wiles* literally means 'cunningness, craftiness, and deception'. Satan doesn't have the power or authority to force us to do anything. The problem is that he's a master liar, intimidator, and deceiver. When we don't know the truth about who we are in Christ and the power we've been given, then – in a very real sense – we are the ones who are giving Satan the power and authority to rule and dominate us. That's why the Bible says we have to stand against the wiles, deception, lies, and deceit of the devil.

2. Since God had given dominion over the earth to man, He couldn't just step in and straighten out the mess (Gen. 1:28). As Creator and owner, He's always had the right and privilege, but outside of total judgement, He didn't have the authority to just come into the affairs of man and change things (Ps. 115:16). Even though mankind used that authority in a way contrary to what God desired, He would have been unjust and untrue to His own statements to come down here and do that. This is why God had to become a man. Jesus – the Word made flesh, the God-Man – had to become a physical person so that He could have authority on this earth.

3. Since there was no person sinless, pure, and able to bring God's righteousness into the earth, He had to come and save us Himself (Ezek. 22:30 and Is. 59:16). God created the physical body for Jesus to inhabit by speaking words over a four-thousand-year period of time through anointed men. Then those words entered into the womb of Mary, and that's how Jesus was conceived (Luke 1:38 and John 1:14). That's why He had authority on earth to do what He did.

1. A. Read Ephesians 6:10-11. Does Satan have the power or authority to force us to do anything? (No)
   B. The Bible says that we have to stand against the _____ of the devil. (Wiles, deception, lies, and deceit)
2. A. Read Genesis 1:28 and Psalm 115:16. Why couldn't God just step in and straighten out the mess? (Because He had given dominion over the earth to man)
   B. Jesus had to become _____ so that He could have authority on this earth. (The Word made flesh, the God-Man, a physical person)
3. A. Read Ezekiel 22:30, Isaiah 59:16, Luke 1:38, and John 1:14. Why did God have to come and save us Himself? (Because there was no person sinless, pure, and able to bring God's righteousness into the earth)
   B. How did God create the physical body for Jesus to inhabit? (By speaking words over a four-thousand-year period of time through anointed men, and then those words entered into the womb of Mary)

4. God couldn't get to Satan directly without violating His Word because He had given authority over the earth to people with physical human bodies. Jesus said the reason He had authority to execute judgement was because He was the Son of Man (John 5:26-27). When Jesus said that the Father had given Him authority to execute judgement because He was the Son of Man, He was making a direct reference to the fact that He had a physical body. He always had power as Creator, but He didn't have the authority to use that power until He took on flesh. He limited His own authority and power by giving it to us, and God never breaks His Word.

5. Jesus entered into the devil's kingdom and destroyed it. He took away all authority and power from Satan and reduced him to a zero with the rim knocked off. If we yield to him, we're doing the same thing Adam and Eve did – *we* are yielding *our* human power and authority. Satan can't do anything to us without our consent and cooperation.

4. A. Read John 5:26-27. Why couldn't God get to Satan directly without violating His Word? (Because He had given authority over the earth to people with physical human bodies)
    B. Jesus said the reason He had authority to execute judgement was because of what? (He was the Son of Man)
5. A. What did Jesus do when He became a man? (He entered into the devil's kingdom and destroyed it)
    B. How are we doing the same thing Adam and Eve did when we yield to Satan? (*We* are yielding *our* human power and authority)

UNDER THE UMBRELLA
Lesson 7 – Additional Information

My teaching entitled "How to Conceive a Miracle" goes into greater depth on this topic. It's the second message from *Lessons from the Christmas Story*.

UNDER THE UMBRELLA
Lesson 7 – Discipleship Questions

1. Ephesians 6:10-11 reveals that we are to stand against what?

2. Who does John 4:24 say is a Spirit?

3. According to Psalm 115:16, the heavens belong to whom?

4. According to Ezekiel 22:30, had God found a man to stand in the gap before Him?

5. Isaiah 59:16 says there was no what?

6. Isaiah 7:14 prophesied that Jesus would be called what?

7. In Luke 1:38, Mary said, "Be it unto me according to …" what?

8. John 1:14 says that the Word was made what?

9. Where did He dwell?

10. What was He full of?

11. What title did Jesus use in John 5:26-27 to express His humanity?

12. According to Colossians 1:16-17, _____ were created by Him.

13. What does 1 Timothy 3:16 reveal God was manifest in?

14. According to 2 Corinthians 2:11, we don't want whom to get an advantage of us?

15. What are we not ignorant of?

UNDER THE UMBRELLA
Lesson 7 – Answer Key

1. The wiles of the devil.
2. God.
3. The Lord.
4. No.
5. Intercessor.
6. Immanuel.
7. Thy word.
8. Flesh.
9. Among us.
10. Grace and truth.
11. Son of Man.
12. All things.
13. The flesh.
14. Satan.
15. His (Satan's) devices.

UNDER THE UMBRELLA
Lesson 7 – Scriptures

Finally, my brethren, be strong in the Lord, and in the power of his might. Put on the whole armour of God, that ye may be able to stand against the wiles of the devil.

Ephesians 6:10-11

God is a Spirit: and they that worship him must worship him in spirit and in truth.

John 4:24

The heaven, even the heavens, are the LORD'S: but the earth hath he given to the children of men.

Psalm 115:16

And I sought for a man among them, that should make up the hedge, and stand in the gap before me for the land, that I should not destroy it: but I found none.

Ezekiel 22:30

And he saw that there was no man, and wondered that there was no intercessor: therefore his arm brought salvation unto him; and his righteousness, it sustained him.

Isaiah 59:16

And God said, Let us make man in our image, after our likeness: and let them have dominion over the fish of the sea, and over the fowl of the air, and over the cattle, and over all the earth, and over every creeping thing that creepeth upon the earth.

Genesis 1:26

Therefore the Lord himself shall give you a sign; Behold, a virgin shall conceive, and bear a son, and shall call his name Immanuel.

Isaiah 7:14

And Mary said, Behold the handmaid of the Lord; be it unto me according to thy word. And the angel departed from her.

Luke 1:38

And the Word was made flesh, and dwelt among us, (and we beheld his glory, the glory as of the only begotten of the Father,) full of grace and truth.

John 1:14

For as the Father hath life in himself; so hath he given to the Son to have life in himself; And hath given him authority to execute judgement also, because he is the Son of man.

John 5:26-27

For by him were all things created, that are in heaven, and that are in earth, visible and invisible, whether they be thrones, or dominions, or principalities, or powers: all things were created by him, and for him: And he is before all things, and by him all things consist.
Colossians 1:16-17

And without controversy great is the mystery of godliness: God was manifest in the flesh, justified in the Spirit, seen of angels, preached unto the Gentiles, believed on in the world, received up into glory.
1 Timothy 3:16

Lest Satan should get an advantage of us: for we are not ignorant of his devices.
2 Corinthians 2:11

IS THIS THE ONE?
Lesson 8

When Jamie and I first started out in the ministry, we really struggled financially. Occasionally, I'd work odd jobs to help make ends meet. One day I came home from a painting job feeling so sick, I could hardly stand up. I just wanted to lie down on the couch and rest. Jamie was in the kitchen fixing me lunch. When she saw me on the couch, she asked, "What are you doing?"

"I feel sick. I don't know if I can eat anything."

We had already been teaching other believers these same truths. "You have to use your body to quit yielding to the devil. Don't cooperate with him. Do the very thing that you don't feel like doing. Resist the devil, and fight against him with your physical actions" (James 4:7).

Jamie came right over and got me up off of that couch. She put my arm around her shoulder and started dragging me through the house, saying, "We need this money. You will go back to that job. You're healed!" She made me get up and start acting healed. She just forced me to practice what I'd been preaching.

Praise God, in ten minutes I was over it and felt well again. I went back to work and got paid that day. Thank You, Jesus.

"ACT ON THE WORD!"

The night before I was to be ordained into the ministry, I hurt my back opening our broken garage door. We were living in Seagoville, Texas, at the time. As I bent over and started lifting the garage door up, it got caught and something just popped in my back. The pain that immediately shot through my body was so excruciating, it knocked me to the ground.

My one-year-old son had been watching me. I told him "Go, tell Mummy," but he just sat there jabbering at me. Eventually, he wandered into the house and brought Jamie out. When she saw me lying there, I hurt so bad that all I could do was whisper, "I hurt my back."

"Well, then, get up." Jamie pulled me up, prayed over me, and said, "Now, you act on the Word of God!" Again, we needed me to be able to work, so she cut me no slack.

It's a long story, but I started doing things with my physical body. My shoulder blades were back so far they were touching each other. The pain was excruciating, but I forced myself to do things I didn't feel like doing. Finally, over a day's period of time, I got to where I could do sit-ups and other things. Although my movement had returned, my shoulders were still pulled back.

I went to bed that night, and when I woke up the next morning, my shoulders were still pulled back. I just kept fighting it all day long. Right before I went to my ordination service,

I declared, "I am going to act healed. I am going there, and I will be ordained." By the time I arrived at church, I was healed. My actions played a major part in receiving and manifesting that healing.

You can't lie in bed acting sick and at the same time release the supernatural power of God. You must learn how to use your physical body to resist the devil and cooperate with the Lord. If you don't step out in faith and act on the Word, you'll limit God (James 2:20).

WE CAN LIMIT GOD

God is a Spirit (John 4:24), and He gave dominion over this earth to physical human beings (Gen. 1:26-28). In doing so, He limited His own dominion and authority. If we don't cooperate with God, we can limit Him.

> **Yea, they turned back and tempted God, and limited the Holy One of Israel.**
>
> Psalm 78:41

Yes, we can limit God. Jesus dealt with this in His own hometown.

> **He could there do no mighty work ... because of their unbelief.**
>
> Mark 6:5-6

It's not that Jesus didn't want to; He couldn't do any mighty work, because of their unbelief. Even the Lord Jesus Christ had to have cooperation from people to release His power into their lives.

Religion says, "God is sovereign. He controls everything." No, He doesn't. God is sovereign in the sense that He's King of kings. But He doesn't control everything that happens on the earth. God isn't limited in the sense that He doesn't have the power. He has the power, but He gave dominion over this earth to physical human beings. Because of His own integrity, He will not overstep that authority and violate His own Word.

Therefore, God has limited His own sovereignty, His own ability to intervene in the affairs of man here on earth. Until He became a physical being Himself, He didn't have the authority to come down to this earth and straighten out the mess man had created.

EARN THE RIGHT

God Himself operates within these laws of authority. God Himself will not violate His own Word.

Because we live in a culture today where authority isn't a big issue, these truths can be hard to comprehend. People basically don't submit themselves to authority. They only do what they are forced and demanded to do, but they don't recognise authority. People violate authority all the time.

I don't mean this in a critical way, but the younger generation – as a whole – doesn't respect authority the way the older generation does. They've been raised in such a way that they can get by with violating everything. A recent study showed that the majority of today's students have cheated before and don't see anything wrong with it. They aren't submitted to authority. They think as long as they don't get caught, everything is fine. That's absolutely wrong. All of life is based on authority.

I teach our Charis Bible College students that they have to earn the right to speak into someone's life. They have to gain their respect before they'll let them minister to their heart. This works on every level.

One reason so much of what's called 'evangelism' today isn't very effective is because it's disrespectful and offensive. People just walk up to a stranger, stick a tract in their face, and say, "You're going to hell. Repent!" Then they try to coerce that person to submit to them and 'pray a prayer'. However, they haven't even used common courtesy to introduce themselves or ask, "How are you? How's your day going?" These so-called 'evangelists' just come up to them and get right in their face. That is absolutely wrong!

"WHO ARE YOU?"

While in Kansas City once, a guy came up to me after a meeting and started railing on my wife. He said, "If you were a man of God, you'd straighten this out. You'd make her do this and that and this other thing." Then he started criticising and giving me all of his opinions about how my wife should dress. If you knew Jamie, you'd know that my wife is a very conservative dresser. She never wears anything inappropriate. There was nothing wrong with her. This guy just had a bunch of legalistic, religious opinions about jewelry, makeup, and hairstyles that he was trying to force on us.

Basically, I stopped him right in the middle of his tirade, asking, "Who are you?"

He told me his name.

"No, I mean who gave you the right to speak to us this way? You have no dominion, no right, and no authority over my wife. God did not die and appoint you to take His place. You're nobody. I don't care what your opinion is!"

Of course, this guy was highly offended. His attitude was, *How dare you speak to me that way*. But since he had the audacity to confront me, rail on my wife, and tell me what to do, I just decided to respond in kind. "Mister, you have no authority in my life."

I would never just walk in and start telling the president of the United States what to do. It's not because I feel inferior. It's not because I don't believe that God has given me some valuable things to say. I just recognise that I'd have to earn that right. He would have to request it. I'm not his superior. I can't just force my way in and start spouting opinions.

It's the same for a mail clerk in a business. You may have some ideas that would work, but you can't just barge into the CEO's office and start telling them what to do. You must remain under authority. Now, if they're a good CEO, they'd encourage your feedback. They'd even occasionally go to the hourly workers and ask, "What do you think?" But really, it's voluntary. You don't have the right – the authority – to just go up to them and start spouting.

I would never go up to one of these ministers I see on television or radio and just start rebuking them and telling them things. I've listened to some of them, and they are absolutely wrong. God has shown me some truths in His Word that could help them, but I respect that person enough to wait to be invited in. I'm not their supervisor. They don't submit to me. We don't have that kind of rapport built up. I'd never do such a thing.

NONE OF YOUR BUSINESS

However, every day someone does that to me. Whether it be in a letter, a phone call, an email, or in person, someone who considers themselves to be the official standard of what's right and wrong reams me up one side and down the other. Yet they've never witnessed to anyone, never seen someone set free, never done anything, and yet they think that they know it all.

If you just understood authority, you would stop these kinds of abuses. You have to earn the right to speak into someone's life.

I've told my Bible school students before, "There are some things I know about some of you sitting here right now. However, these problems are outside of school, and you haven't come to me about them. If we haven't built a rapport to where I feel like you've opened up to me and given me the freedom, then I won't come to you and talk to you about those kinds of things." It's not my place. It's none of my business.

I'll deal with things that affect people while they're at school, but I'm not going to pry into their personal lives. Some folks think, *Well, that's wrong. You ought to get more involved*. Well, I believe it's wrong for you to stick your nose into other people's business. It really does come down to authority.

DEFEATED

God is a God of authority. He set structure in place, and He's not going to circumvent it. When one of my employees disagrees with a superior, I tell them, "Go to your superior, and talk to them about it. Don't circumvent the superior by coming to me and trying to get me to counter their opinion." It works better this way. That's how God is. He established authority, and we need to recognise that God Himself obeys it. He would not intervene in the affairs of man until He became a man. Once He took upon Himself the form of flesh, then He had the authority to take it to the devil. That's good news.

Satan didn't get his authority directly from God. He doesn't have a superior angelic power that he uses over the human race. The devil was stripped of all his angelic power and authority. The power and authority that Satan has used to rule this earth has been man's authority that God gave him.

Understanding that Satan can do nothing in your life without your consent and cooperation puts him down on a plane where he isn't a superior foe. As a master deceiver, he's still a threat because he can lie to you. You must know the truth and be on guard. But you can resist him.

I know I can win this battle. I can take the power and authority God has given me and confront the devil. I'm not ignorant of him, but I'm no longer afraid of him either. I've seen awesome things happen just because I recognise that Satan has been defeated.

GRANDMA'S ROOM

Like most people who were raised in typical America, I honestly didn't think about demons. I'd read about them in the Bible, but I thought all the demons were overseas in some Third-World country. I didn't think there were demons here, or that we could physically encounter them. Then I got turned on to the Lord and began to look more closely at the Bible. I recognised that the spirit realm is as real today as it was two thousand years ago. I realised that many different things were demonic, including sicknesses. My friends and I began casting demons out of people and seeing miraculous things happen.

My grandmother raised me until I was about six years old. Then she went senile and finally died when I was eight. When she died, she left some demons behind in that room she occupied in our house. Right after she passed on, I moved out of the room I was sharing with my brother and into what had been Grandmother's room. A picture of her that we had sitting on the dresser would come alive at night. Her image would come out of the frame and walk around the room. Since I was only eight years old, that scared the fire out of me. I knew this was strange, and it wasn't the way it was supposed to be. But I was afraid to tell my mother and father because they would have thought I was crazy. So I just didn't say anything about it. But as soon as possible, I moved out of that room and back in with my brother. He thought *Well, then, I'll take that other room* and moved in there. It wasn't a month before he moved back in with me. Then my sister took that room. It wasn't a month before she moved out of there too.

For the next twelve years, we kept that room of our house locked up. Nobody ever said anything, but nobody liked being in there. My older sister brought her newborn daughter home when I was fourteen years old. She'd be sound asleep, but if they walked into that room, she would wake up crying. Then they'd walk out and she'd be okay. Walk in and she'd cry, walk out and she was okay. When I had Bible studies, people would go all over the house to pray with others, but nobody would go in that room. After a while, my lightning-fast mind began to figure out that something was wrong in there.

Not long after I became aware that demons were real and they did exercise influence, I decided to go in that room and cast them out of our house. We always kept the door to that room closed, so I went in and shut the door behind me. I started rebuking and binding and doing everything I could think of. All the hair on the back of my neck stood up. I was afraid and had goose bumps all over me.

In the midst of all this, I remember thinking, *O God. I'm so glad I can't see into the spirit realm right now. If I could, I'd see these huge demons towering over me with fangs and claws.* I was envisioning these monstrous demonic powers that were inches away from devouring me, and it was only the name of Jesus that was holding them at bay. I remember praying, "O God. Thank You that I can't see what's going on in the spirit realm."

Immediately, the Lord spoke to my heart, saying, *Andrew, if I were to show you the spirit realm, instead of seeing these huge, powerful demons with fangs and claws, you'd see tiny little imps. You'd be amazed. They're nothing. They just have big mouths. They know how to scream loud and intimidate. They boast of great things, but they can't deliver.* As soon as the Lord changed that image from towering demons to tiny little imps who had no power or authority, faith rose up in my heart. Instead of fear, I felt like the Incredible Hulk. A spirit of might and boldness came over me, and I got rid of those demons in no time flat.

Some folks might think, *That was all in your mind*. Well, I didn't tell a single person, but the next time we had a Bible study, people went right into that room without thinking anything about it. There was definitely a difference.

SATAN'S ONLY POWER

After the devil made all his prideful boasts in Isaiah 14:12-14, saying "I will do this, and I will do that," this passage of Scripture goes on to say,

> **Yet thou shalt be brought down to hell, to the sides of the pit. They that see thee shall narrowly look upon thee, and consider thee, saying, Is this the man that made the earth to tremble, that did shake kingdoms; That made the world as a wilderness, and destroyed the cities thereof; that opened not the house of his prisoners?**
>
> Isaiah 14:15-17

This passage prophesied how people would eventually respond to Satan. Of course, all this has come to pass now that Jesus has literally destroyed the devil through His death, burial, and resurrection. When we see Satan as he really is, we'll say, "Is this the one who intimidated me? Is this the one I allowed to ruin my life? Is this the one I let keep me in bondage – this nothing, this zero?" That's how Satan is. He doesn't have all this power the church has represented him with. The only power Satan has came from man.

Mankind made Satan. We are the ones who empowered him. God created Lucifer – a ministering spirit, an angelic being. Man yielded his God-given dominion, and it's this human authority and power Satan uses. That's why he has to have a body to possess. That's why a pig has more power and authority on this earth than a disembodied demon. Satan is a factor, but it's only because people yield to him. If we know the truth, the truth will make us free (John 8:32). Now, that's good news!

IS THIS THE ONE?
Lesson 8 – Outline

I. God is a Spirit, and He gave dominion over this earth to physical human beings (John 4:24 and Gen. 1:26-28).

    A.   In doing so, He limited His own dominion and authority.

    B.   If we don't cooperate with God, we can limit Him.

Yea, they turned back and tempted God, and limited the Holy One of Israel.

Psalm 78:41

    C.   Even the Lord Jesus Christ had to have cooperation from people to release His power into their lives.

He could there do no mighty work…because of their unbelief.

Mark 6:5-6

    D.   God has the power, but He gave dominion over this earth to physical human beings.

    E.   Because of His own integrity, He will not overstep that authority and violate His own Word.

II. God is a God of authority.

    A.   He set structure in place, and He's not going to circumvent it.

    B.   He would not intervene in the affairs of man until He became a man.

    C.   Once He took upon Himself the form of flesh, then He had the authority to take it to the devil.

III. The power and authority that Satan has used to rule this earth has been man's authority that God gave him.

    A.   Understanding that Satan can do nothing in your life without your consent and cooperation puts him down on a plane where he isn't a superior foe.

    B.   As a master deceiver, he's still a threat because he can lie to you.

    C.   You must know the truth and be on guard – but you can resist him.

IV. Isaiah 14:15-17 prophesied how people would eventually respond to Satan:

> **Yet thou shalt be brought down to hell, to the sides of the pit. They that see thee shall narrowly look upon thee, and consider thee, saying, Is this the man that made the earth to tremble, that did shake kingdoms; That made the world as a wilderness, and destroyed the cities thereof; that opened not the house of his prisoners?**

   A. Of course, all this has come to pass now that Jesus has literally destroyed the devil through His death, burial, and resurrection.

   B. When we see Satan as he really is, we'll say, "Is this the one who intimidated me? Is this the one I allowed to ruin my life? Is this the one I let keep me in bondage – this nothing, this zero?"

   C. The only power Satan has came from man.

   D. Satan is a factor, but it's only because people yield to him.

   E. If you know the truth, the truth will make you free (John 8:32).

IS THIS THE ONE?
Lesson 8 – Teacher's Guide

1. God is a Spirit, and He gave dominion over this earth to physical human beings (John 4:24 and Gen. 1:26-28). In doing so, He limited His own dominion and authority. If we don't cooperate with God, we can limit Him (Ps. 78:41). Even the Lord Jesus Christ had to have cooperation from people to release His power into their lives (Mark 6:5-6). God has the power, but He gave dominion over this earth to physical human beings. Because of His own integrity, He will not overstep that authority and violate His own Word.

2. God is a God of authority. He set structure in place, and He's not going to circumvent it. He would not intervene in the affairs of man until He became a man. Once He took upon Himself the form of flesh, then He had the authority to take it to the devil.

3. The power and authority that Satan has used to rule this earth has been man's authority that God gave him. Understanding that Satan can do nothing in our lives without our consent and cooperation puts him down on a plane where he isn't a superior foe. As a master deceiver, he's still a threat because he can lie to us. We must know the truth and be on guard – but we can resist him.

4. Isaiah 14:15-17 prophesied how people would eventually respond to Satan. Of course, all this has come to pass now that Jesus has literally destroyed the devil through His death, burial, and resurrection. When we see Satan as he really is, we'll say, "Is this the one who intimidated me? Is this the one I allowed to ruin my life? Is this the one I let keep me in bondage – this nothing, this zero?" The only power Satan has came from man. Satan is a factor, but it's only because people yield to him. If we know the truth, the truth will make us free (John 8:32).

1. A. Read John 4:24, Genesis 1:26-28, Psalm 78:41, and Mark 6:5-6. What can happen if we don't cooperate with God? (We can limit Him)
   B. Even the Lord Jesus Christ had to have _____ from people to release His power into their lives (Cooperation)
2. A. God is a God of what? (Authority)
   B. He would not intervene in the affairs of man until when? (He became a man)
3. A. What does understanding that Satan can do nothing in our lives without our consent and cooperation do? (It puts him down on a plane where he isn't a superior foe)
   B. Why is he still a threat? (Because as a master deceiver, he can lie to us)
4. A. Read Isaiah 14:15-17 and John 8:32. Jesus has literally destroyed the devil how? (Through His death, burial, and resurrection)
   B. What must we know that will make us free? (The truth)

IS THIS THE ONE?
Lesson 8 – Additional Information

For additional study on this topic, I recommend "The Sovereignty of God," *Taking the Limits Off God*, and *Spiritual Authority*.

IS THIS THE ONE?
Lesson 8 – Discipleship Questions

1. According to James 4:7, who are we to resist?

2. If we submit to God and actively fight against the devil, what will he do?

3. Who does he flee from?

4. James 2:20 reveals that faith without works is _____.

5. What does John 4:24 say we are to do in spirit and in truth?

6. Genesis 1:26-28 tells us that God gave us dominion over every living thing where?

7. The Israelites turned back and tempted whom in Psalm 78:41?

8. Who did they limit?

9. What caused Jesus to marvel in Mark 6:5-6?

10. What does Isaiah 14:12-17 describe Lucifer as the son of?

11. According to John 8:32, what shall we know?

12. What shall the truth make us?

IS THIS THE ONE?
Lesson 8 – Answer Key

1. The devil.
2. Flee from us.
3. You.
4. Dead.
5. Worship Him.
6. That moves on the earth.
7. God.
8. The Holy One of Israel.
9. The people's unbelief.
10. The morning.
11. The truth.
12. Free.

IS THIS THE ONE?
Lesson 8 – Scriptures

Submit yourselves therefore to God. Resist the devil, and he will flee from you.

James 4:7

But wilt thou know, O vain man, that faith without works is dead?

James 2:20

God is a Spirit: and they that worship him must worship him in spirit and in truth.

John 4:24

And God said, Let us make man in our image, after our likeness: and let them have dominion over the fish of the sea, and over the fowl of the air, and over the cattle, and over all the earth, and over every creeping thing that creepeth upon the earth. So God created man in his own image, in the image of God created he him; male and female created he them. And God blessed them, and God said unto them, Be fruitful, and multiply, and replenish the earth, and subdue it: and have dominion over the fish of the sea, and over the fowl of the air, and over every living thing that moveth upon the earth.

Genesis 1:26-28

Yea, they turned back and tempted God, and limited the Holy One of Israel.

Psalm 78:41

And he could there do no mighty work, save that he laid his hands upon a few sick folk, and healed them. And he marvelled because of their unbelief. And he went round about the villages, teaching.

Mark 6:5-6

How art thou fallen from heaven, O Lucifer, son of the morning! how art thou cut down to the ground, which didst weaken the nations! For thou hast said in thine heart, I will ascend into heaven, I will exalt my throne above the stars of God: I will sit also upon the mount of the congregation, in the sides of the north: I will ascend above the heights of the clouds; I will be like the most High. Yet thou shalt be brought down to hell, to the sides of the pit. They that see thee shall narrowly look upon thee, and consider thee, saying, Is this the man that made the earth to tremble, that did shake kingdoms; That made the world as a wilderness, and destroyed the cities thereof; that opened not the house of his prisoners?

Isaiah 14:12-17

And ye shall know the truth, and the truth shall make you free.

John 8:32

SUCH AS I HAVE
Lesson 9

God has given us a huge authority. As born-again believers, Jesus has given us more authority than even Adam and Eve had. They had authority over this earth. However, after Christ rose from the dead, He had authority in heaven, authority on earth, and authority under the earth – meaning the demonic realm and hell (Phil. 2:10). After Jesus resurrected, but before He ascended, He turned to His disciples and said,

> *All power* [authority, power of rule] *is given unto me in heaven and in earth. Go ye therefore, and teach all nations, baptising them in the name of the Father, and of the Son, and of the Holy Ghost: Teaching them to observe all things whatsoever I have commanded you: and, lo, I am with you alway, even unto the end of the world. Amen.*
>
> Matthew 28:18-20, brackets mine

Since **"therefore"** means "in light of what I've just said," Jesus was basically telling His followers, "The authority and power I have, I now give to you. Go, and continue doing My work, the work that I have begun."

The authority we have as believers in Christ today is superior to the authority Adam had. We have everything back that he lost, and much more. We now have authority over the demonic realm (Matt. 10:1 and 7-8).

OLD VS. NEW

Compared to the Old Testament, there is a huge difference in the way the New Testament talks about Satan. Although the Old Testament hardly mentions him, the New Testament reveals that Satan is the one who caused different kinds of sicknesses, seizures, convulsions, and blindness. The New Testament reveals many things as being demonic in origin.

How come God gave us this knowledge in the New Testament but not in the Old? Simply put, even if the Old Testament saints would have known these things, they couldn't have done anything with them. It wouldn't have done them any good to know that Satan was behind certain things, because they didn't have authority to rebuke or bind him.

Basically, the Old Testament people were told, "Just submit to these laws. With your actions, do these things and don't do these others." By yielding their actions to God in this manner, He was empowered to move in their lives. It also limited what Satan could do. Basically, this was the approach in the Old Testament.

In the New Testament, we now have an authority that has been given to us that enables us to go beyond the surface level. Since we've been given authority over demons, we can go behind the scenes and deal with the demonic powers that are causing sicknesses and diseases and are inspiring people to act a certain way. We can see results that Old Testament people could never have seen.

However, along with this superior authority we've been given comes responsibility. This means that since the Lord gave us such power and authority, if we don't use it, then we stop Him from intervening. God flows through us.

GOD'S POWER

Jesus gave us power and authority over the devil.

> **Then he [Jesus] called his twelve disciples together, and gave them power and authority over all devils, and to cure diseases.**
>
> Luke 9:1, brackets mine

"Power" here means that we have the ability and the might. We also have the authority to use that ability and might. But with that authority comes responsibility.

> **Submit yourselves therefore to God. Resist the devil, and he will flee from you.**
>
> James 4:7

That means if we don't resist the devil, he won't flee from us. Although this is very simple, few believers understand it.

Many Christians aren't using the authority that's been given to them. When Satan bothers them – maybe it's through some sickness, disease, poverty, tragedy, or other demonic attack – they approach God as if they don't have any power or authority. They beg God, saying, "O Lord, please change this situation. Please get the devil off my back." They don't realise that this isn't within God's authority – He's given that to us.

This is exactly what Scripture says. "I give you power and authority over all devils" (Luke 9:1). God gave us authority over the devil. If you're being fought by a demonic force, you have the authority to do something about it. Now, you do have to be spiritual enough to discern its origin. Is it truly spiritual or just something completely natural? If it's truly a demonic attack, then you are responsible to get rid of that demon. It's God's power, but that power has been placed under your authority. If you don't use it, it won't be used.

WE MUST USE IT

Many Christians who come to me for counsel and prayer are just powerless. They don't understand that they have any authority. They're begging God, "Please remove this sickness and prosper me financially. Please save this person." They are begging God to do things that He told them they have the authority to do.

When God said "You resist the devil, and he will flee from you," that means that if you don't resist the devil, he won't flee. God isn't going to take care of the devil for you. He's already defeated Satan and stripped him of his power. God gave you authority, and if you don't exercise it, He's not going to come and rebuke the devil for you. The battle isn't between God and the devil directly; it's between the devil and us. God has equipped us with authority and power, and we have to use it.

Some folks wonder, *Well, if it's God's will for us to be healed, then why did this person die?* God gave us the power to heal. It's not our power. It's His power, but it's under our authority. Jesus never told us to pray and ask God to heal people. He told us to go and...

> *Heal the sick.*
>
> Matthew 10:8

In the Gospels, Jesus never commanded His disciples to *pray* for the sick, but He did command them to *heal* the sick (Luke 9:2 and 10:9). The way it's being done in the church today, we basically pray, "O Father. We know that You can do it. If it's Your will, please – pretty please – do it." We come as beggars, asking. And if we don't see something manifest, if we don't see an instant result, then we wonder, *Why didn't God heal them?* No. God has already released all the healing power it takes for every person on this planet to be healed of every sickness and disease. Jesus took the stripes, and now He's given us the power to heal the sick. He gave us power and authority over all demons to cast them out and cure diseases. Jesus gave that power to us, and it's up to us to use it.

WALKING, LEAPING, AND PRAISING GOD

Consider Peter and John at the temple gate.

> *Now Peter and John went up together into the temple at the hour of prayer, being the ninth hour. And a certain man lame from his mother's womb was carried, whom they laid daily at the gate of the temple which is called Beautiful, to ask alms of them that entered into the temple; Who seeing Peter and John about to go into the temple asked an alms. And Peter, fastening his eyes upon him with John, said, Look on us. And he gave heed unto them, expecting to receive something of them.*
>
> Acts 3:1-5

> *Then Peter said, Silver and gold have I none; but such as I have give I thee: In the name of Jesus Christ of Nazareth rise up and walk. And he took him by the right hand, and lifted him up: and immediately his feet and ankle bones received strength. And he leaping up stood, and walked, and entered with them into the temple, walking, and leaping, and praising God.*
>
> Acts 3:6-8, emphasis mine

Notice in verse 6 that Peter said, **"Such as I have, give I thee."** Peter and John would be kicked out of most churches around the world today for saying, "I have the power to heal you." It's become fashionable for us to say, "Oh, it's not me. I couldn't heal a gnat." Well, the truth is none of us can heal a gnat in our own human power. But we aren't only human. We're born again! And God gave us power and authority – the right and ability to use that power. So Peter was absolutely correct when he said, **"Such as I have, give I thee."**

Notice in this instance that Peter never even prayed a prayer. Most people would think that was terrible. *How dare him heal someone without praying and asking God!* I don't know about you, but I'm after results – and Peter got the right results. His approach to this situation is the proper approach. Peter said, **"Such as I have, give I thee."** Peter knew he had power. He knew he had the authority to use that power. So he took his responsibility and gave it. Because of it, that man was healed.

This is the very reason many people aren't seeing healing today. They're coming to God and begging Him. They don't understand that the power doesn't reside in heaven. God has placed the power to heal on the inside of every born-again believer. He's also given us the authority to use it, which makes us responsible. If someone isn't healed, it's not God who didn't heal them – it's us not using our authority and power.

IT'S OUR TURN

Of course, there may be some other dynamics involved. It's not always the individual's fault receiving the prayer. It could be the fault of the other people around them. Jesus operated in absolute faith, but He had to put out scoffers and unbelievers. Christ operated in faith perfectly, yet…

He could there do no mighty work…because of their unbelief.

Mark 6:5-6

The limit wasn't in Him, but in the people around Him. The limit isn't always in the person receiving the healing. It could be other factors round about. However, it always comes back to some person or group of people who are limiting God because they aren't taking the authority He has given them and exercising it. We are shirking our responsibility, and we're trying to put all the responsibility on God, saying it's His fault whether or not this person gets saved, healed, or prospered. That's absolutely wrong.

We need to understand and recognise that it's not God's turn to heal. It's our turn to believe that He's already healed. We must accept that power, take that authority, and use it. We need to speak to our problems and command things to change.

If we could get this truth down, it would make a huge difference in the way things happen today. The vast majority of the body of Christ believes that God can do whatever He wants, but they don't believe that He's already done it. They don't believe that He's given us the power to do it. Therefore, they don't feel any responsibility to take and use their authority. This is where it's breaking down.

God has already done His part. He's placed the power and authority on the inside of us, which makes us responsible.

WE WERE HEALED

Through the death, burial, and resurrection of the Lord Jesus Christ, God has already done His part. Now it is up to you to respond in faith and receive His provision. It's totally your responsibility to get healed, prospered, and delivered. It's God's power, but He's placed it under your authority.

Although I'm strongly emphasising your responsibility, there's no need to come under any condemnation (Rom. 8:1). The Lord loves you and wants you to understand these truths so you can enjoy the abundant life He's provided. That's why it's so important to understand your responsibility.

You may be asking, "So do I have to make all this happen?" Not out of your self – your human ability. The born-again part of you – your spirit – has God's power within. All things are possible to those who believe (Mark 9:23). If you would understand and believe that God has already done His part and then exercise your authority, you could make things happen.

Since I've understood and applied these truths, I've seen a huge improvement in my life and ministry. I've prayed for people to be healed for many years. In the beginning, I'd see someone healed every once in a while, but I didn't have a clue what I was doing. Even an old blind squirrel will come up with a nut every once in a while if he just keeps trying. I just prayed for so many people that every once in a while, something would happen and we'd see healing manifest.

However, since then, I've come to realise that it's not me petitioning and asking the Lord to heal people, but rather that God has already healed us of all sickness and disease. The Word says that by His stripes we *were* – past tense – healed (1 Pet. 2:24). Now I understand that God has put His power in me, and it's up to me to release it. God has done His part. Now I must take my authority, speak to the mountain, and command people to be healed. Of course, the individual I'm ministering to must believe and cooperate too, but I've seen hundreds of times more people healed than I used to.

JOHN G. LAKE

John G. Lake had a healing ministry back in the early 1900s. He was so effective in ministering healing that the state of Washington actually gave him a medical license. He opened up a hospital in Spokane, where he lived, and saw so many documented cases of people being healed that they literally closed one of the other hospitals in town.

In Lake's hospital, they didn't administer medicine. They just brought the Word to the patients, anointed them, and prayed with them until they saw the healing manifest. He trained others how to minister healing and called them "practitioners." For cases that couldn't come to the hospital, Lake sent out his practitioners to make house calls. Based on James 5:14-15, he'd give them a little bottle of oil and tell them, "Don't come back until they're healed."

This kind of boldness just startles people today. They think, *How could you do that? You don't have any control over this. You don't have that kind of authority. You don't have any responsibility. Just go out and ask God to heal them. He might, He might not. Whatever will be, will be. It's all up to God, you see.* Not true.

John G. Lake and his practitioners knew that God had already done His part to provide healing and that it's our turn to take our authority and use it. The longest time any of those practitioners stayed out ministering was about thirty days. Sometimes they would literally move in with the people and teach them the Word. They'd build them up in faith, minister to them, and see them healed because God had already done His part.

There's a huge difference between us healing the sick and praying for the sick. As a whole, the church has believed that God can do it but not that He has done it. They don't believe that He has already committed that power and authority to us. So when they have a need, they approach God like a beggar. They ask Him to heal so and so, when the truth is that He's already done His part to produce that healing. God has placed supernatural raising-from-the-dead power on the inside of every born-again believer (Eph. 1:19-20), and as believers, it's up to us to command those healings to come to pass. Instead of passively pleading with the Lord and asking Him to do it, we need to become commanders – someone who stands up in faith, takes their authority in Christ, and commands the power of God.

SUCH AS I HAVE
Lesson 9 – Outline

I. As born-again believers, Jesus has given us more authority than even Adam and Eve had.

> ***Jesus came and spake unto them, saying, All power*** [authority, power of rule] ***is given unto me in heaven and in earth. Go ye therefore, and teach all nations, baptising them in the name of the Father, and of the Son, and of the Holy Ghost: Teaching them to observe all things whatsoever I have commanded you: and, lo, I am with you alway, even unto the end of the world. Amen.***
>
> Matthew 28:18-20, brackets mine

    A. Jesus gave us power and authority over the devil (Matt. 10:1 and 7-8).

> ***Then he*** [Jesus] ***called his twelve disciples together, and gave them power and authority over all devils, and to cure diseases.***
>
> Luke 9:1, brackets mine

    B. With that authority comes responsibility.

> ***Submit yourselves therefore to God. Resist the devil, and he will flee from you.***
>
> James 4:7

    C. It's God's power, but that power has been placed under your authority.

    D. The battle isn't between God and the devil directly; it's between the devil and us.

    E. God has equipped us with authority and power, and we have to use it.

II. In the Gospels, Jesus never commanded His disciples to *pray* for the sick, but He did command them to *heal* the sick (Luke 9:2 and 10:9).

    A. God has already released all the healing power it takes for every person on this planet to be healed of every sickness and disease.

    B. Jesus took the stripes, and now He's given us the power to heal the sick.

    C. He gave us power and authority over all demons to cast them out and cure diseases.

    D. Consider Peter and John at the temple gate.

> ***Now Peter and John went up together into the temple at the hour of prayer, being the ninth hour. And a certain man lame from his mother's womb was carried, whom they laid daily at the gate of the temple which is called Beautiful, to ask alms of them that entered into the temple; Who seeing Peter and John about to go into the temple asked an alms. And***

> *Peter, fastening his eyes upon him with John, said, Look on us. And he gave heed unto them, expecting to receive something of them.*
>
> Acts 3:1-5

> *Then Peter said, Silver and gold have I none; but such as I have give I thee: In the name of Jesus Christ of Nazareth rise up and walk. And he took him by the right hand, and lifted him up: and immediately his feet and ankle bones received strength. And he leaping up stood, and walked, and entered with them into the temple, walking, and leaping, and praising God.*
>
> Acts 3:6-8

III. God has placed the power to heal on the inside of every born-again believer.

  A. He's also given us the authority to use it, which makes us responsible.

  B. If someone isn't healed, it's not God who didn't heal them – it's us not using our authority and power.

  C. Of course, there may be some other dynamics involved.

  D. However, it always comes back to some person or group of people who are limiting God because they aren't taking the authority God has given them and exercising it (Mark 6:5-6).

IV. Through the death, burial, and resurrection of the Lord Jesus Christ, God has already done His part.

  A. It's God's power, but He's placed it under your authority.

  B. Although I'm strongly emphasising your responsibility, there's no need to come under any condemnation (Rom. 8:1).

  C. The Lord loves you and wants you to understand these truths so you can enjoy the abundant life He's provided.

  D. If you would understand and believe that God has already done His part and then exercise your authority, you could make things happen.

  E. God has placed supernatural raising-from-the-dead power on the inside of every born-again believer, and as believers it's up to us to command those healings to come to pass (Eph. 1:19-20).

SUCH AS I HAVE
Lesson 9 – Teacher's Guide

1. As born-again believers, Jesus has given us more authority than even Adam and Eve had (Matt. 28:18-20). Jesus gave us power and authority over the devil (Matt. 10:1, 7-8; and Luke 9:1). With that authority comes responsibility (James 4:7). It's God's power, but that power has been placed under our authority. The battle isn't between God and the devil directly; it's between the devil and us. God has equipped us with authority and power, and we have to use it.

2. In the Gospels, Jesus never commanded His disciples to *pray* for the sick, but He did command them to *heal* the sick (Luke 9:2 and 10:9). God has already released all the healing power it takes for every person on this planet to be healed of every sickness and disease. Jesus took the stripes, and now He's given us the power to heal the sick. He gave us power and authority over all demons to cast them out and cure diseases. Consider Peter and John at the temple gate (Acts 3:1-8).

3. God has placed the power to heal on the inside of every born-again believer. He's also given us the authority to use it, which makes us responsible. If someone isn't healed, it's not God who didn't heal them – it's us not using our authority and power. Of course, there may be some other dynamics involved. However, it always comes back to some person or group of people who are limiting God because they aren't taking the authority God has given them and exercising it (Mark 6:5-6).

4. Through the death, burial, and resurrection of the Lord Jesus Christ, God has already done His part. It's God's power, but He's placed it under our authority. Although I'm strongly emphasising our responsibility, there's no need to come under any condemnation (Rom. 8:1). The Lord loves us and wants us to understand these truths so we can enjoy the abundant life He's provided. If we would understand and believe that God has already done His part and then exercise our authority, we could make things happen. God has placed supernatural raising-from-the-dead power on the inside of every born-again believer, and as believers, it's up to us to command those healings to come to pass (Eph. 1:19-20).

---

1. A. Read Matthew 28:18-20, 10:1, 7-8; Luke 9:1; and James 4:7. What has Jesus given us over the devil? (Power and authority)
   B. What does that authority come with? (Responsibility)
2. A. Read Luke 9:2, 10:9; and Acts 3:18. In the Gospels, what did Jesus command us to do – pray for the sick or heal them? (Heal them)
   B. What has God already released? (All the healing power it takes for every person on this planet to be healed of every sickness and disease)
3. A. Read Mark 6:5-6. Where has God placed the power to heal? (On the inside of every born-again believer)
   B. What makes us responsible? (He's also given us the authority to use it)
4. A. Read Romans 8:1 and Ephesians 1:19-20. God has already done His part through what? (The death, burial, and resurrection of the Lord Jesus Christ)
   B. Why does the Lord want us to understand these truths? (So we can enjoy the abundant life He's provided)

SUCH AS I HAVE
Lesson 9 – Additional Information

For additional information about what God has already done and what He's placed inside of you as a born-again believer, I recommend *Spirit, Soul & Body* and *You've Already Got It!* These two teachings are foundational and will really help you receive and experience God's best.

SUCH AS I HAVE
Lesson 9 – Discipleship Questions

1. According to Philippians 2:10, what should bow at the name of Jesus?

2. Who did Jesus tell us to go and teach in Matthew 28:18-20?

3. What are we to teach them?

4. According to Matthew 10:1 and 7-8, Jesus gave His disciples power and commanded them to do what?

5. In Luke 9:1-2, Jesus gave them power and authority over what?

6. Luke 10:9 instructs us to heal the sick and then say what to them?

7. According to Acts 3:1-8, in whose name did Peter command this man to rise up and walk?

8. Romans 8:1 declares that there is now no _____ to those who are in Christ Jesus.

9. According to Mark 9:23, what is possible to them that believe?

10. What does 1 Peter 2:24 say that we, being dead to sins, should live unto?

11. By Jesus' stripes we were what?

12. James 5:14-15 instructs a sick person to call for whom?

13. What shall save/heal the sick?

14. According to Ephesians 1:19-20, His power is to us who _____.

15. This is the same power God wrought in Christ when He raised Him from the dead and set Him where?

SUCH AS I HAVE
Lesson 9 – Answer Key

1. Every knee.

2. All nations.

3. To observe all things whatsoever Jesus has commanded us.

4. Heal the sick, cleanse the lepers, raise the dead, and cast out devils.

5. All devils and to cure diseases.

6. The kingdom of God is come nigh unto you.

7. Jesus Christ of Nazareth.

8. Condemnation.

9. All things.

10. Righteousness.

11. Healed.

12. The elders of the church.

13. The prayer of faith.

14. Believe.

15. At His own right hand in the heavenly places.

SUCH AS I HAVE
Lesson 9 – Scriptures

That at the name of Jesus every knee should bow, of things in heaven, and things in earth, and things under the earth.

Philippians 2:10

And Jesus came and spake unto them, saying, All power is given unto me in heaven and in earth. Go ye therefore, and teach all nations, baptising them in the name of the Father, and of the Son, and of the Holy Ghost: Teaching them to observe all things whatsoever I have commanded you: and, lo, I am with you alway, even unto the end of the world. Amen.

Matthew 28:18-20

And when he had called unto him his twelve disciples, he gave them power against unclean spirits, to cast them out, and to heal all manner of sickness and all manner of disease.

Matthew 10:1

And as ye go, preach, saying, The kingdom of heaven is at hand. Heal the sick, cleanse the lepers, raise the dead, cast out devils: freely ye have received, freely give.

Matthew 10:7-8

Then he called his twelve disciples together, and gave them power and authority over all devils, and to cure diseases. And he sent them to preach the kingdom of God, and to heal the sick.

Luke 9:1-2

Submit yourselves therefore to God. Resist the devil, and he will flee from you.

James 4:7

And heal the sick that are therein, and say unto them, The kingdom of God is come nigh unto you.

Luke 10:9

Now Peter and John went up together into the temple at the hour of prayer, being the ninth hour. And a certain man lame from his mother's womb was carried, whom they laid daily at the gate of the temple which is called Beautiful, to ask alms of them that entered into the temple; Who seeing Peter and John about to go into the temple asked an alms. And Peter, fastening his eyes upon him with John, said, Look on us. And he gave heed unto them, expecting to receive something of them.

Acts 3:1-5

Then Peter said, Silver and gold have I none; but such as I have give I thee: In the name of Jesus Christ of Nazareth rise up and walk. And he took him by the right hand, and lifted him up: and immediately his feet and ankle bones received strength. And he leaping up stood, and walked, and entered with them into the temple, walking, and leaping, and praising God.

Acts 3:6-8

And he could there do no mighty work, save that he laid his hands upon a few sick folk, and healed them. And he marvelled because of their unbelief. And he went round about the villages, teaching.

Mark 6:5-6

THERE is therefore now no condemnation to them which are in Christ Jesus, who walk not after the flesh, but after the Spirit.

Romans 8:1

Jesus said unto him, If thou canst believe, all things are possible to him that believeth.

Mark 9:23

Who his own self bare our sins in his own body on the tree, that we, being dead to sins, should live unto righteousness: by whose stripes ye were healed.

1 Peter 2:24

Is any sick among you? let him call for the elders of the church; and let them pray over him, anointing him with oil in the name of the Lord: And the prayer of faith shall save the sick, and the Lord shall raise him up; and if he have committed sins, they shall be forgiven him.

James 5:14-15

And what is the exceeding greatness of his power to us-ward who believe, according to the working of his mighty power, Which he wrought in Christ, when he raised him from the dead, and set him at his own right hand in the heavenly places.

Ephesians 1:19-20

COMMAND YE ME
Lesson 10

Peter stood up in faith, took his authority in Christ, and commanded the power of God.

Such as I have give I thee: In the name of Jesus Christ of Nazareth rise up and walk. And he took him by the right hand, and lifted him up: and immediately his feet and ankle bones received strength. And he leaping up stood, and walked, and entered with them into the temple, walking, and leaping, and praising God.

Acts 3:6-8

Most people say, "Well, I'd never do that," which is why you aren't getting the results that Peter and John did. This is one of the major reasons we aren't seeing the power of God manifest more today.

Many Christians are in need of a miracle. It's critical. Maybe you need healing in your body, a financial provision, or restoration in your marriage. Whatever it is, you are praying and asking God, but you aren't taking any authority over the Enemy, you aren't speaking against the problem, and you aren't commanding the infirmity to leave. You're acting like a beggar instead of the commander Christ has authorised and empowered you to be.

OLD SINNER OR SAVED BY GRACE?

Religion says, "You can't do anything. You're a worm. You are nothing." That's true if you're talking about your carnal, natural, fleshly self. Jesus said,

Without me ye can do nothing.

John 15:5

That is absolutely true. Apart from Christ, we are and can do nothing. However, we are not without Jesus. We are born again. The Spirit of the Living God dwells on the inside of us. We're not only human. Jesus Himself lives in and through us (Gal. 2:20).

Christians who don't recognise that in, Christ they've become brand-new creations aren't taking their God-given authority. They don't understand the authority of the believer. They come to God as beggars, saying, "I'm an old sinner saved by grace."

I'm not an old sinner saved by grace. I was an old sinner, but then I got saved by grace. Now I've become the righteousness of God in Christ Jesus (2 Cor. 5:21). It's true that without God, I'm nothing, but I'm not without God. He lives on the inside of me. Now I have the authority and power to command the power of God.

UNDER YOUR COMMAND

Now, this authority that Jesus has given us only enforces spiritual law. If God hasn't provided something, then we can't just command it. Taking and using the authority Jesus has given isn't us "making" God do things.

> **Thus saith the LORD, the Holy One of Israel, and his Maker, Ask me of things to come concerning my sons, and** concerning the work of my hands command ye me.
>
> Isaiah 45:11, emphasis mine

The last part of this verse is a strong statement that many people choke on. They can't receive it because they think to do so would be to take authority over God and tell Him, "Lord, You obey me. I command You to do this." Certainly, that's ridiculous.

I am not God. I'm not superior to Him. It's not me that is the power source. God isn't waiting on my every whim, and He isn't obeying what I tell Him to do. That's not what Isaiah 45:11 is talking about. The Lord said, "Concerning the work of My hands, you command Me." This means that God has told me to command the work of His hands – which is everything He's already provided in Christ – into manifestation.

It's like electricity. The power company is the source – they generate the power. You aren't the power source. You could stick a light bulb in your mouth, but it'll never come on. The power company generates the power and delivers it to your home. You've signed a contract, and that power is under your command.

If you want the light to come on, you don't call the power company and ask them to come out and turn it on. They've already generated that power and delivered it to you. Now it's up to you to command that power. When you flip that switch, you are commanding that power. You aren't the source, but the power is under your control. It's under your authority. So you use that authority and switch it on.

FLIP THE SWITCH

Now, if the power company doesn't generate the electricity, you could flip that switch all you want. But if there's no power there, nothing is going to happen.

If someone who wasn't yet born again tried to speak to sickness, or a demon, and command it to leave, it wouldn't work. Nothing would happen because they don't have the power of God inside of them. This is what happened to the seven sons of Sceva (Acts 19:11-16). These lost men saw Paul expelling demons in the name of Jesus and tried to do the same. But the demons inside of the man they were trying to deliver rose up and caused him to beat up those seven lost men and send them away bleeding. If you aren't connected to the power source, if you aren't truly born again, you can't do what I'm sharing with you. But if you are truly born again and have received the power of the Holy Spirit according to Acts 1:8, then that power is in you, and it's up to you to command it.

If you called the power company and said, "I have some friends coming over for lunch. Would you please turn on the power? I need it to cook the food, have light, and play soft music." It doesn't matter how much you plead or how serious your need is, the power company isn't going to send somebody out to flip the switch for you. They generate the power, but you must take your position of authority and flip the switch.

Many Christians today are praying and asking God to come over and flip their switches. They don't realise that He's placed that power on the inside of them. They don't recognise their responsibility to flip their own switches. They aren't believing God's Word, which reveals they now have the power, authority, and responsibility to heal the sick. Instead of commanding and releasing this power that's been given to them, they pray and ask God to heal the sick. That's just as silly as asking the electric company to come over and turn on your lights!

"THE DONKEY I RIDE ON"

One of the first times a friend of mine went to Africa to minister, God dealt with him on this very issue. At his meetings, he saw all kinds of great miracles, including many people healed. As a result of this, the African people were just overwhelmed. As my friend walked through the city streets, people would run up to him screaming, yelling, and wanting to touch him. His first reaction was, "It's not me. It's God. Don't look to me!" But before he could say anything, the Lord spoke to his heart, saying, "When I rode into Jerusalem, all the people were throwing palm branches and garments down in My path, singing 'Hosanna – glory to God in the highest!' What would you have thought if that donkey I was riding on would have said, 'Oh, it's not me. It's not me'?" The Lord continued, saying, "It's not you that they are yelling about and trying to touch – it's Me. You're just the donkey that I ride on." Once my friend saw that, he started walking around and letting people touch him.

Some people take offense at this and say, "You just think you're somebody special!" No, I'm nobody special. There is nothing special in me, but I carry the most special Person who has ever walked the face of this earth. The Lord Jesus Christ lives on the inside of me, and He's given me His power and anointing. Just like Peter's shadow touched people and they were healed, I'm believing for a day when my shadow will do the same. I'm believing they will lay sick in the streets and my shadow will fall upon them and heal them. Some people might think, *Well, you arrogant thing!* It's not me; it's who I carry. He's the same Person Peter carried. If it worked for him, it'll work for me.

So many Christians are so focused on the physical, carnal, natural side of who they are that they don't recognise that they aren't only human. They don't realise that they've been given supernatural power and authority. That's why they aren't seeing the power of God.

There is a religious culture today that is against everything I'm teaching. It comes against this authority and tries to make you feel like you're nothing, that you have no power and no authority. It says you are to come to God as a beggar, pleading with Him to do what He's told you in His Word that He's already done. But God's told you to go out and represent Him. Therefore, stop begging and pleading, bawling and squalling, and asking Him to do things that it's not His turn to do. Take a stand, use your authority, and command things to come to pass.

JOE BLOW BELIEVER

Jesus commissioned His disciples and sent them out, saying,

> **Heal the sick, cleanse the lepers, raise the dead, cast out devils: freely ye have received, freely give.**
>
> Matthew 10:8

You can't give away something you don't have. If you don't believe that God has already done His part and put that raising-from-the-dead power on the inside of you, then you can't go out and heal the sick, cleanse the lepers, or raise the dead. I wish I could just make you believe these truths, but I know I'm fighting against hundreds of years of religious traditions that have made the Word of God of none effect (Mark 7:13). God has already healed every person that will ever be healed. That power has already been generated and is now deposited on the inside of every born-again, Spirit-filled, tongue-talking believer. You have that power. It's not up to God to heal the sick. It's up to us to believe, take our authority, release that power, and command these things to happen. We must give – minister – this healing power to other people.

I really enjoy watching our Charis Bible College students and alumni minister at our citywide meetings (*Gospel Truth Seminars*). In the past, when I ministered in churches, after I built the people's faith up with the Word, I'd stay there praying with them for hours. The people would come to me by the hundreds, and I would pray for them and see blind eyes and deaf ears open, many miracles, and healings. After three or four hours of that, I was excited, but I was also worn out. I knew I was limited. I'd see all the people lined up for prayer and know that I wouldn't be able to make it to the end of the line. People couldn't wait that long, so they'd leave because I just couldn't minister to them.

Then we started going into these larger venues, and instead of having two or three hundred people, we started having five hundred, even a thousand, people come to my meetings. There was just no way I could minister to all of them. So the Lord told me to teach these truths to our Bible College students, that they have the power on the inside of them and can command healings to come to pass. Now I have these students and alumni help me minister in these larger meetings. Instead of me only being able to pray for a hundred or so people, together we're praying for four or five hundred people per night. We're seeing blind eyes and deaf ears open, people come out of wheelchairs, and all kinds of miracles. I'm thrilled to know that it isn't just a supernatural gift flowing through one individual that everything has to funnel through. This is for Joe Blow believer!

MINISTER HIS POWER TO OTHERS

One of our prayer ministers had never prayed for another person and seen a physical miracle happen in his life. The very first night he began to pray with people, he ministered to a blind man who received his sight. This fellow who had never prayed for another person in all his life was so excited that he didn't sleep all night. He came back the next day telling everyone on the team all about it.

I'm not against people who have a supernatural gift. There is a place for that in the body of Christ. But some folks have thought that they have to be one of these healing evangelist miracle ministers in order to be able to pray for people. No, that's not so. Every born-again, Spirit-filled believer has been given power and authority to heal the sick, cleanse the lepers, and raise the dead (Matt. 10:8). The Lord has commanded us to give – minister – that power to other people.

COMMAND YE ME
Lesson 10 – Outline

I. Are you acting like a beggar instead of the commander Christ has authorised and empowered you to be?

> **Then Peter said, Silver and gold have I none; but such as I have give I thee: In the name of Jesus Christ of Nazareth rise up and walk. And he took him by the right hand, and lifted him up: and immediately his feet and ankle bones received strength. And he leaping up stood, and walked, and entered with them into the temple, walking, and leaping, and praising God.**
>
> Acts 3:6-8

   A. Christians who don't recognise that in Christ, they've become brand-new creations aren't taking their God-given authority.

   B. I was an old sinner, but then I got saved by grace.

   C. Now I've become the righteousness of God in Christ Jesus (2 Cor. 5:21).

   D. It's true that without God, I'm nothing, but I'm not without God – He lives on the inside of me.

   E. Now I have the authority and power to command the power of God.

II. Now, this authority that Jesus has given us only enforces spiritual law.

   A. If God hasn't provided something, then we can't just command it.

   B. Taking and using the authority Jesus has given isn't us "making" God do things.

   > **Thus saith the LORD, the Holy One of Israel, and his Maker, Ask me of things to come concerning my sons, and** concerning the work of my hands command ye me.
   >
   > Isaiah 45:11, emphasis mine

   C. This means that God has told me to command the work of His hands – which is everything He's already provided in Christ – into manifestation.

III. It's like electricity.

   A. The power company generates the power and delivers it to your home.

   B. You've signed a contract, and that power is under your command.
   C. If you want the light to come on, you don't call the power company and ask them to come out and turn it on.

D. They generate the power, but you must take your position of authority and flip the switch.

IV. Jesus commissioned His disciples and sent them out, saying,

> **Heal the sick, cleanse the lepers, raise the dead, cast out devils: freely ye have received, freely give.**
>
> Matthew 10:8

A. If you don't believe that God has already done His part and put that raising-from-the-dead power on the inside of you, then you can't heal the sick, cleanse the lepers, or raise the dead.

B. God's healing power has already been generated and is now deposited on the inside of every born-again, Spirit-filled, tongue-talking believer.

C. It's not up to God to heal the sick.

D. It's up to us to believe, take our authority, release that power, and command these things to happen.

E. We must give – minister – this healing power to other people.

COMMAND YE ME
Lesson 10 – Teacher's Guide

1. Are we acting like beggars instead of the commanders Christ has authorised and empowered us to be? (Acts 3:6-8.) If we as Christians don't recognise that in Christ, we've become brand-new creations, we aren't taking our God-given authority.

   I was an old sinner, but then I got saved by grace. Now I've become the righteousness of God in Christ Jesus (2 Cor. 5:21). It's true that without God, I'm nothing, but I'm not without God – He lives on the inside of me. Now I have the authority and power to command the power of God.

2. Now, this authority that Jesus has given us only enforces spiritual law. If God hasn't provided something, then we can't just command it. Taking and using the authority Jesus has given isn't us "making" God do things (Is. 45:11); it means that God has told me to command the work of His hands – which is everything He's already provided in Christ – into manifestation.

3. It's like electricity. The power company generates the power and delivers it to our homes. We've signed a contract, and that power is under our command. If we want the light to come on, we don't call the power company and ask them to come out and turn it on. They generate the power, but we must take our position of authority and flip the switches.

4. Jesus commissioned His disciples and sent them out, saying, **"Heal the sick, cleanse the lepers, raise the dead, cast out devils: freely ye have received, freely give"** (Matt. 10:8). If we don't believe that God has already done His part and put that raising-from-the-dead power on the inside of us, then we can't go out and heal the sick, cleanse the lepers, or raise the dead. God's healing power has already been generated and is now deposited on the inside of every born-again, Spirit-filled, tongue-talking believer. It's not up to God to heal the sick. It's up to us to believe, take our authority, release that power, and command these things to happen. We must give – minister – this healing power to other people.

---

1. A. Read Acts 3:6-8 and 2 Corinthians 5:21. Instead of beggars, what should we be acting like? (The commanders Christ has authorised and empowered us to be)
   B. Who isn't taking their God-given authority? (Christians who don't recognise that in Christ, they've become brand-new creations)
2. A. Read Isaiah 45:11. What does this authority that Jesus has given us enforce? (Spiritual law)
   B. God has told us to command into manifestation the work of His hands, which is what? (Everything He's already provided in Christ)
3. A. Who generates the power and delivers it to our homes? (The power company)
   B. They generate the power, but in order to turn the light on, we must do what? (Take our position of authority and flip the switches)
4. A. Read Matthew 10:8. What has already been generated and is now deposited on the inside of every born-again, Spirit-filled, tongue-talking believer? (God's healing – raising-from-the-dead – power)
   B. Who must give – minister – this healing power to other people? (We must)

COMMAND YE ME
Lesson 10 – Discipleship Questions

1. In Acts 3:6-8, the healed man entered with them into the temple how?

2. According to John 15:5, Jesus is the vine and we are the what?

3. What can we do without Him?

4. According to Galatians 2:20, who is crucified with Christ?

5. The life that I now live in the flesh, I live by the faith of whom?

6. According to 2 Corinthians 5:21, Jesus was made sin for us so that we might be made what?

7. What did God say in Isaiah 45:11 that we are to command?

8. Acts 19:11-16 tells about the seven sons of whom?

9. Although they weren't born again themselves, they were trying to use the name of Jesus (whom Paul preached) to do what?

10. According to Acts 1:8, when shall we receive power?

11. When that happens, what shall we be?

12. Where?

13. According to Jesus in Matthew 10:8, why are we to freely give?

14. In Mark 7:13, how were the religious leaders making the Word of God of none effect?

COMMAND YE ME
Lesson 10 – Answer Key

1. Walking, leaping, and praising God.

2. Branches.

3. Nothing.

4. We are.

5. The Son of God.

6. The righteousness of God in Him.

7. The work of His hands.

8. Sceva.

9. Cast out evil spirits.

10. After the Holy Spirit is come upon us.

11. Witnesses unto Jesus.

12. Both in Jerusalem and in all Judea and in Samaria and to the uttermost part of the earth.

13. Because we have freely received.

14. Through their traditions.

COMMAND YE ME
Lesson 10 – Scriptures

Then Peter said, Silver and gold have I none; but such as I have give I thee: In the name of Jesus Christ of Nazareth rise up and walk. And he took him by the right hand, and lifted him up: and immediately his feet and ankle bones received strength. And he leaping up stood, and walked, and entered with them into the temple, walking, and leaping, and praising God.

Acts 3:6-8

I am the vine, ye are the branches: He that abideth in me, and I in him, the same bringeth forth much fruit: for without me ye can do nothing.

John 15:5

I am crucified with Christ: nevertheless I live; yet not I, but Christ liveth in me: and the life which I now live in the flesh I live by the faith of the Son of God, who loved me, and gave himself for me.

Galatians 2:20

For he hath made him to be sin for us, who knew no sin; that we might be made the righteousness of God in him.

2 Corinthians 5:21

Thus saith the LORD, the Holy One of Israel, and his Maker, Ask me of things to come concerning my sons, and concerning the work of my hands command ye me.

Isaiah 45:11

And God wrought special miracles by the hands of Paul: So that from his body were brought unto the sick handkerchiefs or aprons, and the diseases departed from them, and the evil spirits went out of them. Then certain of the vagabond Jews, exorcists, took upon them to call over them which had evil spirits the name of the Lord Jesus, saying, We adjure you by Jesus whom Paul preacheth. And there were seven sons of one Sceva, a Jew, and chief of the priests, which did so. And the evil spirit answered and said, Jesus I know, and Paul I know; but who are ye? And the man in whom the evil spirit was leaped on them, and overcame them, and prevailed against them, so that they fled out of that house naked and wounded.

Acts 19:11-16

But ye shall receive power, after that the Holy Ghost is come upon you: and ye shall be witnesses unto me both in Jerusalem, and in all Judaea, and in Samaria, and unto the uttermost part of the earth.

Acts 1:8

Heal the sick, cleanse the lepers, raise the dead, cast out devils: freely ye have received, freely give.

Matthew 10:8

Making the word of God of none effect through your tradition, which ye have delivered: and many such like things do ye.

Mark 7:13

PROCLAIM AND DEMONSTRATE
Lesson 11

Whatsoever city ye enter…heal the sick that are therein, and say unto them, The kingdom of God is come nigh unto you.

Luke 10:8-9

Jesus told us to heal the sick *and* preach the kingdom of God. However, so many of us have chosen to ignore the first part of our commission. Proclamation and demonstration should always go hand in hand. God's Word needs to be confirmed with signs, wonders, and miracles.

The Spirit-filled side of the church desires to see miracles and healings, but the way so many of them are going about it is to beg and plead with God, saying, "O God, I ask You to pour out Your Spirit. Do a new thing, and send revival." That's not the approach the people in the Bible took. They believed that God had given them the authority. They went out and brought revival, commanded revival, and released revival by seeing miracles happen.

MORE THAN JUST DOCTRINE

Consider the disciples who had been arrested and commanded not to preach the Gospel anymore.

Being let go, they went to their own company, and reported all that the chief priests and elders had said unto them. And when they heard that, they lifted up their voice to God with one accord, and said, Lord…behold their threatenings: and grant unto thy servants, that with all boldness they may speak thy word, by stretching forth thine hand to heal; and that signs and wonders may be done by the name of thy holy child Jesus.

Acts 4:23-24 and 29-30

Notice how they prayed. "God, help us to preach Your Word." How? "By stretching forth Your hand to heal." This is the way the early New Testament church preached the Gospel. It wasn't just doctrine. There was both proclamation and demonstration in the power of the Spirit. They prayed, "Lord, help us to preach Your Word *by* healing the sick and seeing Your power manifest." That's how they went out to minister, and that's the reason they saw better results than most folks are getting today.

There ought to be a difference between how you preach and how false religions preach. They aren't truly born again. They don't accept Jesus as the only begotten Son of God, the only way to the Father. Yet, when many Christians go out and knock on a door, they are no different than a Jehovah's Witness or a Mormon. All they have is a doctrine. Proper doctrine is important, but it's not the only thing that should separate a true believer in Christ from one who isn't. A true Christian is a person who not only has a proper doctrine about who Jesus is, but who can also demonstrate it by the power and gifts of the Holy Spirit. The reason that isn't happening more is because God is being asked to do what He commanded the believer to do.

COMMAND HEALING TO MANIFEST

The Lord told us to go heal the sick. He didn't tell us to pray and ask Him to heal the sick. Jesus told us to do it. God is the power source, but He's placed that power on the inside of us. He gave us the authority to use His name and use His power. If we don't command healing to come, it won't happen. It's not going to come by us begging and asking God to heal.

Perhaps you know someone who has an incurable disease. You've been praying and asking God to heal them. You've been trying to lay hold of God for healing, and you haven't seen the manifestation yet. You're fighting fear, doubt, and frustration. You need to recognise that you're asking God to do what He asked you to do. God told you to go heal the sick. He told you to give – minister – His healing power. Just like Peter and John, you need to take your authority and command healing to manifest.

Cecil Paxton trains people how to receive and minister healing. He used to oversee our Helpline, but now he travels widely, preaching, teaching, and ministering all around the world. Back when he lived in Colorado Springs, a mutual friend of ours had a stroke and went blind. Cecil went over to this guy's house and ministered to him. He used his authority and commanded the man's eyes to open. In an instant, those totally blind eyes opened, and he could see perfectly. Cecil took his authority in Christ, commanded the healing to manifest, and it did.

GOD'S WILL

God desires for every person to respond to Him and receive salvation.

The Lord is not slack concerning his promise, as some men count slackness; but is longsuffering to us-ward, not willing that any should perish, but that all should come to repentance.
2 Peter 3:9

God doesn't will for a single person to die and go to hell. Does that mean everyone will receive salvation? No, obviously not. Jesus said:

Enter ye in at the strait gate: for wide is the gate, and broad is the way, that leadeth to destruction, and many there be which go in thereat: because strait is the gate, and narrow is the way, which leadeth unto life, and few there be that find it.
Matthew 7:13-14

The Bible clearly reveals that God's will doesn't just automatically come to pass.
So much religion and tradition in the church today misrepresents God. It says, "Nothing happens without His direct or indirect approval. God either causes it or allows it." This is not what the Word teaches. The reason this doctrine is so popular – and people latch onto it – is because it gives them an excuse and frees them from all personal responsibility. In other words, you can just pray, "Lord, if it's Your will, please heal this person. If it's Your will, save this marriage." Then if it works – great. If it doesn't, "Then it must not have been God's will." It takes us totally out of the picture. We have no responsibility or accountability in the matter. This is absolutely wrong!

PEOPLE HAVE A CHOICE

Second Peter 3:9 clearly reveals that it's not God's will that anyone perish. Yet people are perishing – lots of them. God doesn't control or just allow these things. He's not the one who "predestined" some people to be saved and others to be lost. There are a number of reasons why people are perishing instead of being saved.

Every individual person has a choice. God isn't going to force anyone to be saved. He honours our free will. Some people – due to the lies and deception of the devil or because they've been hurt and have taken up an offense – are preoccupied with the cares of this life. Because of it they have rejected all of the invitations and interventions of God in their lives. So, by their own free will, they are choosing not to make Jesus their Lord.

You can't just make a person get saved on your faith. That's not what the Word of God teaches.

Acts 16:31 says,

Believe on the Lord Jesus Christ, and thou shalt be saved, and thy house.

In context, this is saying, "Believe on the Lord Jesus Christ, and you will be saved. And as each one of your family members believe on Him, they'll be saved too."

Each person must believe on the Lord Jesus Christ and receive salvation for themselves. No one can do it for them, and they can't do it for someone else. People have a choice in the matter.

MISREPRESENTING THE LORD

Sometimes the problem is that we're misrepresenting the Gospel, the Lord, and His kingdom. We aren't telling people the truth. We're giving them religion and tradition. Or, our words aren't matching our lives.

For whatever reason, many people are led into false religions. Some are being told that to kill people for religious purposes grants them entrance into heaven with a harem of women throughout all eternity. That is absolute foolishness. It's completely wrong and violates the truth of God's Word. Yet there are people full of misplaced hope and zeal doing suicide bombings and other similar activities. False doctrines are sending lots of people to hell.

If God doesn't desire any of this, then why is it happening? God gave us authority, and with it comes responsibility. In order to see people born again, we must preach the Gospel. If people aren't being born again, it's not because God hasn't done everything necessary to provide their salvation. It's not because He doesn't want them saved. Basically, it all comes down to people who haven't taken their authority and used it properly.

Perhaps believers aren't preaching the true Gospel. They're ministering religion and tradition instead. Maybe some Christians presented a negative witness with their lifestyles. Perhaps the lost person had one bad experience with someone who said they were a believer and because of it refuses to really listen to the true claims of Christ. Some way or another, it's people that are messing things up. Satan is inspiring it. He's doing his best to prejudice people against the Gospel, but it's not God's will that any person die and go to hell. Yet it's happening.

That same logic applies to healing, prosperity, and marriages. People say, "Well, if it's God's will, they'll be healed whether you or I pray for them or not." If the same reasoning is applied to salvation, it doesn't make sense. "If it's God's will, people will be saved whether we minister to them or not." That's not true. Believers have a responsibility. They've been given power and authority to preach the Gospel.

PREACH THE GOSPEL

That's what I'm doing. I'm sharing the Word of God with as many people as I can. There are millions of folks being touched by our daily television, radio, and internet ministry. People are hearing the Word of God, and their lives are being changed. They're being born again, baptised in the Holy Spirit, healed, delivered, and set free. It's always been God's will to set them free, but they hadn't heard the truth. Somebody had to come across their paths and share it with them.

> *How then shall they call on him in whom they have not believed? and how shall they believe in him of whom they have not heard? and how shall they hear without a preacher? And how shall they preach, except they be sent ... So then faith cometh by hearing, and hearing by the word of God.*
>
> Romans 10:14-15 and 17

It's not God's will for anyone to perish, but God relies on us as believers to minister His Word to effect change. God has given us both the authority and the responsibility to preach the Gospel. If we don't take that responsibility and use that authority, the Word won't be preached, and people won't get saved. It's not God's will for our nation or this world to be in the mess it's in. His will is for us all to reflect His values, submit to Him, and shine as a glorious church. However, it's not working that way because people aren't responding to Him properly.

Let's stop begging God to do what He has told us to do. Instead of asking Him to send revival and save people, we need to go out and preach the Gospel with signs and wonders. Let's take what Jesus has already provided and make it manifest. It's His power, but it's our authority (which He gave us) that makes it work. God's power is released as we use our authority. Go ahead, flip the switch!

PROCLAIM AND DEMONSTRATE
Lesson 11 – Outline

I. Jesus told us to heal the sick *and* preach the kingdom of God.

> **Whatsoever city ye enter…heal the sick that are therein, and say unto them, The kingdom of God is come nigh unto you.**
>
> Luke 10:8-9

    A. Proclamation and demonstration should always go hand in hand.

    B. God's Word needs to be confirmed with signs, wonders, and miracles.

    C. This is the way the early New Testament church preached the Gospel.

> **Being let go, they went to their own company, and reported all that the chief priests and elders had said unto them. And when they heard that, they lifted up their voice to God with one accord, and said, Lord…behold their threatenings: and grant unto thy servants, that with all boldness they may speak thy word, By stretching forth thine hand to heal; and that signs and wonders may be done by the name of thy holy child Jesus.**
>
> Acts 4:23-24 and 29-30

    D. A true Christian is a person who not only has a proper doctrine about who Jesus is, but who can also demonstrate it by the power and gifts of the Holy Spirit.

II. The reason that isn't happening more is because we are praying and asking God to do what He commanded us to do.

    A. The Lord told us to go heal the sick.

    B. God is the power source, but He's placed that power on the inside of us.

    C. He gave us the authority to use His name and use His power.

    D. If we don't command healing to come, it won't happen.

III. God desires for every person to respond to Him and receive salvation.

> **The Lord is not slack concerning his promise, as some men count slackness; but is longsuffering to us-ward, not willing that any should perish, but that all should come to repentance.**
>
> 2 Peter 3:9

    A. The Bible clearly reveals that God's will doesn't just automatically come to pass.

> **Enter ye in at the strait gate: for wide is the gate, and broad is the way, that leadeth to**

> *destruction, and many there be which go in thereat: Because strait is the gate, and narrow is the way, which leadeth unto life, and few there be that find it.*
>
> Matthew 7:13-14

    B.   Every individual person has a choice.

    C.   God isn't going to force anyone to be saved – He honours our free will.

IV. You can't just make a person get saved on your faith.

> *Believe on the Lord Jesus Christ, and thou shalt be saved, and thy house.*
>
> Acts 16:31

    A.   In context, this is saying, "Believe on the Lord Jesus Christ, and you will be saved. And as each one of your family members believe on Him, they'll be saved too."

    B.   Each person must believe on the Lord Jesus Christ and receive salvation for themselves.

    C.   People have a choice in the matter.

V. God gave us authority, and with it comes responsibility.

    A.   In order to see people born again, we must preach the Gospel.

    B.   If people aren't being born again, it's not because God hasn't done everything necessary to provide their salvation.

    C.   Some way or another, it's people that are messing things up.

    D.   The same logic applies to healing, prosperity, and restoring marriages.

VI. Let's stop begging God to do what He has told us to do.

    A.   Instead of asking Him to send revival and save people, we need to go out and preach the Gospel with signs and wonders.

    B.   Let's take what Jesus has already provided and make it manifest.

    C.   God's power is released as we use our authority.

PROCLAIM AND DEMONSTRATE
Lesson 11 – Teacher's Guide

1. Jesus told us to heal the sick *and* preach the kingdom of God (Luke 10:8-9). Proclamation and demonstration should always go hand in hand. God's Word needs to be confirmed with signs, wonders, and miracles. This is the way the early New Testament church preached the Gospel (Acts 4:23-24 and 29-30). A true Christian is a person who not only has a proper doctrine about who Jesus is, but who can also demonstrate it by the power and gifts of the Holy Spirit.

2. The reason that isn't happening more is because we are praying and asking God to do what He commanded us to do. The Lord told us to go heal the sick. God is the power source, but He's placed that power on the inside of us. He gave us the authority to use His name and use His power. If we don't command healing to come, it won't happen.

3. God desires for every person to respond to Him and receive salvation (2 Pet. 3:9). The Bible clearly reveals that God's will doesn't just automatically come to pass (Matt. 7:13-14). Each individual person has a choice. God isn't going to force anyone to be saved – He honours our free will.

4. We can't just make a person get saved on our faith. In context, Acts 16:31 is saying, "Believe on the Lord Jesus Christ, and you will be saved. And as each one of your family members believe on Him, they'll be saved too." Each person must believe on the Lord Jesus Christ and receive salvation for themselves. People have a choice in the matter.

1. A. Read Luke 10:8-9; Acts 4:23-24, and 29-30. What should always go hand in hand? (Proclamation and demonstration)
   B. What needs to be confirmed with signs, wonders, and miracles? (God's Word)
2. A. What did the Lord tell us? (To go heal the sick)
   B. What did God give us the authority to use? (His name and His power)
3. A. Read 2 Peter 3:9 and Matthew 7:13-14. What does God desire? (For every person to respond to Him and receive salvation)
   B. What does God honour? (Our free will)
4. A. Read Acts 16:31. What must each person do? (Believe on the Lord Jesus Christ and receive salvation for themselves)
   B. What do people have in the matter? (A choice)

5. God gave us authority, and with it comes responsibility. In order to see people born again, we must preach the Gospel. If people aren't being born again, it's not because God hasn't done everything necessary to provide their salvation. Some way or another, it's people that are messing things up. The same logic applies to healing, prosperity, and restoring marriages.

6. Let's stop begging God to do what He has told us to do. Instead of asking Him to send revival and save people, we need to go out and preach the Gospel with signs and wonders. Let's take what Jesus has already provided and make it manifest. God's power is released as we use our authority.

5. A. What comes with the authority God gave us? (Responsibility)
   B. What must we preach in order to see people born again? (The Gospel)
6. A. Instead of asking God to send revival and save people, what do we need to do? (Go out and preach the Gospel with signs and wonders)
   B. What is released as we use our authority? (God's power)

PROCLAIM AND DEMONSTRATE
Lesson 11 – Additional Information

Cecil's wife, Lisa, has a powerful testimony of God's healing power. It's available in audio form as "Lisa Paxton's Testimony" or in booklet form as *Lisa's Story*. You'll be encouraged!

PROCLAIM AND DEMONSTRATE
Lesson 11 – Discipleship Questions

1. According to Luke 10:8-9, what should we eat when we enter into a city and are received?

2. In Acts 4:23-30, the early believers prayed that they would speak God's Word how?

3. They also asked that as they spoke the Word that healings, signs, and wonders would be done by whose name?

4. According to 2 Peter 3:9, who is the Lord longsuffering toward?

5. What does He not want?

6. He is willing that how many should come to repentance?

7. According to Matthew 7:13-14, we should enter in where?

8. This gate leads to what?

9. How many find it?

10. If we believe on the Lord Jesus Christ, Acts 16:31 says that we shall be what?

11. According to Romans 10:14-17, how beautiful are _____ feet.

12. How does faith come?

PROCLAIM AND DEMONSTRATE
Lesson 11 – Answer Key

1. Such things as are set before us.

2. With all boldness.

3. Thy holy child Jesus.

4. Us.

5. That any should perish.

6. All.

7. At the strait gate.

8. Life.

9. Few.

10. Saved.

11. Them that preach the gospel of peace.

12. By hearing the Word of God.

PROCLAIM AND DEMONSTRATE
Lesson 11 – Scriptures

And into whatsoever city ye enter, and they receive you, eat such things as are set before you: And heal the sick that are therein, and say unto them, The kingdom of God is come nigh unto you.

Luke 10:8-9

And being let go, they went to their own company, and reported all that the chief priests and elders had said unto them. And when they heard that, they lifted up their voice to God with one accord, and said, Lord, thou art God, which hast made heaven, and earth, and the sea, and all that in them is.

Acts 4:23-24

And now, Lord, behold their threatenings: and grant unto thy servants, that with all boldness they may speak thy word, By stretching forth thine hand to heal; and that signs and wonders may be done by the name of thy holy child Jesus.

Acts 4:29-30

The Lord is not slack concerning his promise, as some men count slackness; but is longsuffering to us-ward, not willing that any should perish, but that all should come to repentance.

2 Peter 3:9

Enter ye in at the strait gate: for wide is the gate, and broad is the way, that leadeth to destruction, and many there be which go in thereat: Because strait is the gate, and narrow is the way, which leadeth unto life, and few there be that find it.

Matthew 7:13-14

And they said, Believe on the Lord Jesus Christ, and thou shalt be saved, and thy house.

Acts 16:31

How then shall they call on him in whom they have not believed? and how shall they believe in him of whom they have not heard? and how shall they hear without a preacher? And how shall they preach, except they be sent? as it is written, How beautiful are the feet of them that preach the gospel of peace, and bring glad tidings of good things! But they have not all obeyed the gospel. For Esaias saith, Lord, who hath believed our report? So then faith cometh by hearing, and hearing by the word of God.

Romans 10:14-17

BE A WITNESS
Lesson 12

When they therefore were come together, they asked of him, saying, Lord, wilt thou at this time restore again the kingdom to Israel? And he said unto them, It is not for you to know the times or the seasons, which the Father hath put in his own power.

Acts 1:6-7

I remember a guy who wrote a book proposing eighty-eight reasons why the Lord would return in 1988. I talked with some people who honestly believed what he said was true. With all of their hearts, they were counting on the Lord coming back in 1988. Of course, it didn't happen. So then he wrote a book detailing eighty-nine reasons why the Lord would return in 1989 – and people bought that book too. The guy totally missed it, yet a bunch of folks still came out and swallowed the very next thing he had to say. How dumb can you get and still breathe?

Acts 1:6-7 is saying that you can't know the time or the season that Jesus is coming back to fully establish His kingdom. If someone tells you that they know and they're predicting some date, then you can just write "Ichabod" across their forehead (that's Old Testament terminology for "the glory has departed"; 1 Sam. 4:21). I guarantee you they are in deception, and what they're saying is not of God.

Immediately after the Lord said "You don't have power or authority concerning those kinds of things because the Father has reserved them for Himself," He continued saying:

But ye shall receive power, after that the Holy Ghost is come upon you: and ye shall be witnesses unto me both in Jerusalem, and in all Judaea, and in Samaria, and unto the uttermost part of the earth.

Acts 1:8

Jesus told His disciples, *you* will have power to be a witness. Think about it. The Lord would never give you a position without also giving you the authority to execute and accomplish what He told you to do. So, with this power to be a witness comes an authority to be a witness – and all the responsibility that goes along with it.

THROUGH PEOPLE

Peter exercised this power and authority to be a witness when he followed God's leading to Cornelius' house.

There was a certain man in Caesarea called Cornelius, a centurion of the band called the Italian band, A devout man, and one that feared God with all his house, which gave much alms to the people, and prayed to God alway. He saw in a vision evidently about the ninth hour of the day an angel of God coming in to him, and saying unto him, Cornelius. And when he looked on him, he was afraid, and said, What is it, Lord? And he said unto him, Thy prayers and thine alms are come up for a memorial before God. And now send men to Joppa, and call for one Simon, whose surname is Peter. He lodgeth with one Simon a tanner, whose house is by the sea side: he shall tell thee what thou oughtest to do.

Acts 10:1-6

An angel appeared to this centurion and said, "Cornelius, you're a devout man. God has heard your prayers. Now send to Joppa and ask for Peter. He'll come and tell you how to be born again." Why didn't this angel tell Cornelius the Gospel? It would have been much more efficient than sending men on a two-day journey (one way) to bring Peter back. Why didn't this angel just tell him how to be born again? The answer is simple: God gave power and authority to people to preach the Gospel, not to angels. Angels don't have the authority to preach the Gospel – we do. God has limited Himself to preaching the Gospel through people.

God's plan is for us to preach the truth of the Gospel, and for people to hear it and be born again through the incorruptible seed of God's Word. However, Satan has come in through religious teaching, saying, "You don't have to share God's Word. Just *pray* them into the kingdom." So now there are all these Christians who are praying and asking God to save people, and they never share the Gospel with them.

I've actually met people before who say they are "prayer warriors," who never get out of their closet. Their prayer lists are so long, they can't even read it all in an hour. They diligently work through their lists and pray for everybody, but they won't witness to a neighbour. They don't talk to people at the grocery store. They won't speak to the mailman. They don't share the Word with anyone, but they're praying for a "great move of God." That's deception. It doesn't happen that way. You can't bring a person into the kingdom of God through prayer alone.

FAITH COMES BY HEARING

You have to be born again by the incorruptible seed of God's Word.

Being born again, not of corruptible seed, but of incorruptible, by the word of God, which liveth and abideth for ever.

1 Peter 1:23

God's Word is the seed. It must be planted in the ground that is a person's heart. It's also like sowing a seed in the womb of a woman. You can't conceive a child apart from a seed being sown. There was only one virgin birth, and there isn't going to be another. You must get out of your prayer closet and sow the seed of God's Word.

Faith cometh by hearing, and hearing by the word of God.

Romans 10:17

You can't be born again without faith, and that faith comes through the seed of God's Word.

PLANT THE SEED

You don't get pregnant through prayer. You can receive healing through prayer, which may affect your ability to get pregnant, but you don't get pregnant through prayer. I've prayed with many couples that were unable to have children and have seen them conceive supernaturally, but my prayer wasn't what made them pregnant.

One time a woman came forward and asked me to pray that she'd get pregnant. Right before I put my hands on her, I felt impressed to ask, "Are you married?" She answered, "No, I'm not." I pulled my hands back real quick. I wasn't going to have anything to do with this lady getting pregnant if she wasn't married. That's not God's will. Prayer doesn't make you pregnant. You have to plant that seed.

Many Christians are praying for people to be born again, but they're not praying about the planting of the seed. They're not praying for someone to come across their paths and preach the Gospel to them (Matt. 9:38). They aren't asking the Holy Spirit to bring back to their memory the words God has already spoken to them (John 14:26). They're just thinking that they can pray somebody into the kingdom. That violates the power and authority God gave us when He told us to go preach the Gospel. The angel didn't tell Cornelius how to get saved; Peter – a physical human being – had to do that. You need to understand that God gave the power, authority, and responsibility for preaching the Gospel to people.

You may have been praying for someone for umpteen years, but you're frustrated and wondering, *Why isn't God saving this person?* It's because you aren't praying right. You're asking God to save them as if there were something He could do. He's already done His part to provide salvation through the death, burial, and resurrection of Jesus Christ. The Lord commissioned us to preach the Gospel. If that person hasn't received salvation, it's either because they aren't hearing the true Gospel, or they're choosing to reject it. It's not God who isn't saving that individual. There are ways you can pray to speed things up and enable the Holy Spirit to minister to this person more, but just praying and asking God "Please save them" is useless. That's not how the Word teaches us to do it.

THE TRUTH

You may be tempted to be offended right now, feeling like I'm saying, "God is limited in power." No, I'm saying that God has limited Himself by His own Word. He told us to preach the Gospel. He said that people are born again by the incorruptible seed of God's Word. If we don't follow His instructions, then we can't expect the proper results.

If you choose to say "Well, God, I'm not going to talk to them. I don't want to get out there and risk suffering any embarrassment, shame, or persecution that might come by me speaking the Word. I'm just going to pray in my closet and believe that You're going to do a miracle," then you're just spitting in the wind. It isn't going to work, because that's not how the kingdom operates.

I'm telling you the truth in love. If we ask God to save someone but don't do what He commanded us to do – which is preach the Gospel and be a witness – then it isn't going to happen. People must be born again through the Word of God. Prayer doesn't cause people to be born again. Prayer may help once you've already shared the Gospel, but it's not a substitute for doing what God has told you to do. People don't get born again through prayer; they get born again through hearing the truth.

Ye shall know the truth, and the truth shall make you free.

John 8:32

The devil has deceived many of us into just praying and asking God to do what He has commanded us to do. He's commanded us to preach the Gospel. Cornelius had an angel appear to him in response to his prayers, but the angel didn't preach the Gospel to him. Instead, he told him to send men to Joppa to bring Peter back to tell them how to be born again. Angels don't have the authority to preach the Gospel. God didn't commit that to them. It's our responsibility.

GOD LOVES PEOPLE

I pray. I spend a lot of time just fellowshipping and communing with the Lord. The vast majority of my prayer life is worshiping God, thanking the Lord, and asking Him for wisdom and instruction. As far as my ministry to others, I ask God to help me speak His Word with clarity and boldness. I pray that He would give me revelation knowledge and better ways of communicating it to others.

However, I don't spend any time asking God to "move" and save people. I don't pray, "O Lord, please touch their hearts and cause them to be born again." That's because I know that God loves them more than I do. I'm convinced that He wants to touch their lives and see them born again. I don't plead with Him, saying, "Please love these people and move in their lives." Since God is love, He's led me to do everything I can – including broadcasting daily programs on television and radio around the world, giving away lots of free materials on my website, translating my books into multiple languages, and starting new branches of Charis Bible College all the time – to share the truth of God's Word with as many people as possible. The Lord knows that as people receive the truth into their hearts, it will make them free.

Since I know that God already loves people and wants to minister to them, I don't spend any time pleading with Him to "Please love, touch, and move in these people's lives." I'm aware that what I am sharing is very different from the way many folks pray. However, most people aren't getting very good results from their prayer lives. If that's you, maybe you ought to try something different. What I'm telling you about is working.

POLITICS AND PRAYER

When I first started in the ministry, I used to plead with God for an outpouring of His Spirit. I started all-night prayer meetings where we just cried, wailed, and travailed, begging God to send revival. I had divided the city where I lived – Arlington, Texas – up into sections, and was praying over each one of them, saying, "O God, please touch these people. O Lord, we've got to have a move of Your Spirit!" I gave Him all of the statistics in order to impress on Him how important this was, telling Him, "You've got to do something!" I was trying to manipulate, motivate, and twist God's arm.

Finally, as I beat my fist against the wall for emphasis, these words came flying out of my mouth: "God, if You loved the people of Arlington, Texas, half as much as I do, we'd have revival!" As soon as those words left my mouth, I immediately thought, *Something is wrong with this prayer. Here I am presenting to God that I love these people and want to see them ministered to more than He does.* My lightning-fast mind figured out that I was making some serious mistakes.

However, much of the church is still doing this. They're begging, "O God, send revival. O Lord, if You wanted to, You could pour out Your Spirit on our country and things would change." That's not true. God moves on this earth through His people (Eph. 3:20). He moves as His people preach, teach, and act on His Word. He moves through them as they obey the promptings of the Holy Spirit. Satan is the one behind some of these "movements" in the body of Christ today that are getting us into doing everything except preaching the Gospel.

Although it's important for Christians to exercise their civic duty and vote, it's a deception of the devil to put all of our faith, energy, effort, and hope into the political process. Political action has its place in a believer's life, but it's not the primary avenue through which the church should influence a nation. The political process is not the strength of the church – the Gospel is.

The founding fathers of the United States – many of whom were active Christians – said that democracy is totally unsuited for anyone but a moral people. John Adams (our first vice president and second president) said that if we ever cease to be moral, democracy will destroy this nation. That's literally what we see happening today. We're legalising immorality, changing the constitution, and ignoring the clear intent of our founding fathers.

THE STRENGTH OF THE CHURCH

The real strength of the church is in preaching the Gospel. As God's Word changes the hearts of men and women, the political arena will reflect it. The reason so many laws promoting immorality are being proposed right now is because the church hasn't been doing its job. It hasn't been preaching the truth. It's lost the hearts of people, and those hearts are using the political process to pass laws favoring their preferences toward sin. The church would do much more to change America by preaching the Gospel and teaching God's Word than by immersing itself completely into the political process or by its people locking themselves in prayer closets, begging and pleading with God for revival for hours on end.

The Lord told us to go out and preach the Gospel. As people receive the truth into their hearts, the truth will set them free. That's where our strength lies. God told us to influence our nation by ministering His Word because the number one power of the church is the proclamation and demonstration of the Gospel (Rom. 1:16).

Instead of boldly sharing God's truth, many Christians have retreated to their prayer closets. They're afraid to say anything in front of people, lest somebody deem them "politically incorrect." So they run to their prayer closets, begging God for revival and pleading with Him to do what He's told them to do.

> ***It pleased God by the foolishness of preaching*** [the Gospel] ***to save them that believe.***
> 1 Corinthians 1:21, brackets mine

You can't be born again without hearing the Word of God. As believers today, properly emphasise His Word. Boldly share the truth with everyone we can. Don't use politics or "prayer" to shirk your responsibility to preach the Gospel, but be faithful, consistent, and powerful witnesses of our Lord Jesus Christ.

BE A WITNESS
Lesson 12 – Outline

I. Jesus told His disciples, *you* will have power to be a witness.

> *But ye shall receive power, after that the Holy Ghost is come upon you: and ye shall be witnesses unto me both in Jerusalem, and in all Judaea, and in Samaria, and unto the uttermost part of the earth.*
>
> Acts 1:8

    A.   The Lord would never give you a position without also giving you the authority to execute and accomplish what He told you to do.

    B.   So, with this power to be a witness comes an authority to be a witness – and all the responsibility that goes along with it.

II. Peter exercised this power and authority to be a witness when he followed God's leading to Cornelius' house.

> *There was a certain man in Caesarea called Cornelius, a centurion of the band called the Italian band, A devout man, and one that feared God with all his house, which gave much alms to the people, and prayed to God alway. He saw in a vision evidently about the ninth hour of the day an angel of God coming in to him, and saying unto him, Cornelius. And when he looked on him, he was afraid, and said, What is it, Lord? And he said unto him, Thy prayers and thine alms are come up for a memorial before God. And now send men to Joppa, and call for one Simon, whose surname is Peter: He lodgeth with one Simon a tanner, whose house is by the sea side: he shall tell thee what thou oughtest to do.*
>
> Acts 10:1-6

    A.   Angels don't have the authority to preach the Gospel – we do.

    B.   God has limited Himself to preaching the Gospel through people.

    C.   God's plan is for us to preach the truth of the Gospel and for people to hear it and be born again through the incorruptible seed of God's Word.

    D.   You can't pray a person into the kingdom of God.

III. You have to be born again by the incorruptible seed of God's Word.

> *Being born again, not of corruptible seed, but of incorruptible, by the word of God, which liveth and abideth for ever.*
>
> 1 Peter 1:23

    A.   God's Word is the seed.

B. It must be planted in the ground that is a person's heart.

C. You can't be born again without faith, and that faith comes through the seed of God's Word.

Faith cometh by hearing, and hearing by the word of God.

Romans 10:17

IV. Many Christians are praying for people to be born again, but they're not praying about the planting of the seed.

A. There are ways you can pray to speed things up and enable the Holy Spirit to minister to this person more, but just praying and asking God "Please save them" is useless.

B. Prayer may help once we've already shared the Gospel, but it's not a substitute for doing what God has told us to do.

C. The Lord knows that as people receive the truth into their hearts, it will make them free.

Ye shall know the truth, and the truth shall make you free.

John 8:32

V. God moves on this earth through His people (Eph. 3:20).

A. He moves as we preach, teach, and act on His Word.

B. He moves through us as we obey the promptings of the Holy Spirit.

C. God told us to influence our nation by ministering His Word because the number one power of the church is the proclamation and demonstration of the Gospel (Rom. 1:16).

It pleased God by the foolishness of preaching [the Gospel] **to save them that believe.**

1 Corinthians 1:21, brackets mine

D. As believers today, let's properly emphasise His Word and boldly share the truth with everyone we can.

E. Let's not use politics or "prayer" to shirk our responsibility to preach the Gospel, but let's be faithful, consistent, and powerful witnesses of our Lord Jesus Christ.

BE A WITNESS
Lesson 12 – Teacher's Guide

1. Jesus told His disciples, *you* will have power to be a witness (Acts 1:8). The Lord would never give us a position without also giving us the authority to execute and accomplish what He told us to do. So with this power to be a witness comes an authority to be a witness – and all the responsibility that goes along with it.

2. Peter exercised this power and authority to be a witness when he followed God's leading to Cornelius' house (Acts 10:1-6). Angels don't have the authority to preach the Gospel – we do. God has limited Himself to preaching the Gospel through people. God's plan is for us to preach the truth of the Gospel and for people to hear it and be born again through the incorruptible seed of God's Word. We can't bring a person into the kingdom of God through prayer alone.

3. We have to be born again by the incorruptible seed of God's Word (1 Pet. 1:23). God's Word is the seed. It must be planted in the ground that is a person's heart. We can't be born again without faith, and that faith comes through the seed of God's Word (Rom. 10:17).

4. Many Christians are praying for people to be born again, but they're not praying about the planting of the seed. There are ways we can pray to speed things up and enable the Holy Spirit to minister to this person more, but just praying and asking God "Please save them" is useless. Prayer may help once we've already shared the Gospel, but it's not a substitute for doing what God has told us to do. The Lord knows that as people receive the truth into their hearts, it will make them free (John 8:32).

1. A. Read Acts 1:8. Jesus told His disciples they would have power to what? (Be a witness)
   B. The Lord would never give us a position without also giving us what? (The authority to execute and accomplish what He told us to do)
2. A. Read Acts 10:1-6. God has limited Himself to preaching the Gospel through whom? (People)
   B. Can we bring a person into the kingdom of God through prayer alone? (No)
3. A. Read 1 Peter 1:23 and Romans 10:17. What is God's Word? (The incorruptible seed)
   B. We can't be born again without what? (Faith)
4. A. Read John 8:32. Just praying and asking God "Please save them" is what? (Useless)
   B. What happens as people receive the truth into their hearts? (It will make them free)

5. God moves on this earth through His people (Eph. 3:20). He moves as we preach, teach, and act on His Word. He moves through us as we obey the promptings of the Holy Spirit. God told us to influence our nation by ministering His Word because the number one power of the church is the proclamation and demonstration of the Gospel (Rom. 1:16 and 1 Cor. 1:21). As believers today, let's properly emphasise His Word and boldly share the truth with everyone we can. Let's not use politics or "prayer" to shirk our responsibility to preach the Gospel, but let's be faithful, consistent, and powerful witnesses of our Lord Jesus Christ.

5. A. Read Ephesians 3:20, Romans 1:16, and 1 Corinthians 1:21. How does God move on this earth? (Through His people)
   B. What is the number one power of the church? (The proclamation and demonstration of the Gospel)

BE A WITNESS
Lesson 12 – Additional Information

In my teaching *A Better Way to Pray*, I cover this topic of prayer much more comprehensively. If you'd like the results of your prayer life to improve, I strongly encourage you to check it out.

BE A WITNESS
Lesson 12 – Discipleship Questions

1. According to Acts 1:6-8, we shall receive power after _____ has come upon us.

2. What was the child's name in 1 Samuel 4:21?

3. What does this name mean?

4. In Acts 10:1-6, who was described as a devout man?

5. Who came to him in a vision?

6. Who was he told to send for?

7. What shall this man tell him?

8. According to 1 Peter 1:23, what kind of seed is the Word of God?

9. What does Romans 10:17 reveal comes by hearing the Word of God?

10. Who does Matthew 9:38 tell us to pray to?

11. Who is the Comforter mentioned in John 14:26?

12. According to Ephesians 3:20, what do we need to have working in us?

13. In Romans 1:16, Paul shares how he was not ashamed of what?

14. It is the power of God unto what?

15. According to 1 Corinthians 1:21, by what foolishness did it please God to save them that believe?

BE A WITNESS
Lesson 12 – Answer Key

1. The Holy Spirit.

2. Ichabod.

3. The glory has departed.

4. Cornelius.

5. An angel of God.

6. Simon Peter.

7. What he ought to do.

8. Incorruptible.

9. Faith.

10. The Lord of the harvest.

11. The Holy Spirit.

12. Power.

13. The Gospel of Christ.

14. Salvation.

15. The foolishness of preaching.

BE A WITNESS
Lesson 12 – Scriptures

When they therefore were come together, they asked of him, saying, Lord, wilt thou at this time restore again the kingdom to Israel? And he said unto them, It is not for you to know the times or the seasons, which the Father hath put in his own power. But ye shall receive power, after that the Holy Ghost is come upon you: and ye shall be witnesses unto me both in Jerusalem, and in all Judaea, and in Samaria, and unto the uttermost part of the earth.

Acts 1:6-8

And she named the child Ichabod, saying, The glory is departed from Israel: because the ark of God was taken, and because of her father in law and her husband.

1 Samuel 4:21

There was a certain man in Caesarea called Cornelius, a centurion of the band called the Italian band, A devout man, and one that feared God with all his house, which gave much alms to the people, and prayed to God alway. He saw in a vision evidently about the ninth hour of the day an angel of God coming in to him, and saying unto him, Cornelius. And when he looked on him, he was afraid, and said, What is it, Lord? And he said unto him, Thy prayers and thine alms are come up for a memorial before God. And now send men to Joppa, and call for one Simon, whose surname is Peter: He lodgeth with one Simon a tanner, whose house is by the sea side: he shall tell thee what thou oughtest to do.

Acts 10:1-6

Being born again, not of corruptible seed, but of incorruptible, by the word of God, which liveth and abideth for ever.

1 Peter 1:23

So then faith cometh by hearing, and hearing by the word of God.

Romans 10:17

Pray ye therefore the Lord of the harvest, that he will send forth labourers into his harvest.

Matthew 9:38

But the Comforter, which is the Holy Ghost, whom the Father will send in my name, he shall teach you all things, and bring all things to your remembrance, whatsoever I have said unto you.

John 14:26

And ye shall know the truth, and the truth shall make you free.

John 8:32

Now unto him that is able to do exceeding abundantly above all that we ask or think, according to the power that worketh in us.

Ephesians 3:20

For I am not ashamed of the gospel of Christ: for it is the power of God unto salvation to every one that believeth; to the Jew first, and also to the Greek.

Romans 1:16

For after that in the wisdom of God the world by wisdom knew not God, it pleased God by the foolishness of preaching to save them that believe.

1 Corinthians 1:21

HOW TO PRAY FOR THE LOST
Lesson 13

I'd like to share with you some biblical ways to effectively pray for a lost person. This kind of prayer is like water. Once the seed is planted, it must be watered. Prayer isn't a substitute for planting a seed. You can water barren ground all you like, but it won't produce a harvest. You must plant the seed of God's Word for people to be born again. However, these are some good ways to pray to water the seed that's been planted.

As you start praying for a lost person, you need to recognise that God loves them infinitely more than you do.

> **God so loved the world, that he gave his only begotten Son, that whosoever believeth in him should not perish, but have everlasting life**
>
> John 3:16

The Lord doesn't want this person to perish, but to repent, turn to Him, and enjoy everlasting life.

> **The Lord is not slack concerning his promise, as some men count slackness; but is longsuffering to us-ward, not willing that any should perish, but that all should come to repentance.**
>
> 2 Peter 3:9

In light of this, you could start by thanking Him, saying, "Father, I thank You that You love this person so much that You gave Your only begotten Son for them. It's not Your will for them to perish but to come to repentance and turn to You. I thank You, Lord, that You've already provided for their salvation."

> **He** [Jesus] **is the propitiation for our sins: and not for ours only, but also for the sins of the whole world.**
>
> 1 John 2:2, brackets mine

God not only loves the whole world, but He's already died for the sins of the whole world. He's already paid for them. A person who goes to hell is going there with their sins paid for. The reason they go to hell is because they reject the payment – they refuse to believe and receive the Lord Jesus Christ.

LABORERS ACROSS THEIR PATH

You can continue praying, "Father, I thank You that You've already made provision. Jesus, You were the atoning sacrifice for everyone's sins – not only for those who believe but also those who are lost. So, Father, I thank You that You want them to be saved, and You've already provided their salvation." Then you can take your authority and start speaking out things that need to happen. Since God has to flow through a person, you can pray according to Romans 10:17:

Faith cometh by hearing, and hearing by the word of God.

"Father, Your Word says that faith comes by hearing Your Word. So I'm praying that Your Word will come across their path."

Pray ye therefore the Lord of the harvest, that he will send forth labourers into his harvest.

Matthew 9:38

"I ask that You would send forth laborers across their path. I believe that right now someone is coming to them to share Your Word. If they're in a bar, let a preacher walk in and give them the Gospel. If they're at home watching television, I pray that they would come across the Word being presented in a program. If they're driving their car, let them turn the radio on to someone sharing the good news. Father, I ask You to send laborers across their path at their job. May a co-worker sit down next to them and start telling them how much You love them and how they can be born again."

REMEMBER THE WORD

Pray that the Word they've already heard will come back to their remembrance.

But the Comforter, which is the Holy Ghost, whom the Father will send in my name, he shall teach you all things, and bring all things to your remembrance, whatsoever I have said unto you.

John 14:26

"Father, I pray that the Word they heard when they were a kid in Sunday school would come back to them." Somehow, they must receive the incorruptible seed of the Word.

Then, offer yourself as a vessel. It's very ineffective to pray "O God, send laborers across their path" if you're not willing to be one. If you have an opportunity to tell them the truth, take it. I recognise that in certain instances and for whatever reason, that person may have just totally cut you off. Maybe there are certain things that this person won't let you talk to them about. However, if you can speak to them, then do so.

If I was praying for God to bring the Word to someone and then, as I was praying, the Lord said "You go talk to them," I would stop my prayer right there and go talk to that person. Maybe I'd have to call them on the phone, but somehow I would act on God's leading right then. I wouldn't pray about it anymore until I had done as He instructed me to do.

STAND AGAINST THE DEVIL

Also, you can take your authority and stand against the devil.

In whom the god of this world hath blinded the minds of them which believe not, lest the light of the glorious gospel of Christ, who is the image of God, should shine unto them.

2 Corinthians 4:4

This verse reveals that a demonic power operates in people who don't believe, blinding them to the truth so that the light of the Gospel won't shine unto them. God needs someone in a physical body to take their authority and release His power, saying, "I command this demonic blindness and hardened heart to be gone in Jesus' name."

Now, I need to clarify something here. Because you are praying for another person – who has their own free will – you may need to pray these things for them again and again. This isn't praying in unbelief, because they may be negating your prayer by exercising their own free will.

Let's say you pray for this person, breaking the blindness and hardness of heart. God opens up their heart, and all of a sudden this deception is gone, and the Word is coming to them. They're remembering scriptures and people are coming across their path. However, if that person isn't ready to repent and receive, they'll reject this conviction and drawing of the Holy Spirit. Their own free will has more power and authority over them than you do. So even though you've prayed for them and you know it's working, they have the right to reject it. If they do, then you have to pray that prayer again. It's not that you prayed one of those prayers in unbelief. You believe that your prayer was answered, and it was. However, the person just hasn't responded yet.

So you pray in faith again, releasing your faith for God to minister to them and break that blindness so they can see Christ. Hopefully, as they are hit with the Gospel a number of times, it will eventually penetrate and begin to soak in. The reason you have to pray this kind of prayer over and over again is because the person is constantly voiding your prayer by hardening their heart.

REMIT THEIR SINS

Another way you can pray for this person is to remit their sins.

> **Whose soever sins ye remit, they are remitted unto them; and whose soever sins ye retain, they are retained.**
>
> John 20:23

Contrary to what some people have taught, this doesn't mean you can forgive their sins. You don't have the power to forgive sins. However, you can remit them.

When someone with cancer is symptom free, they'll say they are in remission. "Remission" doesn't mean the cancer is gone, just that there are no visible or physical signs of it. So when the Word says that you can remit sins, it means you can deal with the effects sin causes in that person.

In praying for a lost person, you can break off the demonic blindness and hardness of heart. You can pray that laborers would bring God's Word across their path and that it would come back to their remembrance. You can also remit their sins. All of these are biblical and effective ways to pray. Even though they may choose to resist and reject the drawing of the Holy Spirit, you can be confident that through your prayers, God is continuing to work in their life.

HOW TO PRAY FOR THE LOST
Lesson 13 – Outline

I. I'd like to share with you some biblical ways to effectively pray for a lost person.

    A.   This kind of prayer is like water.

    B.   You can water barren ground all you like, but it won't produce a harvest.

    C.   You must plant the seed of God's Word for people to be born again.

    D.   However, these are some good ways to pray to water the seed that's been planted.

II. As you start praying for a lost person, you need to recognise that God loves them infinitely more than you do (John 3:16).

    A.   The Lord doesn't want this person to perish, but to repent, turn to Him, and enjoy everlasting life.

> **The Lord is not slack concerning his promise, as some men count slackness; but is longsuffering to us-ward, not willing that any should perish, but that all should come to repentance.**
>
> 2 Peter 3:9

    B.   In light of this, you could start thanking God, saying, "Father, I thank You that You love this person so much that You gave Your only begotten Son for them. It's not Your will for them to perish but to come to repentance and turn to You. I thank You, Lord, that You've already provided for their salvation."

> **He** [Jesus] **is the propitiation for our sins: and not for ours only, but also for the sins of the whole world.**
>
> 1 John 2:2, brackets mine

    C.   You can continue praying, "Father, I thank You that You've already made provision. Jesus, You were the atoning sacrifice for everyone's sins – not only for those who believe but also those who are lost. So, Father, I thank You that You want them to be saved, and You've already provided it."

III. Then you can take your authority and start speaking out things that need to happen.

    A.   "Father, Your Word says that faith comes by hearing Your Word. So I'm praying that Your Word will come across their path."

> **Faith cometh by hearing, and hearing by the word of God.**
>
> Romans 10:17

B. "I ask that You would send forth laborers across their path."

> *Pray ye therefore the Lord of the harvest, that he will send forth labourers into his harvest.*
> Matthew 9:38

C. Pray that the Word they've already heard will come back to their remembrance.

> *But the Comforter, which is the Holy Ghost, whom the Father will send in my name, he shall teach you all things, and bring all things to your remembrance, whatsoever I have said unto you.*
> John 14:26

D. Then, offer yourself as a vessel.

IV. Also, you can take your authority and stand against the devil.

> *In whom the god of this world hath blinded the minds of them which believe not, lest the light of the glorious gospel of Christ, who is the image of God, should shine unto them.*
> 2 Corinthians 4:4

A. God needs someone in a physical body to take their authority and release His power, saying, "I command this demonic blindness and hardened heart to be gone in Jesus' name."

B. Because you are praying for another person – who has their own free will – you may need to pray these things for them again and again.

C. The reason you have to pray this kind of prayer over and over again is because the person is constantly voiding your prayer by hardening their heart.

D. When the Word says that you can remit sins, it means you can deal with the effects sin causes in that person.

> *Whose soever sins ye remit, they are remitted unto them; and whose soever sins ye retain, they are retained.*
> John 20:23

E. Even though they may choose to resist and reject the drawing of the Holy Spirit, you can be confident that through your prayers, God is continuing to work in their life.

HOW TO PRAY FOR THE LOST
Lesson 13 – Teacher's Guide

1. There are several biblical ways to effectively pray for a lost person. This kind of prayer is like water. We can water barren ground all we like, but it won't produce a harvest. We must plant the seed of God's Word for people to be born again. However, these are some good ways to pray to water the seed that's been planted.

2. As we start praying for a lost person, we need to recognise that God loves them infinitely more than we do (John 3:16). The Lord doesn't want this person to perish, but to repent, turn to Him, and enjoy everlasting life (2 Pet. 3:9). In light of this, we could start thanking Him, saying, "Father, I thank You that You love this person so much that You gave Your only begotten Son for them. It's not Your will for them to perish but to come to repentance and turn to You. I thank You, Lord, that You've already provided for their salvation" (1 John 2:2). We can continue praying, "Father, I thank You that You've already made provision. Jesus, You were the atoning sacrifice for everyone's sins – not only for those who believe but also those who are lost. So, Father, I thank You that You want them to be saved, and You've already provided it."

3. Then we can take our authority and start speaking out things that need to happen. "Father, Your Word says that faith comes by hearing Your Word. So I'm praying that Your Word will come across their path" (Rom. 10:17). "I ask that You would send forth laborers across their path" (Matt. 9:38). Next, we pray that the Word they've already heard will come back to their remembrance (John 14:26). Then, we offer ourselves as a vessel.

1. A. This kind of prayer is like what? (Water)
   B. What must we plant for people to be born again? (The seed of God's Word)
2. A. Read John 3:16, 2 Peter 3:9, and 1 John 2:2. What do we need to recognise as we start praying for a lost person? (That God loves them infinitely more than we do)
   B. The Lord doesn't want this person to perish, but to what? (Repent, turn to Him, and enjoy everlasting life)
3. A. Read Romans 10:17, Matthew 9:38, and John 14:26. What should we pray to come back to their remembrance? (The Word they've already heard)
   B. Then, we should offer ourselves as what? (A vessel)

4. Also, we can take our authority and stand against the devil (2 Cor. 4:4). God needs someone in a physical body to take their authority and release His power, saying, "I command this demonic blindness and hardened heart to be gone in Jesus' name." Because we are praying for another person – who has their own free will – we may need to pray these things for them again and again. The reason we have to pray this kind of prayer over and over again is because the person is constantly voiding our prayer by hardening their heart.

When the Word says that we can remit sins, it means we can deal with the effects sin causes in that person (John 20:23). Even though they may choose to resist and reject the drawing of the Holy Spirit, we can be confident that through our prayers, God is continuing to work in their life.

4. A. Read 2 Corinthians 4:4 and John 20:23. Why might we need to pray these things again and again? (Because we are praying for another person – who has their own free will – and they may be constantly voiding our prayer by hardening their heart)
   B. What does the Word call dealing with the effects sin causes in a person? (Remitting sins)

HOW TO PRAY FOR THE LOST
Lesson 13 – Discipleship Questions

1. According to John 3:16, God so loved whom?

2. That He gave whom?

3. That who should not perish?

4. But have what?

5. According to 2 Peter 3:9, is the Lord slack concerning His promise?

6. First John 2:2 reveals that Jesus is what for our sins?

7. For our sins only?

8. But also for the sins of whom?

9. Matthew 9:38 tells us to pray that the Lord would send forth whom?

10. Send them forth where?

11. Who does John 14:26 reveal will teach us all things Jesus said to us?

12. Who will send Him in Jesus' name?

13. According to 2 Corinthians 4:4, what light does the god of this world work to blind the minds of unbelievers from seeing?

14. John 20:23 speaks of the authority Jesus has given us to do what?

HOW TO PRAY FOR THE LOST
Lesson 13 – Answer Key

1. The world.
2. His only begotten Son.
3. Whosoever believes in Him.
4. Everlasting life.
5. No.
6. The propitiation (atoning sacrifice).
7. No.
8. The whole world.
9. Laborers.
10. Into His harvest.
11. The Holy Spirit.
12. The Father.
13. The light of the glorious Gospel of Christ.
14. Remit and retain sins.

HOW TO PRAY FOR THE LOST
Lesson 13 – Scriptures

For God so loved the world, that he gave his only begotten Son, that whosoever believeth in him should not perish, but have everlasting life.

John 3:16

The Lord is not slack concerning his promise, as some men count slackness; but is longsuffering to us-ward, not willing that any should perish, but that all should come to repentance.

2 Peter 3:9

And he is the propitiation for our sins: and not for our's only, but also for the sins of the whole world.

1 John 2:2

So then faith cometh by hearing, and hearing by the word of God.

Romans 10:17

Pray ye therefore the Lord of the harvest, that he will send forth labourers into his harvest.

Matthew 9:38

But the Comforter, which is the Holy Ghost, whom the Father will send in my name, he shall teach you all things, and bring all things to your remembrance, whatsoever I have said unto you.

John 14:26

In whom the god of this world hath blinded the minds of them which believe not, lest the light of the glorious gospel of Christ, who is the image of God, should shine unto them.

2 Corinthians 4:4

Whose soever sins ye remit, they are remitted unto them; and whose soever sins ye retain, they are retained.

John 20:23

HOW DOES REVIVAL COME?
Lesson 14

Revival is when people are completely in love with God. There's a freshness, a vitality, and an excitement about their relationship with the Lord Jesus Christ. In revival, the miraculous power of God is in manifestation – people are being healed, delivered, saved, and baptised in the Holy Spirit. Churches are full and growing, and folks from all walks of life are turning back to God.

Although I agree that we need revival, it's not going to come the way most people are presently pursuing it. Most people teach that to get revival, we must plead with God, bombard heaven, and grab hold of the horns of the altar, shaking it until God comes out. They tell us that we have to "make" God pour out revival. That's simply not true.

NOT A NEW TESTAMENT PRAYER

God is much more motivated to send revival than you are to receive it. He longs to see this nation revived and wholeheartedly following Him. He desires to see us yielding to the Holy Spirit and applying godly principles from the Word to our lives. The Lord wants us living in revival much more than we want it.

You aren't going to somehow or another get God up to speed with you. That's not what it's about. Yet so much of what is currently being said concerning prayer for revival is all about us begging God to pour out this and pleading with Him to send that.

It's actually these "intercessors" that are praying for revival who are getting a tremendous amount of the credit. From their perspective, if they weren't "standing in the gap," God would just fold His arms and let the whole world go to hell. They don't believe He cares. They think they're causing Him to "repent" by praying, "O God, repent. Turn back to us."

Please don't misunderstand. I used to think that way too. For several years, I begged and pleaded with God for revival with all my heart. I'm not saying that the people who do this are all wrong. Many of them see our genuine need for revival, and they long to see God's power manifest. They're just trying to receive it based on the faulty model they've been given.

Most of these people assume that God is so ticked off at us that He's holding back His Holy Spirit. Since man (or the church, as it may apply) has moved so far away from what He wants him to do, they perceive Him as having turned His back on us. It's like His arms are folded and He's saying, "I've given you over. Forget you!" They picture God with this attitude, and so they beg Him, "Please, pour out Your Spirit on us. Let Your Holy Spirit fall on us again!" And the intercessors jump in there, praying, "O God, have mercy on us. O Lord, don't impute our many sins unto us. We're asking You for mercy – mercy!" They're begging God to turn back to the church and pleading with Him to have mercy on the human race. This is *not* a New Testament prayer!

MOSES

The first few verses of 1 Timothy 2 talk about praying for kings and all those in authority. Then, in verse 5, the Word says:

There is one God, and one mediator between God and men, the man Christ Jesus.

There is now only one mediator – the Lord Jesus Christ.

A *mediator* is someone who stands between two parties that are at odds with each other, seeking to reconcile them. In the Old Testament, there was a gap between God and man. Sin had separated man from God, so mediators – like Moses – were needed. Galatians 3:19 says that the Old Testament Law was…

Ordained by angels in the hand of a mediator [Moses].

Brackets mine

Moses stood between an angry God and a sinful people. In Exodus 32:12, he prayed:

Turn from thy fierce wrath, and repent of this evil [You have threatened to do] **against thy people.**

Brackets mine

That's a strong statement. God was told to repent by one of His creations. It's hard to comprehend, but that's exactly what Moses said. "Repent, oh God. And turn from Your fierce wrath!" What's even more amazing is:

The LORD repented.

Exodus 32:14

"IT IS FINISHED"

Moses stood as a mediator between an angry God and a sinful people. This worked under the Old Covenant because God was angry, sin had separated mankind from Him, and there was a judgement to be meted out. Therefore, it was appropriate for Moses to mediate. However, now that we're in the New Covenant, Jesus has become our Mediator (Heb. 7).

There is one God, and one mediator between God and men, the man Christ Jesus.

1 Timothy 2:5

Jesus forever stood in between a holy God and an unholy people. He paid for our sins on the cross and took upon Himself all the wrath and punishment due us from God. This isn't only temporary – until the next time you sin – it's forever. He paid for all sin for all time – past, present, and even future-tense sin (Heb. 10:10-14). Christ has forever reconciled God and man and has brought the two into an eternal union and harmony (2 Cor. 5:18-19). Whosoever will may receive this gift of God. When Jesus said on the cross **"It is finished,"** He was speaking of God's wrath being satisfied (John 19:30).

Therefore, if Moses were to stand up today and pray "Repent, O God. And turn from your fierce wrath," that would be antichrist. It would be standing against and trying to take the place of what Christ has done. Moses' ministry of mediation was appropriate in the Old Testament because Jesus hadn't come yet. But now that He has come, for us to pray "Repent, O God. Don't pour out Your wrath on this city, nation, or people. Have mercy on us" is antichrist. You are trying to take the place of Christ and accomplish what He's already done.

The way many of us have been praying and pleading with God is literally against what Jesus Christ came to do. It's antichrist. A lack of understanding the New Testament has caused many of us to pray for revival the way they do. Revival doesn't come by begging God. It comes by us recognising that God loves people more than we do and by understanding that He wants us revived much more than even we do. We need to stop begging God to pour out His Spirit and stop passively waiting on a lightning bolt from heaven. Instead, we need to praise the Lord that He wants these results even more than we do. We need to believe God's Word and release our authority by going out and preaching the Gospel.

ALL THE REVIVAL YOU CAN HANDLE

If you go out and raise someone from the dead, you'll have all the revival you can handle. *But, Andrew, you can't raise a person from the dead unless you already have revival!* I disagree. God isn't holding back the flow of His Spirit; we are. It's the body of Christ that is clogging up the pipes and keeping God from flowing. What you need to do is work on your pipe.

You need to work on yourself, saying, "Father, please forgive me for my unbelief. Forgive me for not doing what Your Word says. You said we're supposed to go and heal the sick, cleanse the lepers, and raise the dead. I've been asking You to pour out Your Spirit and do these things without me. I've been pleading with You to move sovereignly. Please forgive me for that." Then take the Word and start meditating on it. Once you see on the inside – with the eyes of your heart – blind eyes and deaf ears opened, demons cast out, and the dead raised, then you'll start seeing it manifest in the physical realm too. You'll have revival.

If you start seeing the sick regularly healed, they'll begin breaking holes in the roof to get into your meetings (Mark 2:4). If your shadow healed the sick it touched (Acts 5:15-16), there would be so many people crowding around. You'd have all the revival you could handle.

I'm a revivalist. I am seeing people revived – blind eyes and deaf ears opened, terminal diseases healed, demons cast out, the dead raised, and people born again and baptised in the Holy Spirit. All around the world, I'm seeing millions of people's lives being changed. But I'm not asking God to do it. I'm praying, "Lord, I know You desire revival. Please help me to be the vessel of Your love and power that I need to be." I yield myself to Him, praying to and fellowshipping with Him, and allowing Him to transform me by His Word and His presence. Then I go out and speak the Word of God. I command healings and miracles to manifest, and I'm seeing revival. People are being revived.

I receive emails daily from Asia, Africa, and Europe testifying how different people have been revived. They're changed by God's Word and the power of the Holy Spirit. It's not by me begging God in some prayer closet. He's not up in heaven with His arms folded, saying, "Beg a little harder. Get another hundred thousand people to pray. And unless you all fast twice a week, I won't do it!" No, it's not like that. God is in heaven with His arms out, trying to release His power, saying, "Is there anyone who will believe Me? Is there anyone who will stand up and start speaking, living, and demonstrating My Word?" If you will do that, you'll have all the revival you can handle. You'll see people's lives begin to change.

DIANA OF THE EPHESIANS

The way many of us are praying, it seems like we have no influence, no authority, and no power to make God's kingdom come to pass here on this earth. We just approach Him like a beggar, saying, "O God, please move. Please have mercy. And please touch us." That isn't accomplishing anything good. It's just making us bitter and angry over "Why hasn't God moved? How come He hasn't poured out His Spirit? Why is God allowing this to go on? Why did He let this person die without first being saved?" God isn't letting this happen. He isn't the one allowing our country to go to hell in a hand basket. God didn't make America basically a "post-Christian" nation. It's not God who hasn't poured out His Spirit. It's many of us who have been begging Him to do what He told us to do. We haven't taken Him at His Word. We haven't been operating in our authority. We've shirked our responsibility by trying to throw it all back on God. This isn't the model we see in the New Testament.

In the New Testament, Jesus never told us to plead with God to heal or to pour out His Spirit. You can't find an example where the Lord conducted His ministry that way. The Apostle Paul didn't either.

There's no example of the Apostle Paul ever asking his people to "intercede" and tear down the stronghold of Diana of the Ephesians. This temple at Ephesus was one of the seven wonders of the world. They had over one thousand priestesses who had sex with the men as they came in to worship. As you might guess, the place was normally packed with people. Paul didn't try to do anything political. He didn't organise the church to pray, begging and pleading that God would stop this idol worship. He didn't get together with people and do "spiritual warfare," binding and rebuking Diana of the Ephesians. What did Paul do? He preached and demonstrated the Gospel.

Paul told them, "Diana of the Ephesians isn't anything. This statue didn't fall from Jupiter. Diana is no god. There's only one true God, and His Son is the Lord Jesus Christ." This is what he did in Corinth, another Roman city known for multiple idols and immoral worship. He preached the truth, and God used that truth to set people free. Paul didn't organise "intercessors" to cover every zone in the region. He didn't have people do "spiritual warfare" or "spiritual mapping." These things that are being done today by the church in an effort to try to change our nation are not what Jesus commanded us to do in the Word of God.

THE NEW TESTAMENT EXAMPLE

In the New Testament, the believers went out and preached the Word everywhere.

> **They went forth, and preached every where, the Lord working with them, and confirming the word with signs following.**
>
> Mark 16:20

They proclaimed and demonstrated God's Word. As they preached the truth, the Holy Spirit bore supernatural witness to that truth. So many people repented and converted to Christ that the temple of Diana in Ephesus fell into disrepair. The people forsook it because they turned from her to God. Diana of the Ephesians hasn't even been a factor in two thousand years until the "intercessors" resurrected her a few years ago.

I'm not trying to be mean – I just want to challenge your thinking with God's Word. Show me in the New Testament where we send people to foreign countries to do nothing but pray and tear down spiritual strongholds. Show me in the Word of God where we send people on missions trips, but forbid them to preach the Gospel, saying, "Don't witness, because you might get censored, punished, or persecuted." That's what's being done today. We are spending millions of dollars to send people to foreign countries just to let them walk around and pray. You can't find a scriptural model for this. You might be able to twist and pervert a verse or two, but if you just take the Word at face value – reading it and believing it as is – you can't find any examples of this.

However, you can find scripture where they prayed for boldness.

> **Now, Lord, behold their threatenings: and grant unto thy servants, that with all boldness they may speak thy word, By stretching forth thine hand to heal; and that signs and wonders may be done by the name of thy holy child Jesus.**
>
> Acts 4:29-30

Paul asked his friends to pray that he'd be bold despite his challenging circumstances.

> **Praying…for me, that utterance may be given unto me, that I may open my mouth boldly, to make known the mystery of the gospel, For which I am an ambassador in bonds: that therein I may speak boldly, as I ought to speak.**
>
> Ephesians 6:18-20

The early New Testament believers prayed that they would be bold, faithful witnesses despite opposition, but they didn't ask God to just "sovereignly" pour out His Spirit on unbelievers without them preaching, demonstrating, and doing their part. There simply isn't a scriptural example for that. Basically, that's the reason the church isn't having more of a salt-and-light influence on our generation. We aren't really following the New Testament example.

THE POWER OF GOD

When Jesus gave power and authority to the church, it came with responsibility. We need to use our authority and preach God's Word. We need to speak the truth to the people the Lord has put in our lives. As they receive that truth into their hearts, their lives will be changed. Many people have rejected the preaching they've heard, because it wasn't the true Gospel. It was just powerless religion and lifeless tradition. It was just condemnation and judgement. That's not the message of the Gospel. We need to preach the good news of salvation by faith in the Lord Jesus Christ. The Gospel is the power of God (Rom. 1:16).

HOW DOES REVIVAL COME?
Lesson 14 – Outline

I. Revival is when people are completely in love with God.

    A. There's a freshness, a vitality, and an excitement about their relationship with the Lord Jesus Christ.

    B. In revival, the miraculous power of God is in manifestation – people are being healed, delivered, saved, and baptised in the Holy Spirit.

    C. Churches are full and growing, and folks from all walks of life are turning back to God.

    D. The Lord wants us living in revival much more than we want it.

II. So much of what is currently being said concerning prayer for revival is all about us begging God to pour out this and pleading with Him to send that.

    A. Most of these people assume that God is so ticked off at us that He's holding back His Holy Spirit.

    B. They're begging God to turn back to the church and pleading with Him to have mercy on the human race, which is *not* a New Testament prayer.

III. There is now only one mediator – the Lord Jesus Christ.

> **There is one God, and one mediator between God and men, the man Christ Jesus.**
> 1 Timothy 2:5

    A. A *mediator* is someone who stands between two parties that are at odds with each other, seeking to reconcile them.

    B. Moses stood as a mediator between an angry God and a sinful people (Ex. 32:12 and 14).

    C. This worked under the Old Covenant because God was angry, sin had separated mankind from Him, and there was judgement to be meted out.

    D. However, now that we're in the New Covenant, Jesus has become our Mediator (Heb. 7,10:10-14; 2 Cor. 5:18-19; and John 19:30).

    E. The way that much of the church has been praying and pleading with God is literally against what Jesus Christ came to do – it's anti-Christ (trying to take the place of Christ and accomplish what He's already done).

IV. We need to believe God's Word and release our authority by going out and preaching the Gospel.

    A. God isn't holding back the flow of His Spirit; we are – it's the body of Christ that is clogging up the pipes and keeping God from flowing.

    B. What you need to do is work on your pipe.

    C. Start meditating on the Word until you can see on the inside – with the eyes of your heart – blind eyes and deaf ears opened, demons cast out, and the dead raised. Then you'll start seeing it manifest in the physical realm too.

    D. God is in heaven with His arms out, trying to release His power, saying, "Is there anyone who will believe Me? Is there anyone who will stand up and start speaking, living, and demonstrating My Word?"

    E. If you will do that, you'll have all the revival you can handle.

V. In the New Testament, the believers went out and preached the Word everywhere.

> **They went forth, and preached every where, the Lord working with them, and confirming the word with signs following. Amen.**
>
> Mark 16:20

    A. As they preached the truth, the Holy Spirit bore supernatural witness to that truth.

    B. So many people repented and converted to Christ that the temple of Diana in Ephesus fell into disrepair.

    C. The early New Testament believers prayed that they would be bold, faithful witnesses despite opposition.

> **Now, Lord, behold their threatenings: and grant unto thy servants, that with all boldness they may speak thy word, By stretching forth thine hand to heal; and that signs and wonders may be done by the name of thy holy child Jesus.**
>
> Acts 4:29-30

> **Praying…for me, that utterance may be given unto me, that I may open my mouth boldly, to make known the mystery of the gospel, For which I am an ambassador in bonds: that therein I may speak boldly, as I ought to speak.**
>
> Ephesians 6:18-20

    D. We need to preach the good news of salvation by faith in the Lord Jesus Christ – the Gospel is the power of God (Rom. 1:16).

HOW DOES REVIVAL COME?
Lesson 14 – Teacher's Guide

1. Revival is when people are completely in love with God. There's a freshness, a vitality, and an excitement about their relationship with the Lord Jesus Christ. In revival, the miraculous power of God is in manifestation – people are being healed, delivered, saved, and baptised in the Holy Spirit. Churches are full and growing, and folks from all walks of life are turning back to God. The Lord wants us living in revival much more than we want it.

2. So much of what is currently being said concerning prayer for revival is all about us begging God to pour out this and pleading with Him to send that. Most of us who do that assume that God is so ticked off at us that He's holding back His Holy Spirit. We're begging God to turn back to the church and pleading with Him to have mercy on the human race, which is *not* a New Testament prayer.

3. There is now only one mediator – the Lord Jesus Christ (1 Tim. 2:5). A *mediator* is someone who stands between two parties that are at odds with each other, seeking to reconcile them. Moses stood as a mediator between an angry God and a sinful people (Ex. 32:12 and 14). This worked under the Old Covenant because God was angry, sin had separated mankind from Him, and there was judgement to be meted out. However, now that we're in the New Covenant, Jesus has become our Mediator (Heb. 7, 10:10-14; 2 Cor. 5:18-19; and John 19:30). The way that much of the church has been praying and pleading with God is literally against what Jesus Christ came to do – it's antichrist (trying to take the place of Christ and accomplish what He's already done).

1. A. In revival, what is in manifestation? (The miraculous power of God – people are being healed, saved, and baptised in the Holy Spirit)
   B. Who wants us living in revival much more than we want it? (The Lord)
2. A. What do many people assume about God? (That He's so ticked off at us that He's holding back His Holy Spirit)
   B. Begging God to turn back to the church and pleading with Him to have mercy on the human race is *not* what? (A New Testament prayer)
3. A. Read 1 Timothy 2:5; Exodus 32:12, 14; Hebrews 7, 10:10-14; 2 Corinthians 5:18-19; and John 19:30. What is a mediator? (Someone who stands between two parties that are at odds with each other, seeking to reconcile them)
   B. Now that we're in the New Covenant, who has become our Mediator? (Jesus)

4. We need to believe God's Word and release our authority by going out and preaching the Gospel. God isn't holding back the flow of His Spirit; we are – it's the body of Christ that is clogging up the pipes and keeping God from flowing. What we need to do is work on our pipes. Let's start meditating on the Word until we can see on the inside – with the eyes of our hearts – blind eyes and deaf ears opened, demons cast out, and the dead raised. Then we'll start seeing it manifest in the physical realm too. God is in heaven with His arms out, trying to release His power, saying, "Is there anyone who will believe Me? Is there anyone who will stand up and start speaking, living, and demonstrating My Word?" If we will do that, we'll have all the revival we can handle.

5. In the New Testament, the believers went out and preached the Word everywhere (Mark 16:20). As they preached the truth, the Holy Spirit bore supernatural witness to that truth. So many people repented and converted to Christ that the temple of Diana in Ephesus fell into disrepair. The early New Testament believers prayed that they would be bold, faithful witnesses despite opposition (Acts 4:29-30 and Eph. 6:18-20). We need to preach the good news of salvation by faith in the Lord Jesus Christ – the Gospel is the power of God (Rom. 1:16).

4. A. Since God isn't holding back the flow of His Spirit, who is? (We are – it's the body of Christ that is clogging up the pipes and keeping God from flowing)
    B. We'll see blind eyes and deaf ears opened, demons cast out, and the dead raised manifest in the physical realm once we start meditating on the Word and seeing it happen where? (On the inside – with the eyes of our hearts)
5. A. Read Mark 16:20, Acts 4:29-30, Ephesians 6:18-20, and Romans 1:16. In the New Testament, the believers went out and _____ everywhere. (Preached the Word)
    B. What is the Gospel? (The power of God)

HOW DOES REVIVAL COME?
Lesson 14 – Additional Information

My teaching entitled *Grace, the Power of the Gospel* (in audio as *The Gospel: The Power of God*) takes a closer look at this very issue. The book of Romans is the Apostle Paul's masterpiece on the grace of God. In it, he clearly reveals what is the Gospel – this powerful good news message we are to preach.

HOW DOES REVIVAL COME?
Lesson 14 – Discipleship Questions

1. According to 1 Timothy 2:5, how many mediators are there now between God and men?

2. Galatians 3:19 reveals that the Law was ordained by angels in the hand of whom?

3. How did the Lord respond when Moses prayed for Him to turn from His fierce wrath and repent of this evil against His people in Exodus 32:12 and 14?

4. According to Hebrews 10:10-14, by one offering He has perfected for how long them that are sanctified?

5. Second Corinthians 5:18-19 reveals that God has reconciled us to Himself by whom?

6. What ministry has He given to us?

7. What word has He committed to us?

8. What did Jesus say in John 19:30 right before He bowed His head and gave up the ghost?

9. In Mark 2:4, what did this sick man's friends do to get him into the crowded house where Jesus was teaching?

10. According to Acts 5:15-16, how many of the sick and demonised folks were healed?

11. Acts 16:20 says that the early believers went forth and _____ everywhere.

12. How did the Lord confirm the Word?

13. In the midst of the persecution they were experiencing, how did the early believers in Acts 4:29-30 pray to be able to speak forth the Word?

14. How did Paul ask his friends to pray for him in Ephesians 6:18-20, concerning the mystery of the Gospel?

15. According to Romans 1:16, the Gospel is the power of God to salvation to whom?

HOW DOES REVIVAL COME?
Lesson 14 – Answer Key

1. One.

2. A mediator.

3. The Lord repented of the evil that He thought to do unto His people.

4. Forever.

5. Jesus Christ.

6. The ministry of reconciliation.

7. The word of reconciliation.

8. It is finished.

9. They uncovered the roof and let him down in his bed.

10. Every one.

11. Preached.

12. With signs following.

13. With all boldness.

14. That utterance may be given to him to open his mouth and speak boldly.

15. Everyone who believes.

HOW DOES REVIVAL COME?
Lesson 14 – Scriptures

For there is one God, and one mediator between God and men, the man Christ Jesus.
1 Timothy 2:5

Wherefore then serveth the law? It was added because of transgressions, till the seed should come to whom the promise was made; and it was ordained by angels in the hand of a mediator.
Galatians 3:19

Wherefore should the Egyptians speak, and say, For mischief did he bring them out, to slay them in the mountains, and to consume them from the face of the earth? Turn from thy fierce wrath, and repent of this evil against thy people.
Exodus 32:12

And the LORD repented of the evil which he thought to do unto his people.
Exodus 32:14

By the which will we are sanctified through the offering of the body of Jesus Christ once for all. And every priest standeth daily ministering and offering oftentimes the same sacrifices, which can never take away sins: But this man, after he had offered one sacrifice for sins for ever, sat down on the right hand of God; From henceforth expecting till his enemies be made his footstool. For by one offering he hath perfected for ever them that are sanctified.
Hebrews 10:10-14

And all things are of God, who hath reconciled us to himself by Jesus Christ, and hath given to us the ministry of reconciliation; To wit, that God was in Christ, reconciling the world unto himself, not imputing their trespasses unto them; and hath committed unto us the word of reconciliation.
2 Corinthians 5:18-19

When Jesus therefore had received the vinegar, he said, It is finished: and he bowed his head, and gave up the ghost.
John 19:30

And when they could not come nigh unto him for the press, they uncovered the roof where he was: and when they had broken it up, they let down the bed wherein the sick of the palsy lay.
Mark 2:4

Insomuch that they brought forth the sick into the streets, and laid them on beds and couches, that at the least the shadow of Peter passing by might overshadow some of them. There came also a multitude out of the cities round about unto Jerusalem, bringing sick folks, and them which were vexed with unclean spirits: and they were healed every one.
Acts 5:15-16

And they went forth, and preached every where, the Lord working with them, and confirming the word with signs following. Amen.

Mark 16:20

And now, Lord, behold their threatenings: and grant unto thy servants, that with all boldness they may speak thy word, By stretching forth thine hand to heal; and that signs and wonders may be done by the name of thy holy child Jesus.

Acts 4:29-30

Praying always with all prayer and supplication in the Spirit, and watching thereunto with all perseverance and supplication for all saints; And for me, that utterance may be given unto me, that I may open my mouth boldly, to make known the mystery of the gospel, For which I am an ambassador in bonds: that therein I may speak boldly, as I ought to speak.

Ephesians 6:18-20

For I am not ashamed of the gospel of Christ: for it is the power of God unto salvation to every one that believeth; to the Jew first, and also to the Greek.

Romans 1:16

BELIEVE AND RECEIVE
Lesson 15

As believers in the Lord Jesus Christ, it's our responsibility to boldly preach the Gospel and faithfully teach God's Word.

> ***Whosoever shall call upon the name of the Lord shall be saved. How then shall they call on him in whom they have not believed? and how shall they believe in him of whom they have not heard? and how shall they hear without a preacher? And how shall they preach, except they be sent? as it is written, How beautiful are the feet of them that preach the gospel of peace, and bring glad tidings of good things!...So then faith cometh by hearing, and hearing by the word of God.***
>
> Romans 10:13-15 and 17

The manifestation of the Holy Spirit on the Day of Pentecost arrested the people's attention. Seizing the opportunity, Peter stood up and preached Christ. The people responded by asking, "What must we do to be saved?" Peter answered,

> ***Repent, and be baptised every one of you in the name of Jesus Christ for the remission of sins, and ye shall receive the gift of the Holy Ghost. For*** *the promise* ***is unto you, and to your children, and to all that are afar off, even as many as the Lord our God shall call.***
>
> Acts 2:38-39, emphasis mine

Considering the context – the Day of Pentecost – and looking back to Acts 1:4-5 and 8, it's clear that the promise being spoken of here is the outpouring of the Holy Spirit. Almost everyone would agree that the outpouring of the Holy Spirit is part and parcel of true revival. Peter was saying, "What You've seen – this outpouring of the Holy Spirit, this manifestation of the coming of God's Spirit, the indwelling of the Holy Ghost, and the miraculous manifestations this has caused – is not only for you but also for your children, for your children's children, and all those who will follow." Peter was looking into the future to the generations to come, saying that this promise they were experiencing of the outpoured Holy Spirit is for today too.

TARRYING FOR THE HOLY SPIRIT

God never quit pouring out His Holy Spirit. This promise was intended to go from generation to generation to all believers throughout time. Although the baptism in the Holy Spirit and the gifts of the Holy Spirit have only been widely recognised and received by the body of Christ at large for the last century or so, it's not because they weren't available. An honest look at church history will reveal pockets of believers down through the centuries who received the Holy Spirit and operated in His power since the book of Acts. However, somewhere along the way – perhaps around the beginning of what's now called the Dark Ages – the church at large, for whatever reasons, stopped believing for and receiving this promise.

In the early days of Azusa Street and the beginning of the Pentecostal movement, they didn't fully understand how they received this powerful manifestation of the Holy Spirit. They didn't understand exactly what they did – or if they did anything at all – to occasion it. Therefore, one of the dominant doctrines that emerged from those early days of the Pentecostal movement was to "tarry" for the Holy Spirit. They said, "You have to beg and plead with God to pour out and fill you with His Holy Spirit." They would just wait – sometimes years – for this cataclysmic experience where God would touch them and baptise them in the Holy Spirit.

It's almost as if we've swung over to the opposite extreme today. Many people come forward who have never even heard about the baptism in the Holy Spirit. When the minister asks if they'd like to receive, they answer, "Well, I guess so." They don't know why they need the Holy Spirit. They don't know what to expect. There's no anticipation and no desire. I've seen people receive prayer for the baptism in the Holy Spirit, walk back to their seats, and it seems to have zero impact on their lives. That's not good either. It shouldn't be that way.

One good thing about the way the old-time Pentecostals did it was that when they finally received the baptism in the Holy Spirit, it meant something to them. They would pray desperately, wailing and travailing before God, sometimes for years. But once they received, the Holy Spirit had a profound impact on their lives.

We know today that we don't have to "tarry" or wait for God to pour out His Spirit. We don't have to beg and plead for the Lord to send the Holy Ghost. We can just believe and receive the free gift He's given. However, it would be wonderful to see the hunger that the "tarrying" produced.

GO TO JERUSALEM

In Acts 1, Jesus told His disciples to wait.

> **Being assembled together with them,** [Jesus] **commanded them that they should not depart from Jerusalem, but wait for the promise of the Father…ye shall be baptised with the Holy Ghost not many days hence.**
> Acts 1:4 and 5, brackets mine

At the time, Jesus had resurrected, but He hadn't yet ascended. He was still bodily upon the earth. Soon after He ascended, though, He poured out the Holy Spirit on His disciples on the Day of Pentecost. Now that the Holy Spirit has already been given, there's no need to wait any longer.

However, if you're going to take this admonition to wait literally, then you must also go to the city of Jerusalem to do it.

> **Behold, I send the promise of my Father upon you: but tarry ye in the city of Jerusalem, until ye be endued with power from on high…** [Jesus] **commanded them that they should not depart from Jerusalem, but wait for the promise of the Father.**
> Luke 24:49 and Acts 1:4, brackets mine

Jesus told these disciples to wait because there was about fifty more days until Pentecost. However, now that the Holy Spirit has already been poured out, you can just believe and receive.

I've seen thousands and thousands of people receive the baptism in the Holy Spirit, speak in tongues, and have a life-changing experience with God simply by believing and receiving. You don't have to wait and "tarry."

"WE'VE GOT IT"

Most people would agree with what I'm sharing about the baptism in the Holy Spirit. But when it comes to revival, they just shift gears, saying, "Oh, but we have to beg and plead, wail and travail. We must get a million people praying and fasting together so God will send revival and pour out His Spirit." No, you just have to believe. You just have to receive. And as you get revived, you'll have an opportunity to influence and share that life with the people around you. As you, your friends, your family, and your workplace get revived, they go out, too, and it spreads.

The reason we aren't seeing a greater revival isn't because we don't have millions of people praying and asking God to pour out His Spirit; it's because we have very few people who are flowing in revival – believing God's Word, taking their authority, and making the power of God manifest.

Duncan Campbell, an outstanding Scottish preacher in the early-to-mid-twentieth century, preached the Scottish Hebrides Revival. This was a powerful manifestation of the Holy Spirit that was received over a hundred years ago. I actually heard him speak when he was older. He told how there were two little women who prayed for over twenty years. Then there was a pastor and his seven elders who also prayed nearly a year, all asking the Lord to pour out His Spirit. Finally, one day the power of God hit, and they experienced all of these glorious things. He said this happened because of all that begging and pleading with God for over twenty years.

Several years after hearing that, I heard the testimony of a young man who had showed up at that final prayer meeting right before the power hit. He said that these other men had prayed every Saturday night for almost a year. They were begging God for an outpouring of His Spirit. This young man walked in, prayed until two in the morning, and declared, "Either God's Word is true, or it isn't. We've got it. I'm going home."

The revival actually came when they quit begging and started believing. Once they started believing God's Word that they already had it, everything changed and the power was loosed. We've been given power and authority by the Lord. We must step out in faith and use what God has given us, or revival won't manifest.

SILENCE

Imagine that you've given me your Bible. It's a gift and it's in my possession right now. What would you do if I turned to you and asked, "May I please borrow your Bible? I'd like to look up a scripture. I really need to hear from God, and I believe He's speaking to me. Would you please give me your Bible?" I could beg. I could plead. I could even try to condemn you, saying, "If you were really a Christian, you'd share your Bible with me." What would you do? You've already given it to me.

How do you respond to someone who is asking you to give them something they've already got? How do you answer somebody who is begging you to do something you've already done for them? If I was the one being asked those questions, I'm not sure how I'd respond. Probably, I'd just look at them dumbfounded. I wouldn't say anything.

If someone is asking for something they already have, how does a person respond to that? Probably in silence. Sounds a lot like the way God has responded to all of our begging and pleading for an outpouring of the Holy Spirit.

The truth is, God poured out His Holy Spirit on the Day of Pentecost, and He's never withdrawn Him since (Acts 2:38-39). The Lord has never become so ticked off that He just said, "All right, Holy Spirit. Come on back. No more revival. No more manifestations." God didn't cause the church to go through the Dark Ages. He didn't will that there be a period of time where truth would be so bound up that very few would ever see it. God didn't just all of a sudden – "sovereignly" – reach down and touch Martin Luther. He didn't just decide to pour out His Spirit upon the Reformers to do something "new" because, after all, God was tired of a thousand years worth of deadness in the earth. No, the problem wasn't God's giving – it was our believing and receiving.

WAVES?

Martin Luther had a real heart for God. He wasn't satisfied with the religious teaching and the traditionally accepted doctrine of his day. As a pilgrim to the holy city, praying his rosary and climbing up the steps of the holy building, he realised that visiting that place and doing those things didn't make any difference. As he stood there, fed up with it all, the Holy Spirit brought Scripture back to his remembrance.

> *Where is boasting then? It is excluded. By what law? of works? Nay: but by the law of faith. Therefore we conclude that a man is justified by faith without the deeds of the law.*
> Romans 3:27-28

Martin Luther heard the Word and believed it. Then he acted on it by nailing his "Ninety-five Theses" up on the door of his church in Wittenburg, Germany. He stood boldly before the religious leaders at the Diet of Worms giving his defense. Martin Luther proclaimed the Word of God, and the Word acted like wildfire in the hungry hearts of the people. From it, the Reformation sprung up, and the world was forever changed. This wasn't because God just sovereignly said, "All right, I'm ready to do something new on the earth." No, it was because a single person – a physical human being – believed, received, and acted on the Word of God.

Religion teaches that God moves in waves. Back in the 1940s and 50s there was the healing movement that came through the body of Christ. Healing revivals, healing evangelists, and tent meetings sprung up everywhere. Then there was the charismatic movement and the Word of faith movement. Now there's this and that movement, and people are saying, "Look, God is doing a new thing! He's pouring out His Spirit again." No, that's not how God works.

The healing revival sprung up because someone saw healing in the Word, believed God, and started releasing this power into the earth by using their authority. They stepped out in faith on the Word and saw the Holy Spirit demonstration. That healing power has been available ever since the death, burial, and resurrection of Christ, but the church just hadn't been receiving it.

ALWAYS AVAILABLE

Back in the 1940s, most of the church believed that miracles, signs, and wonders had all passed away with the apostles. This was the dominant theological position being taught. However, a young Oral Roberts received healing from tuberculosis and stuttering after being bedridden for over five months. As he studied the Word, he became personally convinced that it's God's will to heal today. So this young minister stepped out on that Word by renting a hall in Enid, Oklahoma.

In this first meeting, Oral asked God for three things. The first was a certain minimum number of people in attendance. So, before he ever even went out on the stage, Oral stood behind the curtain and counted the people. Then he went out and immediately took up an offering. Oral had told God, "I'm not going to go in debt. So if this is You, You're going to have to bring in enough money to at least cover these expenses." After the offering was counted, the second requirement was met – nearly to the penny. The third thing Oral asked for was at least one notable miracle. He said, "God, I'm going to preach and proclaim that it's still Your will to heal today. If this is really You, then we have to see at least one notable miracle." After preaching his sermon, he called people forward, and the healings began to manifest. From then on, it was full steam ahead.

Oral Roberts and many others began proclaiming the Word of God concerning healing. As people believed the Word and received healing, a revival broke out. Some people think, *Well, God just sovereignly moved.* No, the Lord has always desired for us to receive healings, manifest miracles, and experience revival ever since He walked on this earth. Jesus Himself said,

> **Verily, verily, I say unto you, He that believeth on me, the works that I do shall he do also; and greater works than these shall he do; because I go unto my Father.**
>
> John 14:12

We can debate what the **"greater works"** are, but what are you going to do with **"the works that I do shall he do also"**?

God always intended for His church to operate in the supernatural. It's not God that just skipped from around 200 until 1940. No, it's people who quit appropriating His power. Christians got into unbelief. They stopped operating in faith. Finally somebody broke through this barrier and started believing again. Then they preached and proclaimed God's Word. When they took their authority and used it, healing manifested. However, the whole counsel of God has always been available to those who would believe.

God doesn't just move for a decade in this and then move for a decade in that. "Ten years ago He moved in healing. Now He's forgotten healing and is moving in righteousness. This next decade He's going to work on marriages. There's a new wave coming!" Nonsense. That's just man's attempt to justify his powerlessness.

WORK ON YOUR RECEIVER

The Lord is today all that He ever was and all that He'll ever be.

> **Jesus Christ the same yesterday, and today, and for ever.**
>
> Hebrews 13:8

He wants to move in and through your life in miracles, healings, deliverance, and prosperity. Everything that God is, is now available to you through His Word. You don't have to beg and plead and then just passively sit back and wait to see what God will do. The Bible calls that unbelief.

Without faith it is impossible to please him: for he that cometh to God must believe that he is, and that he is a rewarder of them that diligently seek him.

Hebrews 11:6

God honours those who honour Him (1 Sam. 2:20). Believe that God is. He's a rewarder of those who diligently seek Him. Pray, "Father, I am seeking You. Your Word tells me that You have provided all these things. By faith, I receive. Thank You, Lord!" As you seek Him and continue building yourself up in faith, the power of God will manifest, and you'll operate in all the revival you want. You're the one who determines how much revival you have – not God.

You don't have to pray and just passively wait, saying, "I've been praying twenty years for revival, and we haven't got it yet. I don't know why God hasn't done it." That's just as wrong as someone saying, "I've been praying twenty years for the baptism in the Holy Spirit, but God hasn't given it to me yet." No, God has already given; you just haven't received it yet. It's not God's *giver* that's having the problem – it's your *receiver*. You need to work on your receiving, not God's giving.

BELIEVE AND RECEIVE
Lesson 15 – Outline

I. As believers in the Lord Jesus Christ, it's our responsibility to boldly preach the Gospel and faithfully teach God's Word.

> *Whosoever shall call upon the name of the Lord shall be saved. How then shall they call on him in whom they have not believed? and how shall they believe in him of whom they have not heard? and how shall they hear without a preacher? And how shall they preach, except they be sent? as it is written, How beautiful are the feet of them that preach the gospel of peace, and bring glad tidings of good things!…So then faith cometh by hearing, and hearing by the word of God.*
>
> Romans 10:13-15 and 17

> *Repent, and be baptised every one of you in the name of Jesus Christ for the remission of sins, and ye shall receive the gift of the Holy Ghost. For the promise is unto you, and to your children, and to all that are afar off, even as many as the Lord our God shall call.*
>
> Acts 2:38-39

    A.   God never quit pouring out His Holy Spirit.

    B.   This promise was intended to go from generation to generation to all believers throughout time.

    C.   We can just believe and receive the free gift He's given (Luke 24:49 and Acts 1:4-5).

II. The reason we aren't seeing a greater revival is because we have very few people who are flowing in revival – believing God's Word, taking their authority, and making the power of God manifest.

    A.   We must step out in faith and use what God has given us, or revival won't manifest.

    B.   God poured out His Holy Spirit on the Day of Pentecost, and He's never withdrawn Him since (Acts 2:38-39).

    C.   Martin Luther heard the Word and believed it.

> *Where is boasting then? It is excluded. By what law? of works? Nay: but by the law of faith. Therefore we conclude that a man is justified by faith without the deeds of the law.*
>
> Romans 3:27-28

    D.   The Reformation sprung up, and the world was forever changed because a single person – a physical human being – believed, received, and acted on the Word of God.

III. The healing revival sprung up because someone saw healing in the Word, believed God, and started releasing this power into the earth by using their authority.

   A. They stepped out in faith on the Word and saw the Holy Spirit demonstrated.

   B. That healing power has been available ever since the death, burial, and resurrection of Christ, but the church just hadn't been receiving it.

   C. The Lord has always desired for us to receive healings, manifest miracles, and experience revival ever since He walked on this earth.

   Verily, verily, I say unto you, He that believeth on me, the works that I do shall he do also; and greater works than these shall he do; because I go unto my Father.
   John 14:12

   D. God always intended for His church to operate in the supernatural.

IV. The whole counsel of God has always been available to those who would believe.

   A. The Lord is today all that He ever was and all that He'll ever be.

   Jesus Christ the same yesterday, and today, and for ever.
   Hebrews 13:8

   B. He wants to move in and through your life in miracles, healings, deliverance, and prosperity.

   C. Everything that God is, is now available to you through His Word.

V. As you seek Him and continue building yourself up in faith, the power of God will manifest, and you'll operate in all the revival you want.

   Without faith it is impossible to please him: for he that cometh to God must believe that he is, and that he is a rewarder of them that diligently seek him.
   Hebrews 11:6

   A. You're the one who determines how much revival you have – not God.

   B. God has already given; you just haven't received it yet.

   C. You need to work on your receiving, not God's giving.

BELIEVE AND RECEIVE
Lesson 15 – Teacher's Guide

1. As believers in the Lord Jesus Christ, it's our responsibility to boldly preach the Gospel and faithfully teach God's Word (Rom. 10:13-15, 17; and Acts 2:38-39). God never quit pouring out His Holy Spirit. This promise was intended to go from generation to generation to all believers throughout time. We can just believe and receive the free gift He's given (Luke 24:49 and Acts 1:4-5).

2. The reason we aren't seeing a greater revival is because we have very few people who are flowing in revival – believing God's Word, taking their authority, and making the power of God manifest. We must step out in faith and use what God has given us, or revival won't manifest. God poured out His Holy Spirit on the Day of Pentecost, and He's never withdrawn Him since (Acts 2:38-39). Martin Luther heard the Word and believed it (Rom. 3:27-28). The Reformation sprung up, and the world was forever changed because a single person – a physical human being – believed, received, and acted on the Word of God.

3. The healing revival sprung up because someone saw healing in the Word, believed God, and started releasing this power into the earth by using their authority. They stepped out in faith on the Word and saw the Holy Spirit demonstrated. That healing power has been available ever since the death, burial, and resurrection of Christ, but the church just hadn't been receiving it. The Lord has always desired for us to receive healings, manifest miracles, and experience revival ever since He walked on this earth (John 14:12). God always intended for His church to operate in the supernatural.

1. A. Read Romans 10:13-17, Acts 2:38-39, Luke 24:49, and Acts 1:4-5. As believers in the Lord Jesus Christ, it's our responsibility to what? (Boldly preach the Gospel and faithfully teach God's Word)
   B. The promise of the Holy Spirit was intended for whom? (To all believers throughout time)
2. A. Review Acts 2:38-39 and read Romans 3:27-28. Why aren't we seeing a greater revival? (Because very few people are flowing in revival – believing God's Word, taking their authority, and making the power of God manifest)
   B. Since when has God poured out – and never withdrawn – His Holy Spirit? (Since the Day of Pentecost)
3. A. Read John 14:12. How did the healing revival spring up? (Because someone saw healing in the Word, believed God, and started releasing this power into the earth by using their authority)
   B. That healing power has been available ever since when? (The death, burial, and resurrection of Christ)

4. The whole counsel of God has always been available to those who would believe. The Lord is today all that He ever was and all that He'll ever be (Heb. 13:8). He wants to move in and through our lives in miracles, healings, deliverance, and prosperity. Everything that God is, is now available to us through His Word.

5. As we seek Him and continue building ourselves up in faith, the power of God will manifest, and we'll operate in all the revival we want (Heb. 11:6). We're the ones who determine how much revival we have – not God. God has already given; we just haven't received it yet. We need to work on our receiving, not God's giving.

---

4. A. Read Hebrews 13:8. God wants to move in and through our lives how? (In miracles, healings, deliverance, and prosperity)
   B. What is now available to us through His Word? (Everything that God is)
5. A. Read Hebrews 11:6. Who determines how much revival we have – us or God? (Us)
   B. What do we need to work on? (Our receiving)

BELIEVE AND RECEIVE
Lesson 15 – Discipleship Questions

1. According to Romans 10:13-17, who shall be saved?

2. Preachers of the Gospel of peace bring glad tidings of what?

3. What gift is promised in Acts 2:38-39 to those who repent and are baptised in the name of Jesus Christ for the remission of sins?

4. John baptised with water, but what does Acts 1:4-5 say they shall be baptised with not many days hence?

5. What does Acts 1:8 reveal that we receive after the Holy Spirit is come upon us?

6. What did Jesus say in Luke 24:49 that the promise of His Father would endue us with?

7. What law does Romans 3:27-28 speak of?

8. Is a man justified by faith with or without the deeds of the Law?

9. Who shall do the works mentioned by Jesus in John 14:12?

10. In addition to the works Jesus did, what works did He promise these believers would also do?

11. According to Hebrews 13:8, Jesus Christ is what yesterday, today, and forever?

12. According to Hebrews 11:6, is it possible to please God without faith?

13. What is God to those that diligently seek Him?

14. What did Eli do to Elkanah and his wife in 1 Samuel 2:20?

BELIEVE AND RECEIVE
Lesson 15 – Answer Key

1. Whosoever calls upon the name of the Lord.

2. Good things.

3. The gift of the Holy Spirit.

4. The Holy Spirit.

5. Power.

6. Power from on high.

7. The law of faith.

8. Without.

9. He that believes on Jesus.

10. Greater works.

11. The same.

12. No.

13. A rewarder.

14. He blessed them.

BELIEVE AND RECEIVE
Lesson 15 – Scriptures

For whosoever shall call upon the name of the Lord shall be saved. How then shall they call on him in whom they have not believed? and how shall they believe in him of whom they have not heard? and how shall they hear without a preacher? And how shall they preach, except they be sent? as it is written, How beautiful are the feet of them that preach the gospel of peace, and bring glad tidings of good things! But they have not all obeyed the gospel. For Esaias saith, Lord, who hath believed our report? So then faith cometh by hearing, and hearing by the word of God.

Romans 10:13-17

Then Peter said unto them, Repent, and be baptised every one of you in the name of Jesus Christ for the remission of sins, and ye shall receive the gift of the Holy Ghost. For the promise is unto you, and to your children, and to all that are afar off, even as many as the Lord our God shall call.

Acts 2:38-39

And, being assembled together with them, commanded them that they should not depart from Jerusalem, but wait for the promise of the Father, which, saith he, ye have heard of me. For John truly baptised with water; but ye shall be baptised with the Holy Ghost not many days hence.

Acts 1:4-5

But ye shall receive power, after that the Holy Ghost is come upon you: and ye shall be witnesses unto me both in Jerusalem, and in all Judaea, and in Samaria, and unto the uttermost part of the earth.

Acts 1:8

And, behold, I send the promise of my Father upon you: but tarry ye in the city of Jerusalem, until ye be endued with power from on high.

Luke 24:49

Where is boasting then? It is excluded. By what law? of works? Nay: but by the law of faith. Therefore we conclude that a man is justified by faith without the deeds of the law.

Romans 3:27-28

Verily, verily, I say unto you, He that believeth on me, the works that I do shall he do also; and greater works than these shall he do; because I go unto my Father.

John 14:12

Jesus Christ the same yesterday, and today, and for ever.

Hebrews 13:8

But without faith it is impossible to please him: for he that cometh to God must believe that he is, and that he is a rewarder of them that diligently seek him.

Hebrews 11:6

*And Eli blessed Elkanah and his wife, and said, The LORD give thee seed of this woman for the loan which is lent to the L*ORD*. And they went unto their own home.*

1 Samuel 2:20

GOD HAS GIVEN YOU POWER
Lesson 16

God created man in his own image, in the image of God created he him; male and female created he them. And God blessed them, and God said unto them, Be fruitful, and multiply, and replenish the earth, and subdue it: and have dominion over the fish of the sea, and over the fowl of the air, and over every living thing that moveth upon the earth.

Genesis 1:27-28

The Lord blessed us and gave us the ability to procreate. He said to Adam and Eve, "You be fruitful. You multiply. You replenish the earth." This power and authority God gave us comes with responsibility.

The Lord gave us the ability to create children. He doesn't send them to us via some stork. It's God's power, but He set certain things in motion. Therefore, you can pray until you're blue in the face, but a woman isn't going to get pregnant until she has a relationship with a man. That's the way God intended this to operate, and that's the way it works.

OUR RESPONSIBILITY

If a woman was just praying and praying and praying to be pregnant and have a child but had no physical relationship with a man, we'd look at her and think, *How dumb can you get and still breathe? Didn't anybody tell her the facts of life? Doesn't she understand how things work?* Yet this is exactly what many Christians are doing in other areas of life. They are asking God for healing, but they aren't doing what the Word says. God's Word says to speak to the mountain:

Whosoever shall say unto this mountain, Be thou removed, and be thou cast into the sea; and shall not doubt in his heart, but shall believe that those things which he saith shall come to pass; he shall have whatsoever he saith.

Mark 11:23

That's one of God's laws. Yet people aren't doing what the Word says, and they wonder, *Why hasn't God healed me yet?* That's just as foolish as a woman who prays constantly to get pregnant without having any relationship with a man and then, when nothing happens, says, "Why hasn't God given me a child yet?" God gave us power and authority in this area.

I know a couple that had twelve kids. When I asked the husband "How many children are you going to have?" he answered, "If God wants us to have kids, we'll have kids. It's just totally up to God." There are certain forms of birth control that I don't advocate because in actuality they create abortions. However, if nothing else, a little self-control would help. If you don't exercise some self-control in this area, thinking *If it's God's will, we'll have children, but if it's not, we won't,* then you're totally ignoring your responsibility. God blessed us and gave us power to procreate.

If people never had children unless it was God's will, then prostitutes wouldn't get pregnant. If all children were just supernaturally ordained of God, unwed mothers wouldn't conceive. It's not God's will for people who aren't married to bear children. If God was directly controlling this aspect of people's lives, He wouldn't let children be born addicted to drugs or with HIV. God gave the power to procreate to physical human beings, and if you cooperate with how He made this universe to function, you can create a child.

WE MUST COOPERATE

It's God's power, but He put it under our control. We have power and authority in this area. If you want the results, then you have to do the right things to cooperate with those laws of how to conceive and birth children. Most people understand this, and they would ridicule someone who thinks they can just pray for a child to appear. God doesn't just supernaturally drop children out of heaven. That's not how they come.

Just praying and asking God to supernaturally drop healing, salvation, or revival from heaven is not how they come. There are spiritual laws that in order to cooperate with them, we must use our authority as human beings. If we don't step out in faith to cooperate with God in these areas, they won't come to pass.

This is so simple that you'd have to have somebody help you to misunderstand it. Yet we've had a lot of help. I've talked to many people who have asked, "If God is really God, then He could have healed this person. Why did He let them die?"

God isn't like that. He doesn't just say, "All right, you have power to heal. You go out and heal the sick." Then, if we aren't doing it because we don't know or because we're more dominated by unbelief than faith, God doesn't look down and say, "These folks are never going to get the job done. Since they're not believing My Word or doing it the way I said, I'm just going to heal this person anyway." That would violate His own integrity.

God told us, "You have the power. You go out. You heal the sick. You cleanse the lepers. You raise the dead (Matt. 10:8)." If we don't do our part, God isn't going to step in and do what He's told us to do. No amount of begging or pleading will change that situation. We in the body of Christ need to discover what God has given to us. We need to find out what's under our authority and start using it the way He intended. Let's take our responsibility and lay aside our unbelief. Let's reject all these religious doctrines that absolve us of our responsibility and say, "Whatever will be, will be. It's just up to God who gets saved and healed. He does all things sovereignly." Let's stop backing out of our responsibility and placing the blame on God. He's not the one failing – it's us.

POWER TO GET WEALTH

In the area of provision, God has given us power to get wealth.

> **Thou shalt remember the LORD thy God: for it is he that giveth thee power to get wealth, that he may establish his covenant which he sware unto thy fathers, as it is this day.**
>
> Deuteronomy 8:18

Anytime God gives us power, He also gives us authority so we can release the power and use it. With this authority comes responsibility. This is why God doesn't give us money directly. The

Scripture doesn't say that God gives us money. He gave us power – an anointing, an ability – to get wealth.

First of all, God doesn't have any money. He doesn't use money. In heaven, there is no currency of exchange. Neither does He make money. If you're praying "O God. I need $100," or whatever currency it is that you need, God doesn't have any of those, and He's not going to counterfeit them either. That's against the law. God isn't going to break the law and start counterfeiting money. He's not going to make money and put it in your pocket. The Bible says,

> **Give, and it shall be given unto you; good measure, pressed down, and shaken together, and running over, shall men give into your bosom.**
>
> Luke 6:38

Since God doesn't have money directly, He sends it to you through people. God impresses other people, and people will be involved in getting you His supply.

THE WORK OF YOUR HANDS

Many people are ignorant of this truth. So they pray, "God, if You're God, You can do anything. Put money in my wallet." Then they open up their wallets, and when there's no more money in there than before, they say, "Well, God isn't faithful. The Word doesn't work. It's just not true." Then they start blaming God because they are ignorant.

God isn't going to create money and put it in your wallet. That's against the law. God gave you power to get wealth, so you must learn to use your authority to release that power. In order to see God's provision for you manifest, you must cooperate with the spiritual laws governing prosperity.

God has promised to bless all the work of your hands.

> **The LORD shall command the blessing upon thee...in all that thou settest thine hand unto...The LORD shall...bless all the work of thine hand.**
>
> Deuteronomy 28:8 and 12

However, if you aren't setting your hands to something, God doesn't have anything to bless. You can't just sit at home doing nothing and expect the Lord to prosper you. It doesn't work that way. You aren't going to see God begin to prosper you if you aren't working. In fact, the Word says:

> **This we commanded you, that if any would not work, neither should he eat.**
>
> 2 Thessalonians 3:10

"GO GET A JOB UNTIL"

God is into work. He's into you doing something productive. That's why welfare – as it's currently being practiced in our country – isn't a godly concept. I'm not saying that any person who's receiving welfare is ungodly. I'm not saying that God hates them or that they're in sin. But I am saying that it isn't God's system.

Anyone might need help on occasion. There's nothing wrong with you taking the help of other people, or a government, if you are in a situation where you temporarily need it. But to be a second-, third-, or fourth-generation welfare recipient where you just sit at home and let the government pay you for doing nothing is an ungodly concept.

If you're going to get into God's divine flow of provision, then you need to start doing some things to release that power and see this anointing begin to generate the income you need. God has given you the power to get wealth, but you need to do something. You need to work. You need to set your hand to something productive.

One of our partners worked as the CEO of a corporation. However, his company downsised and he was laid off. So he started drawing unemployment for a period of time. He wanted to work, so he put in résumés all over town. But this was during an economically challenging time and he was overqualified. Therefore, no one hired him.

So when he was a few weeks away from getting his house repossessed and losing everything, he came to me and asked, "What do I do?"

I answered, "Go get a job."

He said, "I'm trying."

I continued, "No, I mean go get a job *until*. There's nothing wrong with you believing for another CEO job or something similar. But until your better-paying job comes in, get a job stocking shelves or flipping burgers."

This guy was highly offended. "I'm a CEO. I couldn't do something like that. Besides, I need more money than that. My house is about to be repossessed." He was something like $4,000 to $5,000 behind and hadn't worked in over a year.

I told him, "If you would have been stocking shelves or flipping burgers for the past year, you would have had enough money to keep this house from being repossessed while you still sought the job you're believing for. There's nothing wrong with you not wanting to stay there, but you've got to do something. By doing nothing, you are abdicating your responsibility and keeping the blessing of God – that He wants to give you – from manifesting. You can pray and pray, and you might get a miracle that will tide you over to the next week or month. But then you'll have another crisis next month and the month after that and the month after that. You aren't going to see the supernatural flow of finances start manifesting in your life until you recognise God gave you power and authority to get wealth. You need to stand up and use that power and authority by doing something."

THIMBLE OR BUCKET?

Many people are waiting on their ship to come in, but they've never sent one out. They're waiting on a crop to grow up, but they haven't sown any seed. They're believing God for a great supply, but they haven't cooperated with His spiritual laws concerning prosperity. The Word says,

> **Give, and it shall be given unto you; good measure, pressed down, and shaken together, and running over, shall men give into your bosom. For with the same measure that ye mete withal it shall be measured to you again.**
>
> Luke 6:38

Are you using a tiny little thimble, throwing God five bucks here and there, thinking that you're really being generous, when the truth is the tithe off of your paycheck would be $200, $300, or $400? Are you tipping God and wondering, *How come my finances aren't coming in? I'm praying and believing for prosperity.* The Lord said He would give back to you with the same measure that you used. If you're using a thimble, then He's going to use a thimble to give back to you. And if you need a bucket full of finances, it's going to take a long time for God to measure that back to you with the same measure you gave out.

This is how the kingdom works. God doesn't give you money – He gives you the power to get money. Then there are things you must do to release that power. One of them is to set your hand to something. Stocking shelves or flipping burgers is better than getting welfare. "But, Andrew, I'm actually making more money off of welfare than I could working one of those jobs." The difference is, God can't bless welfare. But He can bless stocking shelves or flipping burgers. He could promote you to a manager position. While there, you could meet someone who could give you a promotion or even offer you another job. But when you're doing nothing, you're hindering the power of God from flowing in your own life.

It's not God who fails to answer our prayers – it's us who fail to take our authority and use it properly.

GOD HAS GIVEN YOU POWER
Lesson 16 – Outline

I. The Lord blessed us and gave us the ability to procreate.

> *God created man in his own image, in the image of God created he him; male and female created he them. And God blessed them, and God said unto them, Be fruitful, and multiply, and replenish the earth, and subdue it: and have dominion over the fish of the sea, and over the fowl of the air, and over every living thing that moveth upon the earth.*
> Genesis 1:27-28

    A. This power and authority God gave us comes with responsibility.

    B. Therefore, you can pray until you're blue in the face, but a woman isn't going to get pregnant until she has a relationship with a man.

II. God's Word says to speak to your mountain.

> *Whosoever shall say unto this mountain, Be thou removed, and be thou cast into the sea; and shall not doubt in his heart, but shall believe that those things which he saith shall come to pass; he shall have whatsoever he saith.*
> Mark 11:23

    A. It's God's power, but He put it under our control.

    B. There are spiritual laws that in order to cooperate with them, we must use our authority as human beings.

    C. If we don't step out in faith to cooperate with God in these areas, they won't come to pass.

    D. We need to find out what's under our authority and start using it the way God intended.

III. In the area of provision, God has given us power to get wealth.

> *Thou shalt remember the LORD thy God: for it is he that giveth thee power to get wealth, that he may establish his covenant which he sware unto thy fathers, as it is this day.*
> Deuteronomy 8:18

    A. God gave us power – an anointing, an ability – to get wealth.

    B. Since God doesn't have money directly, He sends it to you through people.

> *Give, and it shall be given unto you; good measure, pressed down, and shaken together,*

and running over, shall men give into your bosom. For with the same measure that ye mete withal it shall be measured to you again.

Luke 6:38

    C.   God impresses other people, and people will be involved in getting you His supply.

    D.   God gave you power to get wealth, so you must learn to use your authority to release that power.

IV. In order to see God's provision for you manifest, you must cooperate with the spiritual laws governing prosperity.

    A.   God has promised to bless all the work of your hands.

The LORD shall command the blessing upon thee…in all that thou settest thine hand unto…The LORD shall…bless all the work of thine hand.

Deuteronomy 28:8 and 12

    B.   However, if you aren't setting your hands to something, God doesn't have anything to bless.

    C.   You aren't going to see God begin to prosper you if you aren't working.

This we commanded you, that if any would not work, neither should he eat.

2 Thessalonians 3:10

    D.   If you're going to get into God's divine flow of provision, then you need to start doing some things to release that power and see this anointing begin to generate the income you need.

    E.   The Lord said He would give back to you with the same measure that you used (Luke 6:38).

    F.   It's not God who fails to answer our prayers – it's us who fail to take our authority and use it properly.

GOD HAS GIVEN YOU POWER
Lesson 16 – Teacher's Guide

1. The Lord blessed us and gave us the ability to procreate (Gen. 1:27-28). This power and authority God gave us comes with responsibility. Therefore, we can pray until we're blue in the face, but a woman isn't going to get pregnant until she has a relationship with a man.

2. God's Word says to speak to our mountains (Mark 11:23). It's God's power, but He put it under our control. There are spiritual laws that in order to cooperate with them, we must use our authority as human beings. If we don't step out in faith to cooperate with God in these areas, they won't come to pass. We need to find out what's under our authority and start using it the way God intended.

3. In the area of provision, God has given us power to get wealth (Deut. 8:18). God gave us power – an anointing, an ability – to get wealth. Since God doesn't have money directly, He sends it to us through people (Luke 6:38). God impresses other people, and they will be involved in getting us His supply. God gave us power to get wealth, so we must learn to use our authority to release that power.

4. In order to see God's provision for us manifest, we must cooperate with the spiritual laws governing prosperity. God has promised to bless all the work of our hands (Deut. 28:8 and 12). However, if we aren't setting our hands to something, God doesn't have anything to bless. We aren't going to see God begin to prosper us if we aren't working (2 Thess. 3:10). If we're going to get into God's divine flow of provision, then we need to start doing some things to release that power and see this anointing begin to generate the income we need. The Lord said He would give back to us with the same measure that we used (Luke 6:38). It's not God who fails to answer our prayers – it's us who fail to take our authority and use it properly.

1. A. Read Genesis 1:27-28. The Lord blessed us and gave us what ability? (The ability to procreate)
   B. What did this power and authority God gave us come with? (Responsibility)
2. A. Read Mark 11:23. What does God's Word say we are to speak to? (Our mountains)
   B. What must we use our authority as human beings to cooperate with? (Spiritual laws)
3. A. Read Deuteronomy 8:18 and Luke 6:38. What did God give us to get wealth? (Power – an anointing, an ability)
   B. How does God send money to us? (Through people)
4. A. Read Deuteronomy 28:8, 12; 2 Thessalonians 3:10; and review Luke 6:38. In order to see God's provision for us manifest, we must cooperate with what? (The spiritual laws governing prosperity)
   B. What would the Lord give back to us with? (The same measure that we used)

GOD HAS GIVEN YOU POWER
Lesson 16 – Additional Information

For additional information on finances, I recommend my teachings entitled *Financial Stewardship*, *Blessings and Miracles*, and *The Power of Partnership*.

GOD HAS GIVEN YOU POWER
Lesson 16 – Discipleship Questions

1. According to Mark 11:23, where should we not doubt?

2. What shall we believe?

3. According to Matthew 10:8, how are we to minister to the sick?

4. How are we to minister to the lepers?

5. How are we to minister to the (prematurely) dead?

6. How are we to deal with devils?

7. Deuteronomy 8:18 instructs us to remember whom?

8. What power has He given us?

9. For what purpose?

10. According to Luke 6:38, what happens when we give?

11. Who gives into our bosom?

12. With what measure shall it be measured to us again?

13. What does Deuteronomy 28:8 and 12 say concerning all the work of our hands?

14. Where else does the Lord command His blessing upon us?

15. According to 2 Thessalonians 3:10, those who don't work shouldn't what?

GOD HAS GIVEN YOU POWER
Lesson 16 – Answer Key

1. In our hearts.
2. That those things we say will come to pass.
3. Heal them.
4. Cleanse them.
5. Raise them.
6. Cast them out.
7. The Lord our God.
8. The power to get wealth.
9. That He may establish His covenant.
10. It shall be given unto us.
11. Men.
12. The same measure with which we gave.
13. The Lord has blessed it.
14. In our storehouses and in our land.
15. Eat.

GOD HAS GIVEN YOU POWER
Lesson 16 – Scriptures

So God created man in his own image, in the image of God created he him; male and female created he them. And God blessed them, and God said unto them, Be fruitful, and multiply, and replenish the earth, and subdue it: and have dominion over the fish of the sea, and over the fowl of the air, and over every living thing that moveth upon the earth.

Genesis 1:27-28

For verily I say unto you, That whosoever shall say unto this mountain, Be thou removed, and be thou cast into the sea; and shall not doubt in his heart, but shall believe that those things which he saith shall come to pass; he shall have whatsoever he saith.

Mark 11:23

Heal the sick, cleanse the lepers, raise the dead, cast out devils: freely ye have received, freely give.

Matthew 10:8

But thou shalt remember the LORD thy God: for it is he that giveth thee power to get wealth, that he may establish his covenant which he sware unto thy fathers, as it is this day.

Deuteronomy 8:18

Give, and it shall be given unto you; good measure, pressed down, and shaken together, and running over, shall men give into your bosom. For with the same measure that ye mete withal it shall be measured to you again.

Luke 6:38

The LORD shall command the blessing upon thee in thy storehouses, and in all that thou settest thine hand unto; and he shall bless thee in the land which the LORD thy God giveth thee.

Deuteronomy 28:8

The LORD shall open unto thee his good treasure, the heaven to give the rain unto thy land in his season, and to bless all the work of thine hand: and thou shalt lend unto many nations, and thou shalt not borrow.

Deuteronomy 28:12

For even when we were with you, this we commanded you, that if any would not work, neither should he eat.

2 Thessalonians 3:10

THE DEVIL WILL FLEE FROM YOU
Lesson 17

Submit yourselves therefore to God. Resist the devil, and he will flee from you.

James 4:7

God has given us power and authority over the devil.

Then he called his twelve disciples together, and gave them power and authority over all ***devils, and to cure diseases.***

Luke 9:1, emphasis mine

God gave us power and authority over *all* devils – and *all* means *all*. There are *no* demons excluded from this. I meet people constantly who say, "Well, the devil is doing this to me, and the devil is doing that." If you know that the devil is your problem, then you can solve that problem by believing God's Word and exercising your authority. Instead of going around saying, "O God, please get the devil off my back. O Lord, the devil is trying to cause me to do this." You aren't going to get freed from Satan's harassment by praying and asking God to remove the devil. That power and authority has been given to you.

Resist the devil, and he will flee from you.

James 4:7, emphasis mine

This doesn't say that he will flee from God. He'll flee from you. It's God's power, but that power is in you. God Himself isn't going to come down and make the devil flee from you. You have to resist the devil.

SATAN IS A COWARD

Resist means "to actively fight against." Resistance is active. You have to stir yourself up and get mad. The godly use of anger is to be mad at the devil, mad at sickness, mad at disease, and mad at poverty. You have to stir yourself up. You can't just tolerate it. As long as you can tolerate something, you will. But when you get to the place where you say "I've had it. Enough is enough. This is it," and you rise up with godly anger and faith to exercise your authority, a positive spiritual dynamic is released. When you get sick and tired of being sick and tired and you put your foot down and resist the devil, he flees from you.

At heart, Satan is a coward. He really is. He's just a bully – intimidating, yelling, and threatening. Even though he says all these things, the truth is he's a coward. If you've ever been around a bully, you'll know that they're always trying to take advantage of other people by manipulating and controlling them. As a boy, I learned that if you stand up to a bully, they'll respect you and leave you alone. You might lose a battle and get beat up, but you'll only fight once. After that, they'll respect you and leave you alone. At heart, a bully doesn't really want to fight. They just want to intimidate and control. If they realise that you're going to stand up and fight every time they try to do something to you, they'll back down. Even if they win the fight, they don't want to put forth that much effort. That's the way Satan is.

When you get angry and resist the devil, he's just like a bully. The moment he knows it's going to cost him something – that you're going to stand there toe to toe in the name of Jesus and go at it with him – Satan will flee from you. But you must resist!

"DEAR DEVIL..."

Saying "Dear devil, please leave me alone" is not resisting. My friends and I were ministering deliverance once to a woman who had sold her soul to the devil. Satan had led her to actually drink other people's urine, among other things, in establishing these demonic pacts. We instructed her that she needed to address the devil and take back the place she had given him. We told her she needed to do this by speaking directly to Satan and renouncing him. So we knelt around a coffee table and started praying. Then we said, "Now you speak to the devil."

This woman said, "Dear devil..." We had to stop her right there and say, "Whoa. Wait a minute. This isn't resisting the devil." You don't resist the devil by saying, "Dear devil, please leave me alone." You must *resist* the devil. God gave you power and authority, and you have to activate it by stirring yourself up, becoming violently resolved (Matt. 11:12), and just putting your spiritual foot down by saying, "Satan, get out of my life!" You might be thinking, *But, Andrew, I'm just not the assertive type.* Well, then, suffer. That's the way it works.

God isn't going to rebuke the devil for you. You have to stand up and resist him. And if you resist the devil, he *will* flee from you. God gave you this authority, and you can't beg Him to do what He's told you to do. It won't work.

One time, the Lord appeared to Kenneth Hagin and was giving him instructions. As Jesus was speaking, this little devil started running, jumping, and yelling in between them. Kenneth tried to pay attention and look around this demon, but he couldn't really focus on what the Lord was saying. He wondered why God was allowing this to go on.

Finally, Hagin became so upset over this that he declared "In the name of Jesus, I command you to leave!" and this little demon took off and was gone. The Lord looked at Kenneth and said, "If you hadn't have done that, I couldn't."

TWO SIDES OF THE COIN

God told you to resist the devil, and he will flee from you. Many of you know that it's the devil trying to destroy your life today. He's trying to kill you with sickness and disease, or he's stealing your prosperity from you. You know what's happening isn't God's will, but you're praying, "O Lord, please solve this. Please do something." You aren't taking your authority. If you are dealing with demonic opposition, then you have to step up to the plate, take the authority God has given you, and command the devil to flee.

There are two sides to this coin – submitting to God and resisting the devil. You can't just go around binding and rebuking anything you want. Some people think, *Well, it's the devil who gave me this wife, and I want a new one. So I'm taking authority and commanding my new wife to come along and to get this one out of the way.* That's not going to happen, because God didn't give you that kind of power and authority. Taking your current wife out of the way so you can marry another isn't His will. You must submit yourself to God and resist the devil, and then he'll flee from you.

These truths concerning authority will only work for you when you are submitted to God. When you're seeking Him with your whole heart and you perceive the devil hindering you, then you can take your authority and command those things to change. If you're just upset because someone cut in front of you in traffic, and you say "I hope they have a wreck down the road," that isn't going to come to pass. God didn't give you authority to curse people like that. You aren't submitted to Him. But when you are submitted to God, then you can resist the devil – actively fight against him – and he will flee from you.

When I was still in a denominational church, my friends and I stumbled into casting out demons. We saw a woman, who normally would have been put into a mental hospital for the rest of her life, set free. We knew her problem wasn't physical or natural, but demonic. We also knew that the authorities wouldn't understand, so we locked her in a room for seven days and took shifts ministering to her. We'd praise God, sing songs about the blood of Jesus, and read Scripture. We didn't know what we were doing, but we literally just beat the devil out of this woman – not with our hands but by singing about the blood and speaking against the devil. We just stayed in there until we saw this woman delivered of demons. Once word got out how she had been restored to her right mind, people started coming to us from all over.

"WHAT'S YOUR NAME?"

A homosexual fellow came to us to be delivered. We didn't really know what we were doing, and to make matters worse, we read this book that taught us all kinds of fallacies – like, you can't cast out a demon by yourself; you must have two people, you have to get the demon's name, and you must have the person puke in a bucket. We did some stupid stuff.

So we spent three weeks preparing this homosexual for deliverance, which you don't have to do. There's a group right here in our city that thinks it's godly to require people seeking deliverance to fill out a forty-page questionnaire and then endure a forty-five day waiting period before the group casts the demons out. That's not the method Jesus used!

Back when we thought we had to always get the demon's name, a friend of mine asked a demon, "What's your name, in Jesus' name?"

The demon answered, "Liar."

Immediately, my friend asked, "Are you telling me the truth?"

"I'M NOT LEAVING WITH THESE DEMONS"

This homosexual fellow we had been prepping came during a Wednesday night service at our church. I was leading the meeting by myself because the associate pastor, who was my partner in casting out demons, was out of town that night. An usher came and got me out of the service, saying, "This guy wants to see you." When I went back and saw him, he had come with another homosexual who wanted to be delivered too.

The fellow we'd been prepping said, "I'm ready to be delivered tonight."

I answered, "Well, we can't do it tonight. I'm by myself."

He responded, "I'm not leaving with these demons."

"Well, I'm not casting them out."

"You'd better do something, because I'm not leaving with these demons."

So I took this guy and his friend into a back room in this denominational church. Jamie came with us to give some prayer support. She wasn't my wife at the time. We were just in a Bible study together. In fact, Jamie wasn't even baptised in the Holy Spirit yet. We had no idea what we were doing.

Once we got to the back room, this guy said, "You better plead the blood over this place or do something, because these demons are coming out."

When I began praying "Father, in the name of Jesus," this guy fell to the floor and started barking, slithering like a snake, and throwing chairs up against the glass wall. It was quite a commotion! When the usher heard this, he went in and stopped the service, saying, "We need to pray for Andrew. He's back there witnessing to somebody." They didn't have a clue what was going on.

"SHUT UP AND COME OUT!"

In this back room, there was a stack of chairs about ten high. The other demonised guy was on top of the stack, plastered against the wall, scared to death. Jamie was praying and doing everything she knew to do.

I didn't know how to proceed, but since we were already in it, I started asking, "What's your name? In the name of Jesus, tell me your name." As I went through this, one demon would name itself and then another and then another. I felt like I was being made a fool because I didn't know if the first demon had come out or not before the second one had named itself. It was ridiculous! Finally, this scripture came to mind.

> **Jesus rebuked him, saying, Hold thy peace, and come out of him.**
>
> Mark 1:25

I thought, *That would be good.* So I said, "In the name of Jesus, I command you all to shut up and come out of him!" Instantly, power was released and this guy lay on the floor just like he was dead. Gently, I shook him to see if he was okay. He just rolled over and whispered, "I'm free. I'm delivered. I'm free." I thought, *If it's as simple as commanding the demons to come out in Jesus' name, why did I go through all this other stuff?*

Although we didn't know what we were doing, we stumbled onto this truth. We used to beg and plead, asking "O God, please get rid of this." I learned, through doing, that God has given me authority, and I don't have to go through all this stuff. I don't have to ask them their names, make people fill out a forty-page questionnaire, or require them to wait several weeks to get ready. I have authority over the devil, and if the person is willing to cooperate, I can go in and command, and those demons will obey me.

I can't ask God to cast the devil out, because that's what He has told me to do. I have to take my authority and be confident that when I speak, it's going to work. I have to have faith in God's Word – that I do have authority over all devils and to cure diseases (Luke 9:1).

SIMPLE ADJUSTMENTS, BIG DIFFERENCE

Since God has given you this power and authority, you also have the responsibility to exercise it. You can't go back to God and beg Him to do what He has commanded you to do. You must take your authority and use it.

There is no problem with God. Prayer works. It's just that wrong prayer doesn't work. You must pray, speak, and act in line with the authority God has given you.

If you would just make these simple adjustments that I've been sharing with you throughout this book, you'll see a big difference. Speak to your problems and command God's Word into manifestation. Pray the Word of God across people's paths who need to be born again. Stop begging the Lord for an outpouring of His Spirit, and start healing the sick, cleansing the lepers, and raising the dead. Do what the Word says, and you'll see His power manifest. Then you'll have all the revival you can handle.

THE DEVIL WILL FLEE FROM YOU
Lesson 17 – Outline

I. God has given us power and authority over the devil.

> **Submit yourselves therefore to God. Resist the devil, and he will flee from you.**
>
> James 4:7

   A. God gave us power and authority over *all* devils – and *all* means *all*.

   > **Then he called his twelve disciples together, and gave them power and authority over all devils, and to cure diseases.**
   >
   > Luke 9:1

   B. You aren't going to get freed from Satan's harassment by praying and asking God to remove the devil.

   C. That power and authority has been given to you.

II. You have to resist the devil.

   A. *Resist* means "to actively fight against."

   B. Resistance is active.

   C. The godly use of anger is to be mad at the devil, mad at sickness, mad at disease, and mad at poverty.

   D. When you get angry and resist the devil, he's just like a bully.

   E. The moment he knows it's going to cost him something – that you're going to stand there toe to toe in the name of Jesus and go at it with him – Satan will flee from you.

III. You don't resist the devil by saying, "Dear devil, please leave me alone."

   A. God gave you power and authority, and you have to activate it by stirring yourself up, becoming violently resolved (Matt. 11:12), and just putting your spiritual foot down by saying, "Satan, get out of my life!"

   B. God isn't going to rebuke the devil for you.

   C. If you resist the devil, he *will* flee from you.

   D. If you are dealing with demonic opposition, then you have to step up to the plate, take the authority God has given you, and command the devil to flee.

IV. There are two sides to this coin – submitting to God and resisting the devil.

    A. You can't just go around binding and rebuking anything you want.

    B. These truths concerning authority will only work for you when you are submitted to God.

    C. When you are seeking Him with your whole heart and you perceive the devil hindering you, then you can take your authority and command those things to change.

    D. When you are submitted to God, then you can resist the devil – actively fight against him – and he will flee from you.

Jesus rebuked him, saying, Hold thy peace, and come out of him.
Mark 1:25

V. Since God has given you this power and authority, you also have the responsibility to exercise it.

    A. You can't go back to God and beg Him to do what He has commanded you to do.

    B. You must pray, speak, and act in line with the authority God has given you.

    C. Do what the Word says, and you'll see His power manifest.

    D. Then you'll have all the revival you can handle.

THE DEVIL WILL FLEE FROM YOU
Lesson 17 – Teacher's Guide

1. God has given us power and authority over the devil (James 4:7). God gave us power and authority over *all* devils – and *all* means *all* (Luke 9:1). We aren't going to get freed from Satan's harassment by praying and asking God to remove the devil. That power and authority has been given to us.

2. We have to resist the devil. *Resist* means "to actively fight against." Resistance is active. The godly use of anger is to be mad at the devil, mad at sickness, mad at disease, and mad at poverty. When we get angry and resist the devil, he's just like a bully. The moment he knows it's going to cost him something – that we're going to stand there toe to toe in the name of Jesus and go at it with him – Satan will flee from us.

3. We don't resist the devil by saying, "Dear devil, please leave me alone." God gave us power and authority, and we have to activate it by stirring ourselves up, becoming violently resolved (Matt. 11:12), and just putting a spiritual foot down by saying, "Satan, get out of my life!" God isn't going to rebuke the devil for us. If we resist the devil, he *will* flee from us. If we are dealing with demonic opposition, then we have to step up to the plate, take the authority God has given us, and command the devil to flee.

---

1. A. Read James 4:7 and Luke 9:1. What has God given us over the devil – in fact, over all devils? (Power and authority)
   B. We aren't going to get _____ by praying and asking God to remove the devil. (Freed from Satan's harassment)
2. A. What does resist mean? (To actively fight against)
   B. The godly use of anger is to be mad at whom or what? (Mad at the devil, mad at sickness, mad at disease, and mad at poverty)
3. A. Read Matthew 11:12. Will God rebuke the devil for us? (No)
   B. If we are dealing with demonic opposition, then we have to what? (Step up to the plate, take the authority God has given us, and command the devil to flee)

4. There are two sides to this coin – submitting to God and resisting the devil. We can't just go around binding and rebuking anything we want. These truths concerning authority will only work for us when we are submitted to God. When we are seeking Him with our whole hearts and we perceive the devil hindering us, then we can take our authority and command those things to change. When we are submitted to God, then we can resist the devil – actively fight against him – and he will flee from us (Mark 1:25).

5. Since God has given us this power and authority, we also have the responsibility to exercise it. We can't go back to God and beg Him to do what He has commanded us to do. We must pray, speak, and act in line with the authority God has given us. If we do what the Word says, we'll see His power manifest. Then we'll have all the revival we can handle.

4. A. Read Mark 1:25. These truths concerning authority will only work for us when?
 (When we're submitted to God)
 B. What can we do when we are seeking God with our whole hearts and we perceive the devil hindering us?
 (We can take our authority and command those things to change)
5. A. What must we do in line with the authority God has given us? (Pray, speak, and act)
 B. If we do what the Word says, what will we see? (His power manifest)

THE DEVIL WILL FLEE FROM YOU
Lesson 17 – Additional Information

For more information about the godly use of anger, please check out my teaching entitled *Anger Management*.

THE DEVIL WILL FLEE FROM YOU
Lesson 17 – Discipleship Questions

1. According to James 4:7, who are we to submit to?

2. How should we deal with the devil?

3. Who did Jesus call together in Luke 9:1?

4. What did He give them over all devils?

5. And to cure what?

6. According to Matthew 11:12, what suffers violence?

7. From when to when has it suffered violence?

8. Who takes it by force?

9. In Mark 1:25, what did Jesus do to the demon?

10. What two commands did the Lord speak to him?

THE DEVIL WILL FLEE FROM YOU
Lesson 17 – Answer Key

1. God.

2. Resist him.

3. His twelve disciples.

4. Power and authority.

5. Diseases.

6. The kingdom of heaven.

7. From the days of John the Baptist until now.

8. The violent.

9. He rebuked him.

10. Hold your peace, and come out of him.

THE DEVIL WILL FLEE FROM YOU
Lesson 17 – Scriptures

Submit yourselves therefore to God. Resist the devil, and he will flee from you.

James 4:7

Then he called his twelve disciples together, and gave them power and authority over all devils, and to cure diseases.

Luke 9:1

And from the days of John the Baptist until now the kingdom of heaven suffereth violence, and the violent take it by force.

Matthew 11:12

And Jesus rebuked him, saying, Hold thy peace, and come out of him.

Mark 1:25

LAW ENFORCEMENT
Lesson 18

We exercise authority when we take our responsibility and do what God has told us to do. However, this doesn't mean we can just "command" anything we want. All authority can do is enforce law.

In the natural realm, we call policemen "law enforcement officers." They only have authority to enforce what's already been established as a law. Police officers don't make up the law. They aren't absolute dictators who can do whatever they want. They are limited. All they can do is enforce laws that are already in effect. It's the same in the spiritual realm.

Every born-again believer has this supernatural, God-given power. However, there are spiritual laws governing how it works. Like a police officer, all we can do is enforce the law that's already in effect. We can't use God's power in a selfish way, because there isn't any law where God promises to give us what we're lusting for. Instead, we need to learn what the laws of God's kingdom are and then recognise that our authority is simply enforcing these spiritual laws.

In the natural realm, some people try to violate the laws of the land. This is why there's a need for law enforcement officers – people who go out and enforce those laws. In the spiritual realm, there are demons who are constantly trying to oppose us, inflict their evil will upon us, and prevent us from experiencing the fullness of God's provision. We must enforce the spiritual laws of God's kingdom that have been given to us.

A LEGAL BINDING CONTRACT

Most people don't see the kingdom of God as operating under law. Instead, they see it as being directly under the Lord, and He often changes His moods. They'll say things like, "You never know what God is going to do" and "You can't put God in a box." God is definitely bigger than – and outside of – the little "box" you've tried to contain Him in, but He has also established spiritual laws that even He will not break.

Thou hast magnified thy word above all thy name.

Psalm 138:2

Although many scriptures reveal the power of the name of Jesus (Phil. 2:9-11), God has magnified His Word even above His name. A person's name is no better than their word. If they don't keep their word, their name isn't accounted for anything. However, the name of Jesus is powerful because He never breaks His Word. When God says something, it becomes a legal binding contract.

My covenant will I not break, nor alter the thing that is gone out of my lips.

Psalm 89:34

When God speaks something out of His mouth, His Word is a covenant. It's a contract He will not break.

Jesus upholds…

All things by the word of his power.

Hebrews 1:3

In other words, our entire universe is held together by the integrity and power of God's Word. If He were to ever break a promise or otherwise violate His Word, this whole world, the universe, and you and I would all self-destruct. It's God's integrity that holds everything together.

THE LAW OF FAITH

So when God speaks something out of His mouth, it becomes a contract – a law. Once He's said it, He won't change it. In order to effectively use your authority, you must know what His laws are.

When a new police officer is hired, they immediately study what the laws are that they are to enforce. Their police chief doesn't say, "Oh, just go out there without knowing anything and see if it works. Maybe the people will submit." No, that's not their attitude at all. The police officer is thoroughly grilled in what the ordinances and statutes are, what is permissible, and what is not.

A law enforcement officer has to know the law because they can't go beyond it. They can't just do things on their own. A police officer does have authority, but that authority ends at the end of the law. If there isn't a law prescribing what they're trying to enforce, then they can't do it.

It's the same in the spiritual realm. You can't just pick and choose according to your own selfish whims. You must know what the laws are that govern the kingdom of God and then abide by them. If you try to enforce something outside of those laws, it won't work. You can't just use your God-given authority to do your own thing.

Romans 3 speaks of **"the law of faith"**:

Where is boasting then? It is excluded. By what law? of works? Nay: but by the law of faith.

Romans 3:27

Faith has a law. There is a law of faith.

LAW OR PHENOMENON?

In the physical realm, there are natural laws. Among many others, there is the law of gravity and the law of thrust and lift. A law is something that's both constant and universal. If gravity operated in the United States, but not in some other country, then it would be a phenomenon, not a law. A law means that it's consistent for everybody on the planet. It's the same for everyone, and it's always that way.

Gravity doesn't just spike every once in a while. However, occasionally you'll see things that might make you think that. A few years ago, a plane was landing in Colorado Springs. As it was making a turn to come in to land, all of a sudden it accelerated and just dove into the ground. It made a crater, and the largest piece of the plane they could find was a one- or two-foot square. It just exploded and everyone was killed. The investigators did three or four years worth of research, but never found a pilot error or mechanical reason for the crash. However, neither did they say, "Well, gravity just increased ten times and all of a sudden made that plane crash like that." No, they didn't even consider that a possibility, because gravity is a law – it's consistent. They didn't say, "Well, the law of thrust and lift just ceased to operate." No, it's a law – it always operates that way.

If you are ever going to have an efficient, effective, powerful relationship with God, you must break out of the mindset that God is inconsistent. You must get out of the thinking that says, "Sometimes God wills to do this, and sometimes He wills to do that. You never know what kind of mood God is in. He might heal this one but not this other. He may want them to suffer that way for the rest of their life." That's not how God is, and it isn't the way His kingdom operates.

God is the one who created the heaven and the earth. It's so orderly and systematic that you can find out exactly where Mars, Jupiter, and all the other planets were five years, or even five thousand years, ago. Everything is like clockwork, perfect and consistent. You can accurately project when an eclipse will occur because it's so predictable.

I'm amazed how people can think that God – who created such order in the universe – would do things sporadically and haphazardly in our lives. Order didn't come from chaos. God Himself is orderly. He created laws – both natural and spiritual. God Himself is consistent and predictable because He operates by His own spiritual laws.

You need to find out what His spiritual laws are. Then, once you do, take your authority as a believer and enforce them. If you're ignorant of God's Word, then you won't be very effective in exercising your authority, because Satan will just talk you out of it.

IGNORANT OF WHAT'S BEEN PROVIDED

Back in the days when people still traveled across the Atlantic by ship, a man scraped everything he had together to buy a ticket to the United States. All he had left was just a tiny little bit of money, with which he bought some crackers and cheese. For the entire month-long voyage across the Atlantic, all he had to eat were crackers and cheese. He watched as all the other passengers feasted sumptuously on the daily bounty of food and drink in the dining room. However, he didn't have any money for food, so he just ate a little bit of his crackers and cheese.

Toward the end of the voyage, one of the porters came up to this man and asked, "Sir, I noticed that you have never joined us in the dining room. Was there something we've done that offended you? Why didn't you eat with us on this voyage?"

The man answered, "Oh, no. I'm not offended at all. I would have loved to have eaten with you. The food looked so good, but I just didn't have any money left. All I had was enough to buy some crackers and cheese."

Dumbfounded, the porter looked at this man and said, "But didn't you realise that the meals came with the ticket? They were included in the price that you paid."

This man was ignorant of what was rightfully his, and because of it, he did without. However, the truth was that he could have daily dined sumptuously on anything he wanted of the feasts that were prepared throughout the entire trip.

So many Christians are the same way. They are ignorant of the abundant life God has given us. Therefore, they live without enjoying many of the salvation benefits Jesus died on the cross to provide. Because they are unaware of what the Word says, Satan has them convinced, "You aren't really going to prosper. You'll just have barely enough to get by."

Are you aware of what the Word promises you concerning prosperity? Deuteronomy 28 says that God has commanded His blessing upon all the work of your hands. Psalm 35:27 reveals that God delights in the prosperity of His servants. If you don't know these spiritual laws, you won't enforce them. You won't demand Satan to quit stealing from you and to turn loose of your God-given provision. You won't experience what's rightfully yours in Christ. In order for you to use your authority and experience God's blessings, you need to know what the spiritual laws are and what has been provided for you.

THIS CONFIDENCE WE HAVE

Just yesterday, a mutual friend coerced me to pray for a certain woman with arthritis. I tried to get her to a place of faith by telling her about all the different people I had personally seen healed of arthritis, and that arthritis was no problem for God. She just looked at me and said, "Well, I believe that God can heal, but I don't believe that you can heal." Of course, it's God's power and not mine, but He has given me the authority to use it. Not understanding this, she was immediately put off and began resisting how I was trying to minister to her. Then she stated, "It all depends upon whether or not it's God's will to heal me." She believed God could do it, but she didn't believe that healing is a law – something He's already done.

Through the death, burial, and resurrection of the Lord Jesus Christ, God has already healed every person that will ever be healed. By the stripes Jesus took across His back two thousand years ago, we *were* – past tense – healed (1 Pet. 2:24). God isn't healing people right now. He did His part a long time ago. The law was passed, and now healing belongs to us. However, it's up to us as believers to know what God's will is and command it to come to pass.

> **This is the confidence that we have in him, that, if we ask any thing according to his will, he heareth us: And if we know that he hear us, whatsoever we ask, we know that we have the petitions that we desired of him.**
>
> 1 John 5:14-15

This is the confidence we have – if we ask anything *according to His will*, we know that He hears us, and if we know that He hears us, then *we know we have these petitions*. The whole thing hinges on "What is God's will?"

Some people say, "Well, you never know what God's will is." That kind of thought undermines this whole principle. If you think that God just sometimes wills for a person to be saved, healed, or prospered and sometimes He doesn't, then you don't know what God's will is. If you think God is totally unpredictable, then you'll never use your authority effectively, because you aren't sure what the laws are.

NO EXCEPTIONS

A police officer can't effectively enforce the law if they think that sometimes it's okay to speed and other times it's not. Is it okay to rob a bank sometimes but other times not? Is it permissible to murder occasionally? No, that's not the way the law is. The law isn't sometimes in effect and other times not. The law is constant – it's the same all the time for everybody.

In the natural realm, we say, "Nobody is above the law." That means that politicians, police officers, whoever it is, will be held accountable if they break the law. It doesn't always work out that way, but that's the philosophy we desire to live by.

It's the same in the spiritual realm. There are no exceptions. There aren't some people that the Word works for and others that it doesn't. It's not that God just likes some people and causes His power to work for them but others He doesn't. That's not it at all. God has established laws, and we need to learn how to cooperate with them.

We can be confident that we will receive anything we ask according to His will (1 John 5:14-15). How can we know God's will? God's Word reveals His will.

> **Beloved, I wish** [will, want, desire] **above all things that thou mayest prosper and be in health, even as thy soul prospereth.**
>
> 3 John 2, brackets mine

God's wish, will, and desire is that you may prosper and be in health, even as your soul prospers. This is a law of God. He wants you to prosper and be healthy. God wants you to be a world overcomer (1 John 5:5).

GOOD GOD, BAD DEVIL

John 10:10 reveals both God's will and Satan's will very clearly:

> **The thief cometh not, but for to steal, and to kill, and to destroy: I am come that they might have life, and that they might have it more abundantly.**

Satan comes to steal, kill, and destroy, but God comes to give you life more abundantly. If something is life and good, it's God. But if something is bad – stealing, killing, and destroying – it's the devil. Although this is a bit simplistic, it's true. Good God. Bad devil. Good things come from God, and bad things come from the devil (James 1:17).

The Lord has ordained laws for your good, so you can access the abundant life He's provided for you. However, you must learn what these laws are so you can cooperate with them and demand Satan to quit stealing, killing, and destroying the blessings that are rightfully yours.

In the natural realm, if someone stole something of yours, you have the right to press charges. You could demand for that person to be picked up by the police and prosecuted. If they're found guilty, some kind of punishment or prison, retribution or reimbursement, could be assessed. However, it's all dependent upon the person who was wronged exercising their rights and pressing charges. In a sense, you have to take your authority and say, "I'm going to receive what's rightfully mine."

It's the same in the spiritual realm. Just like every other believer, you have God-given rights and privileges. He has established His will for you, but it's up to you to claim what God has done for you. You must press the issue. You have to take your authority and enforce those spiritual laws that have been made for your benefit. Ignorance of the spiritual laws will keep you from pressing charges. It will prevent you from keeping Satan out of the picture. The devil just runs wild when you think you don't have any authority or power.

Many Christians just don't know what is rightfully theirs. Thinking they have to be sick, poor, and discouraged, they say, "This is just the way that it is. I can't do anything about it." They don't know that Jesus Christ has redeemed us from these things.

CONSTANT AND UNIVERSAL

In the same way that the physical world operates under natural laws, God has created His kingdom to operate under spiritual laws. These laws are constant and universal, so it's to your benefit to learn what they are and then cooperate with them.

You can't just pick and choose, saying, "Since I have authority as a believer, I'm going to command that I get this house or that car. It's under my power and authority, so I command it and say it's so." No, you have to cooperate with the laws of God. As a matter of fact, there are laws of God that specifically tell you not to covet your neighbour's house, car, or wife. God doesn't have a law that promises you can use His power for selfish purposes to claim, "This person will die so I can marry their mate." That's not going to work, because the Lord hasn't provided it for you. There aren't any spiritual laws in the kingdom of God that work for selfish purposes.

LAW ENFORCEMENT
Lesson 18 – Outline

I. We exercise authority when we take our responsibility and do what God has told us to do.

    A. However, this doesn't mean we can just "command" anything we want.

    B. All authority can do is enforce law.

    C. In the spiritual realm, there are demons who are constantly trying to oppose us, inflict their evil will upon us, and prevent us from experiencing the fullness of God's provision.

    D. We must enforce the spiritual laws of God's kingdom that have been given to us.

II. Most people don't see the kingdom of God as operating under law.

    A. Although many scriptures reveal the power of the name of Jesus (Phil. 2:9-11), God has magnified His Word even above His name.

> ***Thou hast magnified thy word above all thy name.***
>
> Psalm 138:2

    B. The name of Jesus is powerful because He never breaks His Word.

    C. When God says something, it becomes a legal binding contract.

> ***My covenant will I not break, nor alter the thing that is gone out of my lips.***
>
> Psalm 89:34

    D. Our entire universe is held together by the integrity and power of God's Word (Heb. 1:3).

    E. So when God speaks something out of His mouth, it becomes a contract – a law.

III. In order to effectively use your authority, you must know what God's laws are.

    A. You must know what the laws are that govern the kingdom of God and then abide by them.

    B. If you try to enforce something outside of those laws, it won't work.

> ***Where is boasting then? It is excluded. By what law? of works? Nay: but by the law of faith.***
>
> Romans 3:27

C. A law is something that is both constant and universal. It's consistent for everybody on the planet; it's the same for everyone, and it's always that way.

D. God Himself is consistent and predictable because He operates by His own spiritual laws.

E. You need to find out what His spiritual laws are and then take your authority as a believer and enforce them.

IV. If you're ignorant of God's Word, then you won't be very effective in exercising your authority, because Satan will just talk you out of it.

A. Many Christians are ignorant of the abundant life God has given us.

B. Therefore, they live without enjoying many of the salvation benefits Jesus died on the cross to provide.

> *This is the confidence that we have in him, that, if we ask any thing according to his will, he heareth us: And if we know that he hear us, whatsoever we ask, we know that we have the petitions that we desired of him.*
>
> 1 John 5:14-15

C. If you think that God just sometimes wills for a person to be saved, healed, or prospered and sometimes He doesn't, then you don't know what God's will is (1 Pet. 2:24).

D. God's Word reveals His will.

> *Beloved, I wish* [will, want, desire] *above all things that thou mayest prosper and be in health, even as thy soul prospereth.*
>
> 3 John 2, brackets mine

> *The thief cometh not, but for to steal, and to kill, and to destroy: I am come that they might have life, and that they might have it more abundantly.*
>
> John 10:10

E. The Lord has ordained laws for your good, so you can access the abundant life He's provided for you – however, you must learn what these laws are so you can cooperate with them and demand Satan to quit stealing, killing, and destroying the blessings that are rightfully yours.

LAW ENFORCEMENT
Lesson 18 – Teacher's Guide

1. We exercise authority when we take our responsibility and do what God has told us to do. However, this doesn't mean we can just "command" anything we want. All authority can do is enforce law. In the spiritual realm, there are demons who are constantly trying to oppose us, inflict their evil will upon us, and prevent us from experiencing the fullness of God's provision. We must enforce the spiritual laws of God's kingdom that have been given to us.

2. Most people don't see the kingdom of God as operating under law. Although many scriptures reveal the power of the name of Jesus (Phil. 2:9-11), God has magnified His Word even above His name (Ps. 138:2). The name of Jesus is powerful because He never breaks His Word. When God says something, it becomes a legal binding contract (Ps. 89:34). Our entire universe is held together by the integrity and power of God's Word (Heb. 1:3). So when God speaks something out of His mouth, it becomes a contract – a law.

3. In order to effectively use our authority, we must know what God's laws are. They govern His kingdom, and we must abide by them. If we try to enforce something outside of those laws, it won't work (Rom. 3:27). A law is something that is both constant and universal. It's consistent for everybody on the planet; it's the same for everyone, and it's always that way. God Himself is consistent and predictable because He operates by His own spiritual laws. We need to find out what His spiritual laws are and then take our authority as a believer and enforce them.

1. A. All authority can do is what? (Enforce law)
   B. What must we enforce? (The spiritual laws of God's kingdom that have been given to us)
2. A. Read Philippians 2:9-11; Hebrews 1:3; Psalm 138:2, and 89:34. Most people don't see the kingdom of God as what? (Operating under law)
   B. When God speaks something out of His mouth, what does it become? (A contract – a law)
3. A. Read Romans 3:27. A law is something that is both what? (Constant and universal)
   B. Why is God Himself consistent and predictable? (Because He operates by His own spiritual laws)

4. If we're ignorant of God's Word, then we won't be very effective in exercising our authority, because Satan will just talk us out of it. Many of us are ignorant of the abundant life God has given us. Therefore, we live without enjoying many of the salvation benefits Jesus died on the cross to provide (1 John 5:14-15). If we think that God just sometimes wills for a person to be saved, healed, or prospered, and sometimes He doesn't, then we don't know what God's will is (1 Pet. 2:24). God's Word reveals His will (3 John 2 and John 10:10). The Lord has ordained laws for our good, so we can access the abundant life He's provided for us – however, we must learn what these laws are so we can cooperate with them and demand Satan to quit stealing, killing, and destroying the blessings that are rightfully ours.

4. A. Read 1 John 5:14-15, 1 Peter 2:24, 3 John 2, and John 10:10. What reveals God's will? (His Word)
   B. Why must we learn what these laws are? (So we can cooperate with them and demand Satan to quit stealing, killing, and destroying the blessings that are rightfully ours)

LAW ENFORCEMENT
Lesson 18 – Discipleship Questions

1. According to Philippians 2:9-11, what should every tongue confess?

2. To the glory of whom?

3. Psalm 89:34 says that God will not alter what?

4. According to Hebrews 1:3, where did Jesus sit down when He had purged our sins?

5. According to Romans 3:27, where is boasting, then?

6. What does Psalm 35:27 say that those who favor God's righteous cause should do?

7. How often should they say, "Let the LORD be magnified"?

8. The Lord takes pleasure in the prosperity of whom?

9. According to 1 John 5:14-15, what is the confidence that we have in Him?

10. What is it we know that we have?

11. In 3 John 2, God clearly wishes (wills) what?

12. According to 1 John 5:5, who is he that overcomes the world?

13. James 1:17 reveals that what kind of gift comes down from above?

14. From whom?

15. Is there any variableness or shadow of turning with Him?

LAW ENFORCEMENT
Lesson 18 – Answer Key

1. That Jesus Christ is Lord.

2. God the Father.

3. The thing that has gone out of His lips.

4. On the right hand of the Majesty on high.

5. It is excluded.

6. Shout for joy and be glad.

7. Continually.

8. His servant.

9. That if we ask anything according to His will, He hears us.

10. The petitions that we desired of Him.

11. That we may prosper and be in health.

12. He that believes that Jesus is the Son of God.

13. Every good and perfect gift.

14. The Father of lights.

15. No.

LAW ENFORCEMENT
Lesson 18 – Scriptures

I will worship toward thy holy temple, and praise thy name for thy lovingkindness and for thy truth: for thou hast magnified thy word above all thy name.

Psalm 138:2

Wherefore God also hath highly exalted him, and given him a name which is above every name: That at the name of Jesus every knee should bow, of things in heaven, and things in earth, and things under the earth; And that every tongue should confess that Jesus Christ is Lord, to the glory of God the Father.

Philippians 2:9-11

My covenant will I not break, nor alter the thing that is gone out of my lips.

Psalm 89:34

Who being the brightness of his glory, and the express image of his person, and upholding all things by the word of his power, when he had by himself purged our sins, sat down on the right hand of the Majesty on high.

Hebrews 1:3

Where is boasting then? It is excluded. By what law? of works? Nay: but by the law of faith.

Romans 3:27

The LORD shall command the blessing upon thee in thy storehouses, and in all that thou settest thine hand unto; and he shall bless thee in the land which the LORD thy God giveth thee.

Deuteronomy 28:8

The LORD shall open unto thee his good treasure, the heaven to give the rain unto thy land in his season, and to bless all the work of thine hand: and thou shalt lend unto many nations, and thou shalt not borrow.

Deuteronomy 28:12

Let them shout for joy, and be glad, that favour my righteous cause: yea, let them say continually, Let the LORD be magnified, which hath pleasure in the prosperity of his servant.

Psalm 35:27

Who his own self bare our sins in his own body on the tree, that we, being dead to sins, should live unto righteousness: by whose stripes ye were healed.

1 Peter 2:24

And this is the confidence that we have in him, that, if we ask any thing according to his will, he heareth us: And if we know that he hear us, whatsoever we ask, we know that we have the petitions that we desired of him.

1 John 5:14-15

Beloved, I wish above all things that thou mayest prosper and be in health, even as thy soul prospereth.

3 John 2

Who is he that overcometh the world, but he that believeth that Jesus is the Son of God?

1 John 5:5

The thief cometh not, but for to steal, and to kill, and to destroy: I am come that they might have life, and that they might have it more abundantly.

John 10:10

Every good gift and every perfect gift is from above, and cometh down from the Father of lights, with whom is no variableness, neither shadow of turning.

James 1:17

HOW THE POWER FLOWS
Lesson 19

The woman who had an issue of blood powerfully illustrates these truths about how the kingdom of God operates by law.

> *A certain woman, which had an issue of blood twelve years, And had suffered many things of many physicians, and had spent all that she had, and was nothing bettered, but rather grew worse, when she had heard of Jesus, came in the press behind, and touched his garment. For she said, If I may touch but his clothes, I shall be whole. And straightway the fountain of her blood was dried up; and she felt in her body that she was healed of that plague.*
>
> Mark 5:25-29

> *And Jesus, immediately knowing in himself that virtue had gone out of him, turned him about in the press, and said, Who touched my clothes? And his disciples said unto him, Thou seest the multitude thronging thee, and sayest thou, Who touched me? And he looked round about to see her that had done this thing. But the woman fearing and trembling, knowing what was done in her, came and fell down before him, and told him all the truth. And he said unto her, Daughter, thy faith hath made thee whole; go in peace, and be whole of thy plague.*
>
> Mark 5:30-34

Jesus was in the midst of a multitude of people who were thronging Him. That means they were crowding in close, constantly bumping into and touching Him. Many people were reaching out, touching Him, and trying to receive their healing. However, this little woman with the issue of blood came, touched the hem of His garment, and instantly the power of God flowed right through Jesus' body, through His garment, and into this woman. Immediately, she was healed of an infirmity that had plagued her for twelve long years. As soon as this happened, Jesus turned around and asked, "Who touched Me?"

JESUS INCREASED

Some people believe this religious concept that Jesus knew all things. Therefore, they consider this question to be purely rhetorical, saying, "Jesus didn't really mean it. He already knew everything that was going on." That's not accurate at all. The Word says that...

> *Jesus increased in wisdom and stature, and in favour with God and man.*
>
> Luke 2:52

Jesus was fully God, but He was also fully man. Because He was in the flesh – a physical, human body – He had to learn things the same way that you and I do. The Word here says that He increased in wisdom and knowledge.

In His spirit, Jesus was Lord at His birth. That's what the angels said when they made their announcement to the shepherds.

> **For unto you is born this day in the city of David a Saviour, which is Christ the Lord.**
>
> Luke 2:11

So even though in His spirit realm He was God, Jesus didn't come out of the womb speaking Hebrew. He had to learn to eat, walk, and talk. He had to learn who He was. Because Jesus was in a physical body, He had to deal with limitations – not limitations from sin, but limitations due to the fact that God didn't make a physical body to perceive things that haven't been learned through the senses.

So when Jesus was walking through this crowd and this woman touched Him, He perceived the power of God flowing out of Him, but He didn't know who had touched Him.

"WHO TOUCHED ME?"

Most people think that when you approach God for healing (or anything else), He evaluates you to see if you're worthy. They think that once you make your petition, God measures how worthy you are – whether you've been good enough, moral enough, paid your tithes, fasted long enough, have enough people praying for you, and if your situation is desperate enough. Then – based on His personal evaluation – He either releases His power and you get healed, or He retains His power and says, "Nope, you haven't prayed enough, you aren't holy enough, you haven't fasted enough, and/or you have this sin in your life, and until you deal with these things, I won't heal you." People tend to view God this way, that He's up there in heaven evaluating us, and then – depending on His evaluation – He either releases His power or not.

These verses in Mark 5 completely kill this misconception. Jesus didn't know who this woman was. He didn't see her coming. She touched the hem of His garment. He perceived the outflow of power but then asked, "Who touched Me?" Jesus honestly didn't know who had touched Him. Therefore, He didn't evaluate her to see if she was worthy or not. This shows that the power of God flows under law.

When you tap into these spiritual laws, the power of God just flows. The Lord doesn't sise up one person, saying "You're worthy. I'm going to release my power to you," and then looks over another, saying "No, you aren't worthy." It's not like that at all. There are laws that govern how the power of God works. When you cooperate with those laws and put them into effect, the power flows. If you don't, the power doesn't flow. It's nothing about God loving one person more than another; it's just a matter of law. God established His kingdom to operate under spiritual laws. As a believer, you need to find out what those laws are and cooperate with them.

Electricity operates under law. If you're grounded and you grab a live wire, it'll kill you. It's not that the electric company looked at you and said, "Let's teach them a lesson." No, there are just natural laws. You put those laws into effect, and so the power flowed.

On the other hand, a bird can land on a high wire and not be electrocuted, because they aren't grounded. It's not because the electric company loves birds more than they love people. There are just laws that govern how this power flows.

Electricity has been around since God created the earth. It's always been here in the form of thunderstorms and static electricity. People could have used electricity thousands of years ago if they would have understood the laws that governed it. God didn't just "create" electricity a few hundred years ago and "allowed" people to start using it. No, electricity was available to be harnessed for our use. However, our ignorance of those laws kept us from benefiting from it.

GOD DIDN'T SHUT OFF THE POWER

It's the same in the spiritual realm. It wasn't God who let healing, the gifts of the Holy Spirit, and other supernatural aspects of our faith just "pass away" for more than a thousand years. That's not what happened. God didn't shut off the power. People entered the Dark Ages because they didn't retain the knowledge of the things of God.

The early New Testament church operated strongly in the power of God. Then, years later and for whatever reason, the church at large came to this place of believing that God's miracles and supernatural power passed away with the apostles. Then, in the early 1900s, the power of the Holy Spirit began to manifest again in places like Azusa Street. There was an influx of healings, deliverance, speaking in tongues, and miracles that have continued to snowball worldwide up until this present day.

It wasn't God who turned the power off after the first 200 years of Christianity and then turned it back on again 1700 years later. It's not that He operates in cycles and now we're in a "wave" or a "move" of God. That's not how it works any more than it was God who kept people from using electricity, airplanes, and cars a thousand years ago. All the laws were here, but people's ignorance kept them from taking advantage of these laws. Due to their ignorance, people died of heat when they could have had air conditioning if they had known what the laws were. People were hindered from moving over long distances in a short period of time. They had to walk, or ride a camel, donkey, or horse. It wasn't God that kept them in ignorance; they just didn't know these things.

It's not God who isn't healing or blessing you. It's not the Lord who has "willed" you to suffer. God has created laws, but you need to discover what they are. As you learn how to cooperate with and enforce these laws, you'll see God's provision for you manifest.

You might be thinking, *I disagree. That puts all the responsibility on me. You're saying that it's up to me to take hold of what God has provided.* Yes, that's exactly what I'm saying. It's not God who hasn't healed, prospered, or delivered you. It's your own ignorance that keeps you in these bondages. God has already done His part. The Word clearly reveals that the Lord has already healed you, but you have to take advantage of it (1 Pet. 2:24).

UNBELIEF HINDERS RECEIVING

Let's go back to Mark 5 and continue looking at this woman who touched the hem of Jesus' garment. Verse 31 says that there was a multitude of people thronging Him. This could have been as many as three or four hundred people trying to follow Jesus through these city streets. However many it was, there were a lot of people pressing Him. They didn't just want to be near Him; they wanted to draw near because there had been power and virtue flowing out of Him and healing people. A multitude of people were there, of which many needed to be healed and delivered. However, one person out of the many received healing.

This wasn't the only time this happened. The same thing happened in John 5 at the pool of Bethesda. There was a multitude of impotent folk, yet one person received healing. Why is it that one person gets healed when there are many who need it?

Maybe you haven't received your healing. You know of other people who have. How come you don't get healed? One reason is because you don't understand that God has already done His part. You aren't taking your authority and enforcing spiritual laws. You're ignorant of what God has already said and done, so you're passively asking, "God, will You please heal me, if it be Your will? Lord, will You set me free and move in my life?" You can say that many different ways, but the Bible calls it "unbelief." You aren't believing the record.

When God said **"By whose stripes ye were healed"** (1 Pet. 2:24), He put it into the past tense, as an already-accomplished reality. He's already done it. Therefore, you ought to believe the Word and say, "I know it's already done. He put the same power on the inside of me that raised Jesus from the dead (Eph. 1:18-20). I take my authority, and now I speak to my problem and command these things to happen." But instead of taking your authority, you're just going passively to God and asking, "God, will You please heal me, if it be Your will?" That's unbelief and it's the reason you aren't receiving. You're ignorant of God's spiritual laws.

WORDS

This woman in Mark 5 said,

If I may touch but his clothes, I shall be whole.

Mark 5:28

Although there are many different spiritual laws, one of them that governs whether you receive from God or not is the power of your words.

A man's belly shall be satisfied with the fruit of his mouth; and with the increase of his lips shall he be filled. Death and life are in the power of the tongue: and they that love it shall eat the fruit thereof.

Proverbs 18:20-21

Although many different scriptures reveal the importance of our words (Matt. 12:34-37, James 3, and Mark 11), this one clearly reveals that both death and life are in the power of the tongue.

When people are trying to receive healing from the Lord, many of them ignore this law and say, "I've heard people talk about this name-it-and-claim-it, blab-it-and-grab-it group who tell people they can have what they say. They say you're supposed to say you're healed when you don't feel healed. Well, I just don't believe in that stuff." So when somebody asks "How are you?" they say, "Well, I'm dying. I only have a week to live. The doctor told me it's terrible. I feel so bad." They are releasing death with their mouths through their negative speech. Yet they'll go to the Lord in "prayer" and say, "O God, Heal me, if it be Your will." Then when they don't see a physical healing manifest, they get upset with God as if He failed. There are laws that govern how to receive healing. One of them is that people will have what they say (Mark 11:23).

You can't speak death out of your mouth and expect to receive life. It doesn't work that way. You might say, "Well, I just don't believe that." Fine. That's just like a person saying, "I just don't believe that copper is a better conductor of electricity than wood. So I'm going to wire my house with wood, not copper." When they plug the electricity into the connection of wood, I guarantee the power isn't going to flow. It won't run your lights, appliances, or air conditioning. You may not like this, but it's how God established these laws.

WOOD OR COPPER?

Faith flows through words. Words release either death or life, but your ignorance of this law doesn't mean that the law is going to change. You can declare, "I can say whatever I want, and it doesn't make any difference." That's not true. It's not how the spiritual laws of the kingdom operate any more than wood is a better conductor of electricity than copper. It's not up to you to make the laws. You just need to discover what they are and then enforce them. God's Word says that faith speaks (Rom. 10:6).

This woman in Mark 5 started putting some of the spiritual laws of God into effect when she said, "If I may but touch the hem of His garment, I shall be made whole." When she did, the power of God began to flow. Jesus didn't sise her up and evaluate her worthiness. God's power flows when we cooperate with the spiritual laws of His kingdom. Electricity isn't personal when it kills someone. There are just laws at work governing the flow of power. Either you can cooperate and use electricity to your advantage, or those same laws can kill you.

It's the same way in the kingdom of God. There are many people who pray for healing because they don't understand the spiritual laws that govern it. When they don't see healing manifest, they get mad at God, saying, "Lord, if You wanted to, You could have healed this person." No, God has set up the kingdom to operate under laws, and He can't just violate them.

The Lord doesn't want people to die from gravity – falling off bridges, buildings, or cliffs. That's not God's will. However, a Colorado Springs man was climbing on some rocks on a mountain nearby, and he fell about three hundred feet. He was one of our soldiers who survived Iraq, but he didn't survive this fall. It wasn't God's will for this man to die, but what's the Lord going to do? Will He stop the law of gravity to save this man's life? Although God is the one who created the laws that govern this physical world, if He were to suspend gravity because He didn't want this guy to die, there would have been multitudes of other people depending on the law of gravity who would have died.

God created these laws, and He doesn't just suspend them. If you don't cooperate with the law of gravity, you could get killed. If you jump off a ten-story building, gravity will kill you. God intended gravity to be to your advantage and to help you function here on this earth. If you're sitting in a chair right now, you don't have to force yourself to stay down. Gravity is working. The same law that will help you if you cooperate with it will also kill you if you violate it. It's the same way in the spiritual realm.

HOW THE POWER FLOWS
Lesson 19 – Outline

I. The woman who had an issue of blood powerfully illustrates these truths about how the kingdom of God operates by law.

> *A certain woman, which had an issue of blood twelve years, And had suffered many things of many physicians, and had spent all that she had, and was nothing bettered, but rather grew worse, When she had heard of Jesus, came in the press behind, and touched his garment. For she said, If I may touch but his clothes, I shall be whole. And straightway the fountain of her blood was dried up; and she felt in her body that she was healed of that plague.*
>
> Mark 5:25-29

> *And Jesus, immediately knowing in himself that virtue had gone out of him, turned him about in the press, and said, Who touched my clothes? And his disciples said unto him, Thou seest the multitude thronging thee, and sayest thou, Who touched me? And he looked round about to see her that had done this thing. But the woman fearing and trembling, knowing what was done in her, came and fell down before him, and told him all the truth. And he said unto her, Daughter, thy faith hath made thee whole; go in peace, and be whole of thy plague.*
>
> Mark 5:30-34

    A. Jesus honestly didn't know who had touched Him (Luke 2:52 and 2:11).

    B. Therefore, He didn't evaluate her to see if she was worthy or not.

    C. This shows that the power of God flows under law.

II. When you tap into these spiritual laws, the power of God just flows.

    A. God established His kingdom to operate under spiritual laws.

    B. As believers, we need to find out what those laws are and cooperate with them.

    C. As you learn how to cooperate with and enforce these laws, you'll see God's provision for you manifest.

III. God has already done His part.

    A. The Word clearly reveals that the Lord has already healed us, but we have yet to take advantage of it (1 Pet. 2:24).

    B. When God said **"By whose stripes ye were healed"** (1 Pet. 2:24), He put it into the past tense, as an already-accomplished reality.

C. Therefore, you ought to believe the Word and say, "I know it's already done. He put the same power on the inside of me that raised Jesus from the dead (Eph. 1:18-20). I take my authority, and now I speak to my problem and command these things to happen."

IV. Although there are many different spiritual laws, one of them that governs whether you receive from God or not is the power of your words (Matt. 12:34-37, James 3, Mark 11).

> ***A man's belly shall be satisfied with the fruit of his mouth; and with the increase of his lips shall he be filled. Death and life are in the power of the tongue: and they that love it shall eat the fruit thereof.***
>
> Proverbs 18:20-21

A. This woman in Mark 5 said, **"If I may touch but his clothes, I shall be whole"** (Mark 5:28).

B. You will have what you say (Mark 11:23).

C. You can't speak death out of your mouth and expect to receive life – it doesn't work that way.

D. Faith flows through words.

E. Words release either death or life, but your ignorance of this law doesn't mean that the law is going to change.

F. God's Word says that faith speaks (Rom. 10:6).

V. God created these laws, and He doesn't just suspend them.

A. The same law that will help you if you cooperate with it will also kill you if you violate it (e.g., gravity, electricity).

B. It's the same way in the spiritual realm.

HOW THE POWER FLOWS
Lesson 19 – Teacher's Guide

1. The woman who had an issue of blood powerfully illustrates these truths about how the kingdom of God operates by law (Mark 5:25-34). Jesus honestly didn't know who had touched Him (Luke 2:52 and 2:11). Therefore, He didn't evaluate her to see if she was worthy or not. This shows that the power of God flows under law.

2. When we tap into these spiritual laws, the power of God just flows. God established His kingdom to operate under spiritual laws. As believers, we need to find out what those laws are and cooperate with them. As we learn how to cooperate with and enforce these laws, we'll see God's provision for us manifest.

3. God has already done His part. The Word clearly reveals that the Lord has already healed us, but we have yet to take advantage of it (1 Pet. 2:24). When God said **"By whose stripes ye were healed"** (1 Pet. 2:24), He put it into the past tense, as an already-accomplished reality. Therefore, we ought to believe the Word and say, "I know it's already done. He put the same power on the inside of me that raised Jesus from the dead (Eph. 1:18-20). I take my authority, and now I speak to my problem and command these things to happen."

1. Read Mark 5:25-34; Luke 2:11, and 52. What does the woman who had an issue of blood powerfully illustrate? (These truths about how the kingdom of God operates by law)
2. A. When does the power of God just flow? (When we tap into these spiritual laws)
   B. As believers, we need to find out what those laws are and do what? (Cooperate with them)
3. A. Read 1 Peter 2:24. Who has already done His part? (God)
   B. He put 1 Peter 2:24 into what tense, as an already-accomplished reality (Past tense – **"were healed"**)

4. Although there are many different spiritual laws, one of them that governs whether we receive from God or not is the power of our words (Matt. 12:34-37, James 3, Mark 11, and Prov. 18:20-21). This woman in Mark 5 said, **"If I may touch but his clothes, I shall be whole"** (Mark 5:28). We will have what we say (Mark 11:23). We can't speak death out of our mouths and expect to receive life – it doesn't work that way. Faith flows through words. Words release either death or life, but our ignorance of this law doesn't mean that the law is going to change. God's Word says that faith speaks (Rom. 10:6).

5. God created these laws, and He doesn't just suspend them. The same law that will help us if we cooperate with it will also kill us if we violate it (e.g., gravity, electricity). It's the same way in the spiritual realm.

4. A. Read Matthew 12:34-37; Proverbs 18:20-21; Romans 10:6; Mark 5:28, and 11:23. What will we have? (What we say)
   B. What do words release? (Either death or life)
5. A. Who created these laws? (God)
   B. The same law that will help us if we cooperate with it will also _____ if we violate it. (Kill us)

HOW THE POWER FLOWS
Lesson 19 – Discipleship Questions

1. According to Mark 5:25-34, what did Jesus ask when He perceived that virtue (power) had gone out of Him?

2. Luke 2:52 reveals that Jesus increased in what?

3. He increased in favor with whom?

4. In Luke 2:11, Christ the Lord is also called what?

5. According to Matthew 12:34-37, what does the mouth speak out of?

6. What does a good man, out of the good treasure of his heart, bring forth?

7. What does an evil man, out of the evil treasure of his heart, bring forth?

8. What shall we give an account for on the Day of Judgement?

9. According to James 3:2-12, what are bits and bridles for?

10. A very small helm (rudder) turns what?

11. What is a fire, a world of iniquity?

12. What ought not to be?

13. Can a fountain yield both salt water and fresh?

14. According to Romans 10:6, what does the righteousness that is of faith do?

HOW THE POWER FLOWS
Lesson 19 – Answer Key

1. Who touched My clothes?

2. In wisdom, stature, and favor.

3. Both God and man.

4. Saviour.

5. The abundance of the heart.

6. Good things.

7. Evil things.

8. Every idle word spoken.

9. Horses.

10. A ship.

11. The tongue.

12. Blessing and cursing proceeding out of the same mouth.

13. No.

14. It speaks.

HOW THE POWER FLOWS
Lesson 19 – Scriptures

And a certain woman, which had an issue of blood twelve years, And had suffered many things of many physicians, and had spent all that she had, and was nothing bettered, but rather grew worse, When she had heard of Jesus, came in the press behind, and touched his garment. For she said, If I may touch but his clothes, I shall be whole. And straightway the fountain of her blood was dried up; and she felt in her body that she was healed of that plague.

Mark 5:25-29

And Jesus, immediately knowing in himself that virtue had gone out of him, turned him about in the press, and said, Who touched my clothes? And his disciples said unto him, Thou seest the multitude thronging thee, and sayest thou, Who touched me? And he looked round about to see her that had done this thing. But the woman fearing and trembling, knowing what was done in her, came and fell down before him, and told him all the truth. And he said unto her, Daughter, thy faith hath made thee whole; go in peace, and be whole of thy plague.

Mark 5:30-34

And Jesus increased in wisdom and stature, and in favour with God and man.

Luke 2:52

For unto you is born this day in the city of David a Saviour, which is Christ the Lord.

Luke 2:11

Who his own self bare our sins in his own body on the tree, that we, being dead to sins, should live unto righteousness: by whose stripes ye were healed.

1 Peter 2:24

The eyes of your understanding being enlightened; that ye may know what is the hope of his calling, and what the riches of the glory of his inheritance in the saints, And what is the exceeding greatness of his power to us-ward who believe, according to the working of his mighty power, Which he wrought in Christ, when he raised him from the dead, and set him at his own right hand in the heavenly places.

Ephesians 1:18-20

A man's belly shall be satisfied with the fruit of his mouth; and with the increase of his lips shall he be filled. Death and life are in the power of the tongue: and they that love it shall eat the fruit thereof.

Proverbs 18:20-21

O generation of vipers, how can ye, being evil, speak good things? for out of the abundance of the heart the mouth speaketh. A good man out of the good treasure of the heart bringeth forth good things: and an evil man out of the evil treasure bringeth forth evil things. But I say unto you, That every idle word that men shall speak, they shall give account thereof in the day of judgement. For by thy words thou shalt be justified, and by thy words thou shalt be condemned.

Matthew 12:34-37

For in many things we offend all. If any man offend not in word, the same is a perfect man, and able also to bridle the whole body. Behold, we put bits in the horses' mouths, that they may obey us; and we turn about their whole body. Behold also the ships, which though they be so great, and are driven of fierce winds, yet are they turned about with a very small helm, whithersoever the governor listeth. Even so the tongue is a little member, and boasteth great things. Behold, how great a matter a little fire kindleth!

James 3:2-5

And the tongue is a fire, a world of iniquity: so is the tongue among our members, that it defileth the whole body, and setteth on fire the course of nature; and it is set on fire of hell. For every kind of beasts, and of birds, and of serpents, and of things in the sea, is tamed, and hath been tamed of mankind: But the tongue can no man tame; it is an unruly evil, full of deadly poison. Therewith bless we God, even the Father; and therewith curse we men, which are made after the similitude of God. Out of the same mouth proceedeth blessing and cursing. My brethren, these things ought not so to be. Doth a fountain send forth at the same place sweet water and bitter? Can the fig tree, my brethren, bear olive berries? either a vine, figs? so can no fountain both yield salt water and fresh.

James 3:6-12

For verily I say unto you, That whosoever shall say unto this mountain, Be thou removed, and be thou cast into the sea; and shall not doubt in his heart, but shall believe that those things which he saith shall come to pass; he shall have whatsoever he saith.

Mark 11:23

But the righteousness which is of faith speaketh on this wise, Say not in thine heart, Who shall ascend into heaven? (that is, to bring Christ down from above:).

Romans 10:6

COOPERATE WITH GOD
Lesson 20

Some people don't like these truths at all. It's comforting to them to feel that God is the one who willed for this person to die and that one to fail, this person to have a nervous breakdown and that marriage to break up. They find comfort in this mentality because it takes all responsibility away from them and they're able to say, "Whatever will be, will be." I understand that these truths I'm sharing will unsettle some people, but it's the truth that will set them free (John 8:32).

Before my wife and I were married, there was a girl we were both very close friends with. I was with her when she died. She was praying and saying, "God's going to heal me. Now is the time. It has to be now." She was believing for healing. However, we were shocked when she died, because we honestly expected God to heal her. Although it took me almost four years to learn enough of God's Word to figure out what had happened, I realised that we had violated so many spiritual laws and done many things wrong.

GOD'S MESSENGER BOY?

At that time in my life, I was under the false teaching that says, "God puts tragedy in your life to perfect you. He'll bless you with sickness and disease because it's through your hardships that you are made better." This is absolutely untrue, but back then I didn't understand enough of the Word to know any better. So I believed it and accepted it.

I actually attended an out-of-state conference where I heard a man teach that Satan was God's messenger boy. He said, "Anything the devil wants to do in your life, he has to get God's permission. Ultimately, God is the one that's controlling both the good and the bad. So, bad things are actually sent from God to perfect us." When I returned home from this conference, I gave a tape of this message entitled "Satan Is God's Messenger Boy" to my friend. She immediately listened to it.

In the message, this man used the example of a high school boy who was too timid and shy to witness. Even though he wasn't bold enough to speak to others about his faith, he wanted the Lord to use him. So he said, "God, I'll do anything. Put sickness or disease on me so that people will see that I'm not afraid to die."

The very next day, this boy came down with leukemia, and eventually died of it. While sick and dying, he witnessed to people. Since he was a football player, the whole school turned out at his funeral. At the ceremony, four people were born again.

This man used that as an example of how God answered this boy's prayer to be a witness by "blessing" him with leukemia. This girl listened to that tape and prayed the exact same prayer as that boy. "God, give me leukemia so I can be a witness." The next day, she passed out. They rushed her to the hospital. She had acute leukemia, and eventually died of it.

God wasn't the one who answered that prayer. He doesn't put sickness and disease on us. Satan is the one who takes advantage of a "prayer" like that. They dropped all their defenses and opened themselves up to leukemia, believing it was of God.

DOUBLE MINDED

When this girl died, four people were born again at her funeral. I was there. I saw it. Some people thought, *Well, it must not have been God's will to heal her.* How dumb can you get and still breathe? I'm not saying this to be critical of anyone. I was personally involved in this situation. We were so stupid that we were asking God for cancer.

If you start asking God for cancer, believing He is a source of it, it'll come your way. It's not that God sent it, but there are lying spirits that masquerade themselves as angels of light who will claim to be His messenger (2 Cor. 11:14). If you start praying for tragedy in your life, you'll get plenty of it – and you'll think it's from God.

There are laws that govern how God operates. We asked for this sickness and submitted to it, claiming it was the Lord. Therefore, we never fought against it. We never actively resisted the devil, because – in our warped way of thinking – that would have been fighting against God. We thought He was the one who gave this sickness. So there we were, asking for sickness, believing God answered our prayer by giving this girl leukemia, and then on the other hand, asking Him to take it away. That's double minded.

Let not that [double minded] man think that he shall receive any thing of the Lord.
James 1:7, brackets mine

That's violating and voiding the laws of God.

This girl died through my influence. I had a part in it. Some people don't want to accept responsibility. Maybe you know someone who died. Perhaps you've lost a marriage because you didn't understand the laws of God. You didn't know how to stand and fight. Those tragedies and negative things you've experienced weren't God's will – it was your fault or the devil's or someone else's. Many people don't want to accept this responsibility. They'd rather blame God. I understand how you feel because I've been there. However, I accepted responsibility. I realised that I did so many things wrong. I violated God's Word and opened up a door for the devil through false teaching and wrong believing.

I accepted my responsibility and I've changed. I've believed the truth, and the truth has set me free. Since then, I've seen many people healed of leukemia. I can't undo what's done, but I can redeem that situation by going and sharing these truths with other people and seeing them set free.

JESUS COULDN'T?

In Mark 6, Jesus went into His own hometown.

When the sabbath day was come, he began to teach in the synagogue: and many hearing him were astonished, saying, From whence hath this man these things? and what wisdom is this which is given unto him, that even such mighty works are wrought by his hands? Is not

> *this the carpenter, the son of Mary, the brother of James, and Joses, and of Juda, and Simon? and are not his sisters here with us? And they were offended at him.*
>
> Mark 6:2-3

These people knew Him as the carpenter, the son of Joseph and Mary. However, the truth is that He wasn't a carpenter or Joseph's son; Jesus was the Son of God who happened to work as a carpenter for a period of time. These people knew Him in the physical, natural realm, but they didn't know who He truly was. Due to this, they rejected His ministry, thinking, *He's making Himself somebody better than us. He grew up here with my kids. I've seen Him since He was a tiny little boy, and here He is proclaiming that He's the Son of God.* Because of their familiarity with Jesus, they were offended at Him and rejected Him.

> *But Jesus said unto them, A prophet is not without honour, but in his own country, and among his own kin, and in his own house. And he could there do no mighty work, save that he laid his hands upon a few sick folk, and healed them.*
>
> Mark 6:4-5

Notice how Jesus *could* do no mighty work there. It's not that He wouldn't do it – He couldn't.

When many people pray and ask for something and it doesn't come to pass, they think it was God that chose not to do it. God is not free to move independently of us. He has to have a believer – who knows what the laws are and takes their authority – to flow through. We must cooperate with God.

If you pray and don't see something come to pass, you need to evaluate: Have you cooperated with God's laws? Is what you prayed for something He's promised? If you're praying for something that isn't revealed in the Word – stop. It's not good for you, and God hasn't provided it.

When something – like healing – is promised to you in the Word, take your place of authority as a believer and say, "This is a law of God, so I command my body to respond. In the name of Jesus, I am commanding what God has already done to manifest." But you have to know this.

Mark 6:5 says that Jesus *could* do no mighty work. It's not that He wouldn't do it; He couldn't do it. God Himself will not violate our free will. He won't make us receive. He has provided – generated – the power, but we must cooperate and flip the switch. We must learn how to receive what God has already done.

YOUR FREE WILL

It isn't the Lord who is letting people die and go to hell. People are choosing to go to hell, because God gave them a free choice. However, He's doing everything He can to keep that from coming to pass.

No one who is condemned to hell on Judgement Day will be able to put their finger in Jesus' face and say, "It's not fair. You didn't give me a chance!" God has put obstacles and barriers in front of every person who is headed to hell. They've had to climb over their own conscience that has convicted them and told them they were wrong and should repent. People came across their path. There has been obstacle after obstacle. God is faithful to deal with every person who has ever lived, trying to turn them from their destructive ways. But they choose to reject His drawing and ignore Him. Therefore, no one will be able to accuse God. He's not the one sending people to hell. They'll know it was absolutely their choice.

It's the same with healing. It's not God who is letting people be sick. He's already provided for the healing of every single person. However, we're ignorant of His provision and His laws governing how to receive it.

Just as Jesus could do no mighty work in His own hometown, unbelief prevents God from doing what He wants to do in your life (Matt. 13:58). It wasn't Christ's unbelief or lack of willingness, but it was their unbelief that hindered His power. Your unbelief stops God from doing His will.

God will not move in your life without your cooperation. You must be in agreement with Him. That's one of His laws. Your free will is something that the Lord will not violate. You may desire the right end results, but you won't receive them if you disobey every single law along the way. You may wish to enjoy good health, but if you're committing sexual immorality, shacking up with anybody and everybody, through those actions, you are putting a law into effect, the law of sowing and reaping (Gal. 6:7-8), and faith for good health is dead without accompanying works (James 2:17). You can't just pray for something and then act in a contrary way. That's not how the kingdom works.

POWERFUL AND IMPORTANT

I recently prayed with a woman in a hospital. She was very close to death and looked terrible. Since she was barely alive, she couldn't talk or communicate. I tried everything I knew to discern if there was anything I could minister to her or her family, but I couldn't perceive anything. So I just prayed for her the best I knew how and left.

Right before I left town, the family called and told me that she was going downhill fast. The doctor only gave her an hour or two to live. Since I was busy holding a meeting, I sent some friends back to the hospital. After she passed on, my friends were talking to the family. They discovered that this woman had said, "I give up. I'm ready to die." She had quit believing. I was trying to exercise my authority and minister healing, but it was against this woman's will. Healing won't work in a case like that.

God gave us a free choice. Even a medical doctor will tell you that once someone loses the will to live, they'll die. The ailment could even be something minor that could be treated by medicine, but without that will to live, they'll die. However, when some people go beyond medicine's ability to help and the doctors say "There is nothing we can do for them. They're going to die," some people just have a will to live and they fight through. Your personal will is very powerful and important.

One of God's laws is that you can't have your will in one direction and then expect to get the results that would come from going in another. You can't just yield to and serve the devil – giving him total access to you – and reap the benefits of a godly life. It's not because God won't flow or that He's looking at you as being unworthy. Everyone is unworthy in that sense. God doesn't move in your life because you deserve it. However, in order to see His provision – His will – manifest, you do have to cooperate with Him.

COOPERATE WITH GOD
Lesson 20 – Outline

I. It's the truth that will set people free (John 8:32).

    A. If you start asking God for cancer, believing He is a source of it, it'll come your way.

    B. It's not that God sent it, but there are lying spirits that masquerade themselves as angels of light who will claim to be His messenger (2 Cor. 11:14).

    C. If you start praying for tragedy in your life, you'll get plenty of it – and you'll think it's from God.

> ***Let not that** [double minded] **man think that he shall receive any thing of the Lord.***
> James 1:7, brackets mine

    D. When we ministered to my friend with leukemia, we violated God's Word and opened up a door for the devil through false teaching and wrong believing.

    E. I accepted my responsibility, and I've changed.

    F. I can't undo what's done, but I can redeem that situation by going and sharing these truths with other people and seeing them set free.

II. God Himself will not violate our free will.

> ***When the sabbath day was come, he began to teach in the synagogue: and many hearing him were astonished, saying, From whence hath this man these things? and what wisdom is this which is given unto him, that even such mighty works are wrought by his hands? Is not this the carpenter, the son of Mary, the brother of James, and Joses, and of Juda, and Simon? and are not his sisters here with us? And they were offended at him.***
> Mark 6:2-3

    A. Mark 6:5 says that Jesus *could* do no mighty work – it's not that He wouldn't do it; He couldn't do it.

> ***But Jesus said unto them, A prophet is not without honour, but in his own country, and among his own kin, and in his own house. And he could there do no mighty work, save that he laid his hands upon a few sick folk, and healed them.***
> Mark 6:4-5

    B. He won't make you receive.

    C. He has provided – generated – the power, but you must cooperate and flip the switch.

    D. You must learn how to receive what God has already done.

III. Just as Jesus could do no mighty work in His own hometown, unbelief prevents God from doing what He wants to do in your life (Matt. 13:58).

    A.   Your unbelief stops God from doing His will.

    B.   God will not move in your life without your cooperation.

    C.   You must be in agreement with Him.

    D.   You may desire the right end results, but you won't receive them if you disobey every single law along the way.

    E.   You will reap what you sow (Gal. 6:7-8), and faith without works is dead (James 2:17).

IV. You can't just pray for something and then act in a way that's contrary to it.

    A.   God gave us a free choice.

    B.   Your personal will is very powerful and important.

    C.   One of God's laws is that you can't have your will in one direction and then expect to get the results that would come from going in another.

    D.   You can't just yield to and serve the devil – giving him total access to you – and reap the benefits of a godly life.

    E.   God doesn't move in our lives because we deserve it.

    F.   However, in order to see His provision – His will – manifest, we do have to cooperate with Him.

COOPERATE WITH GOD
Lesson 20 – Teacher's Guide

1. It's the truth that will set people free (John 8:32). If we start asking God for cancer, believing He is a source of it, it'll come our way. It's not that God sent it, but there are lying spirits that masquerade themselves as angels of light who will claim to be His messenger (2 Cor. 11:14). If we start praying for tragedy in our lives, we'll get plenty of it – and we'll think it's from God (James 1:7). We violate God's Word and open up a door for the devil through false teaching and wrong believing. Let's accept our responsibility and change. We can't undo what's done, but we can redeem those situations by going and sharing these truths with other people and seeing them set free.

2. God Himself will not violate our free will (Mark 6:2-5). Mark 6:5 says that Jesus *could* do no mighty work – it's not that He wouldn't do it; He couldn't do it. He won't make us receive. He has provided – generated – the power, but we must cooperate and flip the switch. We must learn how to receive what God has already done.

3. Just as Jesus could do no mighty work in His own hometown, unbelief prevents God from doing what He wants to do in our lives (Matt. 13:58). Our unbelief stops God from doing His will. God will not move in our lives without our cooperation. We must be in agreement with Him. We may desire the right end results, but we won't receive them if we disobey every single law along the way. We will reap what we sow (Gal. 6:7-8), and faith without works is dead (James 2:17).

1. A. Read John 8:32, 2 Corinthians 11:14, and James 1:7. What will set people free? (The truth)
   B. How do we violate God's Word and open up a door for the devil?
      (Through false teaching and wrong believing)
2. A. Read Mark 6:2-5. God Himself will not violate our what? (Free will)
   B. What must we learn how to receive? (What God has already done)
3. A. Read Matthew 13:58, Galatians 6:7-8, and James 2:17. What prevents God from doing what He wants to do in our lives? (Unbelief)
   B. God will not move in our lives without our what? (Cooperation)

4. We can't just pray for something and then act in a way that's contrary to it. God gave us a free choice. Our personal will is very powerful and important. One of God's laws is that we can't have our will in one direction and then expect to get the results that would come from going in another. We can't just yield to and serve the devil – giving him total access to us – and reap the benefits of a godly life. God doesn't move in our lives because we deserve it. However, in order to see His provision – His will – manifest, we do have to cooperate with Him.

4. A. We can't have our will in one direction and then expect to get the results that would come from what? (Going in another direction)
     B. We do have to cooperate with God in order to see what manifest? (His provision – His will)

COOPERATE WITH GOD
Lesson 20 – Discipleship Questions

1. According to John 8:32, we shall what the truth?

2. Second Corinthians 11:14 reveals that who is transformed?

3. Into what?

4. According to James 1:7, a double-minded man should not think that he shall receive what?

5. According to Mark 6:2-5, what was the reaction of many who were hearing Jesus begin to teach in the synagogue?

6. Where is a prophet without honour?

7. Other than laying His hands on a few sick folk and healing them, what could Jesus do there?

8. Matthew 13:58 reveals that their unbelief limited Him from doing what?

9. According to Galatians 6:7-8, who is not mocked?

10. What shall we reap?

11. What do people who sow to the flesh reap?

12. What do people who sow to the Spirit reap?

13. What does James 2:17 say is dead if it is alone?

COOPERATE WITH GOD
Lesson 20 – Answer Key

1. Know.

2. Satan.

3. An angel of light.

4. Anything of the Lord.

5. They were astonished and offended.

6. In his own country, among his own kin, and in his own house.

7. No mighty work.

8. Many mighty works.

9. God.

10. Whatsoever we sow.

11. Corruption.

12. Life everlasting.

13. Faith.

COOPERATE WITH GOD
Lesson 20 – Scriptures

And ye shall know the truth, and the truth shall make you free.

John 8:32

And no marvel; for Satan himself is transformed into an angel of light.

2 Corinthians 11:14

For let not that man think that he shall receive any thing of the Lord.

James 1:7

And when the sabbath day was come, he began to teach in the synagogue: and many hearing him were astonished, saying, From whence hath this man these things? and what wisdom is this which is given unto him, that even such mighty works are wrought by his hands? Is not this the carpenter, the son of Mary, the brother of James, and Joses, and of Juda, and Simon? and are not his sisters here with us? And they were offended at him. But Jesus said unto them, A prophet is not without honour, but in his own country, and among his own kin, and in his own house. And he could there do no mighty work, save that he laid his hands upon a few sick folk, and healed them.

Mark 6:2-5

And he did not many mighty works there because of their unbelief.

Matthew 13:58

Be not deceived; God is not mocked: for whatsoever a man soweth, that shall he also reap. For he that soweth to his flesh shall of the flesh reap corruption; but he that soweth to the Spirit shall of the Spirit reap life everlasting.

Galatians 6:7-8

Even so faith, if it hath not works, is dead, being alone.

James 2:17

AS YOU THINK
Lesson 21

You need to learn what God's laws are and then cooperate with them. You can't watch television programs that minister depression, and then operate in joy. You can't take in all of the (bad) news without strengthening unbelief. If you want a pure heart, you can't watch movies that are full of adultery and fornication. You're going to have to think on things that are true, honest, just, pure, lovely, virtuous, praiseworthy, and of good report (Phil. 4:8). Yet people misunderstand these laws.

Your life moves in the direction of your dominant thoughts.

> **As he thinketh in his heart, so is he.**
>
> Proverbs 23:7

You will reap emotions based on what you focus your attention on.

> **For to be carnally minded is death; but to be spiritually minded is life and peace.**
>
> Romans 8:6

That's a law of God. Therefore, you can't experience God's peace if you're constantly meditating on things that are contrary to peace – hatred, strife, and ungodliness. You can't just pray and ask for peace. You must learn to keep your thoughts centered on God and His Word.

> **Thou wilt keep him in perfect peace, whose mind is stayed on thee: because he trusteth in thee.**
>
> Isaiah 26:3

THE KNOWLEDGE OF GOD

Your emotions will follow what you think. That's a law of God. So if you're praying for peace but aren't focused on God, you're just spitting in the wind. It's not going to work. Desiring the things of God is part of the process, but it's not all there is to it.

> **Grace and peace be multiplied unto you through the knowledge of God, and of Jesus our Lord.**
>
> 2 Peter 1:2

Grace and peace are multiplied to you through the knowledge of God and of Jesus Christ our Lord – not through prayer. It isn't a matter of you just pleading with God. The laws of God say that you must think on the right things to receive the right results.

> *Rejoice in the Lord alway: and again I say, Rejoice. Let your moderation be known unto all men. The Lord is at hand. Be careful* [full of care] *for nothing; but in every thing by prayer and supplication with thanksgiving let your requests be made known unto God. And the peace of God, which passeth all understanding, shall keep your hearts and minds through Christ Jesus.*
>
> Philippians 4:4-7, brackets mine

As you keep your mind stayed upon the Lord, the peace of God will keep your heart and mind. The next verse continues, saying:

> *Finally, brethren, whatsoever things are true, whatsoever things are honest, whatsoever things are just, whatsoever things are pure, whatsoever things are lovely, whatsoever things are of good report; if there be any virtue, and if there be any praise, think on these things.*
>
> Philippians 4:8

In other words, this is a command to keep your mind stayed on the Lord and His Word (Is. 26:3).

> *Think on these things.*
>
> Philippians 4:8

These are laws of God. This is how His kingdom works.

THE GOS-PILL

God made you so that your physical and emotional health follows the way you think. If you're thinking on depressing things, you'll be depressed. If you're thinking on the Lord and His Word, you'll be full of life, joy, and peace.

God's Word is…

> *Life unto those that find them, and health to all their flesh.*
>
> Proverbs 4:22

The Word of God brings health.

> *He sent his word, and healed them, and delivered them from their destructions.*
>
> Psalm 107:20

God's prescription for health is His Word. Take it in daily doses, just like medicine. Many people are praying for health, but they're violating the Great Physician's instructions. They aren't taking their medicine.

What if the medical doctor you saw about your condition prescribed to you a method of treatment – taking a certain pill each day – yet you didn't take it. Then, you get upset at the doctor about your treatment, saying, "It's no good. It didn't work." You have no right to criticise the doctor, because you didn't take the pills. You didn't cooperate with the prescribed treatment. The medical doctor gave you a treatment, but you didn't follow it.

God has given us a treatment. He's prescribed to us the Gos-pill (Gospel). He sent His Word to heal us and deliver us from all our destructions (Ps. 107:20). God's Word is health to all our flesh and life to those who find it (Prov. 4:22). This is the Great Physician's prescription.

EXCEEDING ABUNDANTLY ABOVE

In the kingdom of God, there are laws governing faith and healing. Yet we continue to violate these laws. Then we pray for healing and wonder why we aren't receiving. That's ignorance gone to seed!

Please don't take this as condemnation. I'm not trying to condemn anyone. I just want to stop people from condemning God. They say "It's God's will that so and so died, this business didn't work, that marriage broke up, my children are rebellious," and on and on they go. Why do they put the blame on God? "Because I prayed and asked for something, and it didn't come to pass." They just totally ignore this fact that God can't do everything He wants to do. There are laws that govern how His kingdom operates. If we violate those laws, we're actually empowering the devil to come in and steal, kill, and destroy. We need to cooperate with God's laws to receive His abundant life.

Most people think that God is able to do exceeding abundantly above all that we ask or think. However, that's not true. You must read the entire verse to get the true meaning.

> ***Now unto him that is able to do exceeding abundantly above all that we ask or think,*** according to the power that worketh in us.
>
> Ephesians 3:20, emphasis mine

That last phrase puts a limitation on the first one. God isn't free to move in your life independent of you. He has set it up to where He has to flow through people. He doesn't control your life without your consent or agreement. There has to be power working on the inside of you – specifically the power of faith. You have to stir yourself up and make that faith come alive.

Many people just plop themselves down in front of the television. They become discouraged and depressed listening to all of the bad news. They spend virtually no time with God and no time in His Word. Then they just throw a prayer out, and if it doesn't come to pass, "Well, then, God failed."

It is absolutely wrong for us to condemn God. It isn't God who is failing to be good, or failing to answer people's prayers. It's us who fail to understand how to receive. We don't realise that there are laws that govern even God's operation. He's not going to resist the devil for you. God isn't going to do what He told you to do (James 4:7). He commanded you to go heal the sick (Matt. 10:8). He generated the power and placed it on the inside of you – the very same power that raised Christ from the dead (Eph. 1:18-20). He equipped you, but then He told you to go lay hands on the sick and they would recover (Mark 16:18). Many of us are just violating every instruction and admonition in the Word of God and then throwing a prayer out. If it doesn't work, then God failed. That's not true. God is faithful, faithful, faithful!

I'M THE PROBLEM – NOT GOD

I've had bad things happen in my life. People who were close to me died – even after I prayed for their healing. However, in most of these cases, I can see that it was me who missed it. In some situations, I still don't understand exactly why things worked out the way they did, but I've come to this firm conviction that God is always faithful. It's never Him that fails. Somehow, I failed to understand and cooperate with the laws of God.

I find comfort in knowing that I'm the problem – not God. This is one of the great benefits in understanding the authority of the believer. Yet most of us are just the opposite. They can't handle taking responsibility for failure in their lives. Yes, this understanding puts responsibility on us, but it also explains why we don't always see things work. The reason being: God doesn't always have people who will cooperate with His laws.

The release of God's power in your life is directly proportional to how you believe. It's not proportional to your holiness. All of us fail and come short in different ways. The issue is faith. You get what you believe. If you believe that God has already healed you and you begin to exercise your authority, you'll see that healing manifest. But if you believe God can heal but hasn't done it yet, then that healing won't come to pass. Just because you don't like how the kingdom works doesn't mean it changes the laws. This is just how God is.

AS YOU THINK
Lesson 21 – Outline

I. Your life moves in the direction of your dominant thoughts.

> ***As he thinketh in his heart, so is he.***
>
> Proverbs 23:7

    A.   You will reap emotions based on what you focus your attention on.

> ***For to be carnally minded is death; but to be spiritually minded is life and peace.***
>
> Romans 8:6

    B.   You must learn to keep your thoughts centered on God and His Word.

> ***Thou wilt keep him in perfect peace, whose mind is stayed on thee: because he trusteth in thee.***
>
> Isaiah 26:3

    C.   Your emotions will follow what you think.

    D.   Grace and peace are multiplied to you through the knowledge of God and of Jesus Christ our Lord – not through prayer.

> ***Grace and peace be multiplied unto you through the knowledge of God, and of Jesus our Lord.***
>
> 2 Peter 1:2

II. The laws of God say that you must think on the right things to receive the right results.

> ***Rejoice in the Lord alway: and again I say, Rejoice. Let your moderation be known unto all men. The Lord is at hand. Be careful*** [full of care] ***for nothing; but in every thing by prayer and supplication with thanksgiving let your requests be made known unto God. And the peace of God, which passeth all understanding, shall keep your hearts and minds through Christ Jesus.***
>
> Philippians 4:4-7, brackets mine

    A.   As you keep your mind stayed upon the Lord, the peace of God will keep your heart and mind.

> ***Finally, brethren, whatsoever things are true, whatsoever things are honest, whatsoever things are just, whatsoever things are pure, whatsoever things are lovely, whatsoever things are of good report; if there be any virtue, and if there be any praise, think on these things.***
>
> Philippians 4:8

B. In other words, this is a command to keep your mind stayed on the Lord and His Word (Is. 26:3).

III. God made you so that your physical and emotional health follows the way you think.

A. God's Word is **"life unto those that find them, and health to all their flesh"** (Prov. 4:22).

> *He sent his word, and healed them, and delivered them from their destructions.*
> Psalm 107:20

B. God's prescription for health is His Word.

C. Take it in daily doses, just like medicine.

D. Many people are praying for health, but they're violating the Great Physician's instructions.

E. He's prescribed to us the Gos-pill (Gospel).

IV. God isn't free to move in your life independent of you.

> *Now unto him that is able to do exceeding abundantly above all that we ask or think, according to the power that worketh in us.*
> Ephesians 3:20

A. He doesn't control your life without your consent or agreement.

B. There has to be power working on the inside of you – specifically the power of faith.

C. God isn't going to do what He told you to do (James 4:7, Matt. 10:8, Eph. 1:18-20, and Mark 16:18).

D. The release of God's power in your life is directly proportional to how you believe.

AS YOU THINK
Lesson 21 – Teacher's Guide

1. Our lives move in the direction of our dominant thoughts (Prov. 23:7). We will reap emotions based on what we focus our attention on (Rom. 8:6). We must learn to keep our thoughts centered on God and His Word (Is. 26:3). Our emotions will follow what we think. Grace and peace are multiplied to us through the knowledge of God and of Jesus Christ our Lord – not through prayer (2 Pet. 1:2).

2. The laws of God say that we must think on the right things to receive the right results (Phil. 4:4-7). As we keep our minds stayed upon the Lord, the peace of God will keep our hearts and minds (Phil. 4:8). In other words, this is a command to keep our minds stayed on the Lord and His Word (Is. 26:3).

3. God made us so that our physical and emotional health follows the way we think. God's Word is **"life unto those that find them, and health to all their flesh"** (Prov. 4:22 and Ps. 107:20). God's prescription for health is His Word. We take it in daily doses, just like medicine. Many people are praying for health, but they're violating the Great Physician's instructions. He's prescribed to us the Gos-pill (Gospel).

4. God isn't free to move in our lives independent of us (Eph. 3:20). He doesn't control our lives without our consent or agreement. There has to be power working on the inside of us – specifically the power of faith. God isn't going to do what He told us to do (James 4:7, Matt. 10:8, Eph. 1:18-20, and Mark 16:18). The release of God's power in our lives is directly proportional to how we believe.

1. A. Read Proverbs 23:7, Romans 8:6, Isaiah 26:3, and 2 Peter 1:2. Our lives move in what direction? (The direction of our dominant thoughts)
   B. What do our emotions follow? (What we think)
2. A. Read Philippians 4:4-8 and review Isaiah 26:3. We must think on the right things to receive what? (The right results)
   B. As we keep our minds stayed upon the Lord, what will keep our hearts and minds? (The peace of God)
3. A. Read Proverbs 4:22 and Psalm 107:20. How did God make us? (So that our physical and emotional health follows the way we think)
   B. What is God's prescription for health? (His Word – the Gospel)
4. A. Read Ephesians 3:20, James 4:7, Matthew 10:8, Ephesians 1:18-20, and Mark 16:18. What has to be working on the inside of us? (Power – specifically the power of faith)
   B. What is the release of God's power in our lives directly proportional to? (How we believe)

AS YOU THINK
Lesson 21 – Discipleship Questions

1. According to Proverbs 23:7, as we _____ in our hearts, so are we.

2. What does Romans 8:6 say is death?

3. What does it say is life and peace?

4. According to Isaiah 26:3, who will the Lord keep in perfect peace?

5. Second Peter 1:2 says that grace and peace is what to us?

6. How?

7. According to Philippians 4:4-8, when should we rejoice?

8. We should be careful – full of care – for what?

9. What shall keep our hearts and minds through Christ Jesus?

10. What things should we think on?

11. According to Proverbs 4:22, God's Word is life to those who find them and health to all their what?

12. According to Psalm 107:20, what did God send?

13. The Word healed them and delivered them from what?

14. Mark 16:18 says that if a believer drinks any deadly thing, it shall not what?

15. These believers will lay hands on the sick, and they shall what?

AS YOU THINK
Lesson 21 – Answer Key

1. Think.

2. To be carnally minded.

3. To be spiritually minded.

4. The person whose mind is stayed on Him.

5. Multiplied.

6. Through the knowledge of God and of Jesus our Lord.

7. Always.

8. Nothing.

9. The peace of God.

10. Whatsoever things are true, honest, just, pure, lovely, of good report, virtuous, and praiseworthy.

11. Flesh.

12. His Word.

13. Their destructions.

14. Hurt them.

15. Recover.

AS YOU THINK
Lesson 21 – Scriptures

For as he thinketh in his heart, so is he: Eat and drink, saith he to thee; but his heart is not with thee.

Proverbs 23:7

For to be carnally minded is death; but to be spiritually minded is life and peace.

Romans 8:6

Thou wilt keep him in perfect peace, whose mind is stayed on thee: because he trusteth in thee.

Isaiah 26:3

Grace and peace be multiplied unto you through the knowledge of God, and of Jesus our Lord.

2 Peter 1:2

Rejoice in the Lord alway: and again I say, Rejoice. Let your moderation be known unto all men. The Lord is at hand. Be careful for nothing; but in every thing by prayer and supplication with thanksgiving let your requests be made known unto God. And the peace of God, which passeth all understanding, shall keep your hearts and minds through Christ Jesus. Finally, brethren, whatsoever things are true, whatsoever things are honest, whatsoever things are just, whatsoever things are pure, whatsoever things are lovely, whatsoever things are of good report; if there be any virtue, and if there be any praise, think on these things.

Philippians 4:4-8

For they are life unto those that find them, and health to all their flesh.

Proverbs 4:22

He sent his word, and healed them, and delivered them from their destructions.

Psalm 107:20

Now unto him that is able to do exceeding abundantly above all that we ask or think, according to the power that worketh in us.

Ephesians 3:20

Submit yourselves therefore to God. Resist the devil, and he will flee from you.

James 4:7

Heal the sick, cleanse the lepers, raise the dead, cast out devils: freely ye have received, freely give.

Matthew 10:8

The eyes of your understanding being enlightened; that ye may know what is the hope of his calling, and what the riches of the glory of his inheritance in the saints, And what is the exceeding greatness of his power to us-ward who believe, according to the working of his mighty power, Which he wrought in Christ, when he raised him from the dead, and set him at his own right hand in the heavenly places.

Ephesians 1:18-20

They shall take up serpents; and if they drink any deadly thing, it shall not hurt them; they shall lay hands on the sick, and they shall recover.

Mark 16:18

HONOUR GOD
Lesson 22

When you cooperate with God's spiritual laws, His power flows. When you disobey them, it stops the power of God from operating. Again, we see this very clearly in Mark 5 with the woman with the issue of blood.

> *A certain woman, which had an issue of blood twelve years, And had suffered many things of many physicians, and had spent all that she had, and was nothing bettered, but rather grew worse.*
>
> Mark 5:25-26

This lady had gone to physicians for twelve years. Although their treatments had depleted every penny she had, they hadn't helped her a bit.

DOCTORS AREN'T INFALLIBLE

If a woman like this came to me seeking healing from God and gave me every penny she had, yet was still not healed, someone would be on the news accusing me of being a crook and a charlatan. Since people just expect the power of God to always work instantly, they would come against a preacher. However, they wouldn't give a second thought about giving all of their money – hundreds of thousands of dollars – to medical doctors who have been known to make mistakes and even kill people. I'm not against doctors; I'm just saying they aren't infallible. However, hardly anyone ever considers that.

In the natural realm, people understand that there are laws, that sometimes problems arise, and not everything works out the way it's expected. Yet when it comes to the things of God, people just expect them to work with ease, completely problem free. However, there are spiritual laws that govern the kingdom of God. It's not that the Lord has a hard time doing things – it's people. People are dealing with different issues. So there may be a problem in them receiving through me – not because God is a problem, but because I don't know everything, and they don't either.

Sometimes, when I'm praying with someone, we'll see 50 percent of their healing manifest. So I'll go back and keep praying with them. Other people have come up and asked me, "If it's really God, why do you have to pray for them again and again, standing and believing? If it's God, then they'd just be healed." That's someone who doesn't understand that there are spiritual laws. God's people are just barely beginning to scratch the surface of understanding how things work. Sometimes it takes time, not because God has problems, but because I'm having a problem, or the person receiving is having a problem. No one understands everything yet.

The woman with the issue of blood had suffered many years from physicians and their treatments, yet nobody thought anything about it. I'm sure her friends believed she was doing the right thing. As these doctors bled her of everything she had financially without helping her one bit, they'd encourage her to go back to them and try again. However, these same friends probably called her "fanatical" and "extreme" once she had heard of Jesus and decided to pursue receiving her healing supernaturally through Him.

FAITH COMES BY HEARING

This woman was determined. **"She had heard of Jesus"** (Mark 5:27) and what He had done for others, which brings us to another law of God. You cannot believe and receive from God without first somehow hearing of Jesus and His Word.

> *How then shall they call on him in whom they have not believed? and how shall they believe in him of whom they have not heard?...So then faith cometh by hearing, and hearing by the word of God.*
>
> Romans 10:14 and 17

Many people who are trying to believe and receive from God aren't getting into His Word. Faith comes through the Word of God. If you want to increase and release your faith, you need to increase your revelation knowledge of God's Word. That's how simple it is, but there are people who violate this law all the time. They're just expecting to get what they've asked for because they're in a desperate situation. They don't know the first thing about believing God. They don't study the Word. They just sit in front of the television watching all kinds of junk, wondering why they don't have faith.

Both faith and unbelief come by hearing. If you listen to all of the negativity that's on television and radio instead of seeking God, you'll be full of unbelief and you won't receive. That's just a law of God. Some people don't like that and say, "Well, that just doesn't fit my lifestyle." Maybe you ought to change your lifestyle to fit the Word.

I'm amazed at some of the people who come to me wanting God to intervene in their lives. Just in talking to them, it's obvious they haven't spent an hour in the Word in a year. They don't pray or seek God. They haven't been attending church, studying the Word, or listening to Bible teachings. They're living their lives totally for themselves, bound by the discouragement and despair that comes from keeping their minds on evil things. Yet they want all of the benefits of keeping their minds stayed on God. I get upset when people criticise and slander God as if He's the one who failed. The Lord isn't failing. They're the ones who have failed to understand and cooperate with His laws.

SPEAK AND ACT

This woman in Mark 5 was committed that she was going to receive something from God.

> *For she said, If I may touch but his clothes, I shall be whole.*
>
> Mark 5:28

She spoke her faith and then acted on it. That's one of the laws of God. If she would have stayed on the edge of the crowd, saying "I believe, I receive. I believe, I receive," without acting on it, she would not have received.

In order to act on her faith, she had to overcome what other people thought. That's another spiritual law. Jesus said,

> *How can ye believe, which receive honour one of another, and seek not the honour that cometh from God only?*
>
> John 5:44

In other words, being a "man-pleaser" will hinder your faith. It'll keep you from believing. Jesus said, "You can't believe if you are seeking the honour that comes from other people instead of from God." If you're worried about what everybody else is going to say, it'll stop you from receiving.

FOCUS ON THE LORD

According to Old Testament Law, the Jews considered anyone with an issue of blood to be unclean (Lev. 15:19-33). If someone touched something that an unclean person had touched – such as a saddle, bowl, basin, or clothes – they also became unclean. So anyone who touched an unclean person also became unclean. Due to this, the Jews required an unclean person to stand on the edge of a crowd and yell out "Unclean, unclean" so that people would stay away from them.

When this woman crawled through the crowd and touched the hem of Jesus' garment, she touched people. She could have suffered the wrath of these people, been condemned, and stoned to death. When Jesus pointed her out in front of all these folks, it took a lot of courage for her to come forward.

This woman came to a place where she didn't care what anybody else said. She disdained the personal risk involved in coming to Jesus. She became more focused on the Lord and what He had to say than what these other folks had to say. Many people don't receive from God, because they're "man pleasers."

> *The fear of man bringeth a snare.*
>
> Proverbs 29:25

That's a law of God. If you are afraid of other people and what they're going to say, it'll hinder your faith. It'll keep you from receiving what you're believing for. You must come to the place in your heart where you say:

> *Let God be true, but every man a liar.*
>
> Romans 3:4

You must come to the place where you can honestly declare, "God, You are all I care about. I'm going to do what you tell me regardless of the flack that I receive for it." You must believe with all your heart. You can't harbor reservations and fears.

A GOD PLEASER ALONE

I ministered to a woman once who was sent home from the doctors to die. She had three large cancerous tumors that were open and spurting blood. After prayer, they shrunk to the sise of quarters that were easily removed by the doctor as an outpatient procedure.

Although the cancer was miraculously healed by the Lord without the doctors, once they saw the results, they wanted this woman to have radiation treatments just in case there was any cancer remaining. I told her not to do it, that God had healed her, not the doctors. She didn't need to expose herself to all the problems that radiation treatments would bring. But she chose to go ahead with the treatments and nearly died from the complications.

After that, once again, I encouraged her that well people don't get radiation treatments and that they weren't necessary. But this woman was so worried about what her mother, husband, children, and church people had to say. She knew the Lord had completely healed her and that she didn't need any further medical care, but she just couldn't bring herself to go against what these other people said. So she went in for the next round of treatments and died as a direct result of the radiation.

Fearing what other people think brings a snare (Prov. 29:25). This is a law of God. You can't truly believe if you are worried about what other people think (John 5:44). You must be a God pleaser alone.

These are just a few of the laws that govern the kingdom of God. As believers exercising our authority, we don't just pick and choose and make God do certain things; all we do is enforce the laws He's already set in place. We discover what God has already provided and how He said it works, and then we cooperate with and enforce those laws.

HONOUR GOD
Lesson 22 – Outline

I. When you cooperate with God's spiritual laws, His power flows.

    A.   When you disobey them, it stops the power of God from operating.

    B.   Again, we see this very clearly in Mark 5 with the woman with the issue of blood.

> ***A certain woman, which had an issue of blood twelve years, And had suffered many things of many physicians, and had spent all that she had, and was nothing bettered, but rather grew worse.***
>
> Mark 5:25-26

    C.   This woman was determined.

> ***She had heard of Jesus.***
>
> Mark 5:27

II. You cannot believe and receive from God without first somehow hearing of Jesus and His Word.

> ***How then shall they call on him in whom they have not believed? and how shall they believe in him of whom they have not heard? and how shall they hear without a preacher? ... So then faith cometh by hearing, and hearing by the word of God.***
>
> Romans 10:14-17

    A.   If you want to increase and release your faith, you need to increase your revelation knowledge of God's Word.

    B.   Both faith and unbelief come by hearing.

    C.   Maybe you ought to change your lifestyle to fit the Word.

III. This woman in Mark 5 was committed that she was going to receive something from God.

> ***For she said, If I may touch but his clothes, I shall be whole.***
>
> Mark 5:28

    A.   She spoke her faith and then acted on it.

    B.   In order to act on her faith, she had to overcome what other people thought.

> *How can ye believe, which receive honour one of another, and seek not the honour that cometh from God only?*
>
> John 5:44

    C.   If you are afraid of other people and what they're going to say, it'll hinder your faith.

> *The fear of man bringeth a snare.*
>
> Proverbs 29:25

    D.   You must believe with all your heart.

> *Let God be true, but every man a liar.*
>
> Romans 3:4

    E.   You can't harbor reservations and fears.

IV. As believers exercising our authority, we don't just pick and choose and make God do certain things.

    A.   All we do is enforce the laws He's already set in place.

    B.   We discover what God has already provided and how He said it works, and then we cooperate with and enforce those laws.

HONOUR GOD
Lesson 22 – Teacher's Guide

1. When we cooperate with God's spiritual laws, His power flows. When we disobey them, it stops the power of God from operating. Again, we see this very clearly in Mark 5 with the woman with the issue of blood (Mark 5:25-26). This woman was determined because "She had heard of Jesus" (Mark 5:27).

2. We cannot believe and receive from God without first somehow hearing of Jesus and His Word (Rom. 10:14-17). If we want to increase and release our faith, we need to increase our revelation knowledge of God's Word. Both faith and unbelief come by hearing. Maybe we ought to change our lifestyle to fit the Word.

3. This woman in Mark 5 was committed that she was going to receive something from God (Mark 5:28). She spoke her faith and then acted on it. In order to act on her faith, she had to overcome what other people thought (John 5:44). If we are afraid of other people and what they're going to say, it'll hinder our faith (Prov. 29:25). We must believe with all our hearts (Rom. 3:4). We can't harbor reservations and fears.

4. As believers exercising our authority, we don't just pick and choose and make God do certain things; all we do is enforce the laws He's already set in place. We discover what God has already provided and how He said it works, and then we cooperate with and enforce those laws.

1. A. Read Mark 5:25-27. What happens when we cooperate with God's spiritual laws? (His power flows)
   B. What happens when we disobey them? (It stops the power of God from operating)
2. A. Read Romans 10:14-17. If we want to increase and release our faith, we need to increase what? (Our revelation knowledge of God's Word)
   B. What comes by hearing? (Both faith and unbelief)
3. A. Read Mark 5:28, John 5:44, Proverbs 29:25, and Romans 3:4. What will hinder our faith? (If we are afraid of other people and what they're going to say)
   B. We must _____ with all our hearts. (Believe)
4. A. What do we need to discover? (What God has already provided and how He said it works)
   B. Then we need to do what? (Cooperate with and enforce those laws)

HONOUR GOD
Lesson 22 – Discipleship Questions

1. According to Mark 5:25-28, how many years had the woman had the issue of blood?

2. How much had she spent trying to get well?

3. What did she touch believing she would be made whole?

4. According to Romans 10:14, how can they believe in Him of whom they have not____.

5. Romans 10:17 says that faith comes as we _____ the Word of God.

6. According to John 5:44, seeking the honour that comes from other people will hinder what?

7. We need to seek the honour that comes from whom instead?

8. What does Leviticus 15:19-33 say that a woman with an issue of blood was (under the Law)?

9. According to Proverbs 29:25, what brings a snare?

10. Who should we put our trust in?

11. Then what shall we be?

12. Romans 3:4 says to let God be _____ and every man a liar.

HONOUR GOD
Lesson 22 – Answer Key

1. Twelve years.

2. All that she had.

3. Jesus' garment.

4. Heard.

5. Hear.

6. Our believing.

7. God.

8. Unclean.

9. The fear of man.

10. The Lord.

11. Safe.

12. True.

HONOUR GOD
Lesson 22 – Scriptures

And a certain woman, which had an issue of blood twelve years, And had suffered many things of many physicians, and had spent all that she had, and was nothing bettered, but rather grew worse, When she had heard of Jesus, came in the press behind, and touched his garment. For she said, If I may touch but his clothes, I shall be whole.

Mark 5:25-28

How then shall they call on him in whom they have not believed? and how shall they believe in him of whom they have not heard? and how shall they hear without a preacher?

Romans 10:14

So then faith cometh by hearing, and hearing by the word of God.

Romans 10:17

How can ye believe, which receive honour one of another, and seek not the honour that cometh from God only?

John 5:44

And if a woman have an issue, and her issue in her flesh be blood, she shall be put apart seven days: and whosoever toucheth her shall be unclean until the even. And every thing that she lieth upon in her separation shall be unclean: every thing also that she sitteth upon shall be unclean. And whosoever toucheth her bed shall wash his clothes, and bathe himself in water, and be unclean until the even. And whosoever toucheth any thing that she sat upon shall wash his clothes, and bathe himself in water, and be unclean until the even. And if it be on her bed, or on any thing whereon she sitteth, when he toucheth it, he shall be unclean until the even. And if any man lie with her at all, and her flowers be upon him, he shall be unclean seven days; and all the bed whereon he lieth shall be unclean.

Leviticus 15:19-24

And if a woman have an issue of her blood many days out of the time of her separation, or if it run beyond the time of her separation; all the days of the issue of her uncleanness shall be as the days of her separation: she shall be unclean. Every bed whereon she lieth all the days of her issue shall be unto her as the bed of her separation: and whatsoever she sitteth upon shall be unclean, as the uncleanness of her separation. And whosoever toucheth those things shall be unclean, and shall wash his clothes, and bathe himself in water, and be unclean until the even. But if she be cleansed of her issue, then she shall number to herself seven days, and after that she shall be clean. And on the eighth day she shall take unto her two turtles, or two young pigeons, and bring them unto the priest, to the door of the tabernacle of the congregation. And the priest shall offer the one for a sin offering, and the other for a burnt offering; and the priest shall make an atonement for her before the LORD for the issue of her uncleanness. Thus shall ye separate the children of Israel from their uncleanness; that they die not in their uncleanness, when they defile my tabernacle that is among them. This is the law of him that hath an issue, and of him whose seed goeth from him, and is defiled

therewith; And of her that is sick of her flowers, and of him that hath an issue, of the man, and of the woman, and of him that lieth with her that is unclean.
Leviticus 15:25-33

The fear of man bringeth a snare: but whoso putteth his trust in the LORD shall be safe.
Proverbs 29:25

God forbid: yea, let God be true, but every man a liar; as it is written, That thou mightest be justified in thy sayings, and mightest overcome when thou art judged.
Romans 3:4

NO NEW TESTAMENT MODEL
Lesson 23

Satan isn't using a superhuman, angelic power and authority; it's just mankind's God-given power and authority that we yielded to him when we obeyed him and disobeyed God. So it's actually nothing but a human power and authority that is being used against us. Therefore, the devil can't do anything against us without our consent and cooperation.

Understanding these truths radically changes our view of spiritual warfare. We recognise that the devil is a defeated foe. Jesus completely stripped him of all power and authority through the cross. However, the warfare we face today is in enforcing the Lord's victory. It's fighting against the wiles of the devil – his deception, lies, trickery, cunningness, and craftiness (Eph. 6:11).

All the warfare scriptures in the New Testament reveal that the battle is in our minds.

> *For though we walk in the flesh, we do not war after the flesh: (For the weapons of our warfare are not carnal, but mighty through God to the pulling down of strong holds;) Casting down imaginations, and every high thing that exalteth itself against the knowledge of God, and bringing into captivity every thought to the obedience of Christ.*
>
> 2 Corinthians 10:3-5

Notice what these weapons accomplish: They cast down strongholds, imaginations, every high thing that exalts itself against the knowledge of God, and bring every thought captive. All of this has to do with your thinking. The battlefield is your mind. Satan is fighting you with thoughts, and you can counter him with the thoughts God gives you.

"SPIRITUAL WARFARE"

This isn't the way most people teach "spiritual warfare." Many folks say, "There's a system of demonic powers hovering over every city. They can block your prayers and prevent them from getting to God. Since the Lord dwells out in space somewhere and the demonic powers are in the physical atmosphere, you have to get your prayers up through them." You may think this sounds silly, but it really is a prevalent doctrine in the body of Christ today. People really believe that they have to clear a hole over people's houses and/or cities so their prayers can get through to God. This is not what the Word of God teaches.

God's Word teaches that the Lord in all of His power and glory indwells each believer. You don't need your prayers to get through the atmosphere, above the ceiling, or even above your nose. The reason you bow your head to pray is so that you can look at God – He lives right there inside you.

These popular, but erroneous, concepts simply don't take into account the New Testament believer being God possessed. He dwells on the inside of us. Therefore, we don't have to deal with principalities and powers blocking our prayers from getting to God. The way these demons fight us is through our thoughts. The spiritual warfare in the Christian life is in our minds.

There's actually a group here where I live that teaches that when they first arrived in town, the heavens were "brass" – meaning that people's prayers were hindered and weren't getting through. So through this group's "spiritual warfare" and "intercession," they "opened up the heavens" and cleared things up. They say that's the reason their church has grown and the reason we've seen great things happen in our city. They claim that's why the crime rate dropped for a couple of years in a row. They believe that it's all the intercession and prayer that was making all of this come to pass.

What happened the next year when the crime rate shot back up and there were more murders than ever before? Did the heavens close back up? Did they quit praying effectively? What happened? I recognise that there are many things that influence this and that Christians do affect the world around them. But it's not all the demons hovering over a city that makes crime and murders happen.

BATTLE FOR THE MIND

Why are there lots of homicides in certain places? It's because of the demonic activity in the minds of people, not in the heavenlies. They have lost the battle for their minds and have given themselves over to Satan. They are watching and listening to all kinds of hatred, violence, and murder on television, movies, and video games. Since our society as a whole no longer supports and reinforces godly moral values, we're allowing these things to happen.

Yes, there are demonic powers in the air. Scripture plainly reveals this. But the way we deal with them is by coming against the unrenewed minds of people. We need to preach and teach the truth of God's Word to people. We can't just control demonic powers in the heavenlies through our prayers and therefore indirectly control other people. We can't make people behave because we bind a certain demonic power. That's not the model that the Scripture presents. The way the Bible teaches us to do it is to tell people the truth. As they believe and obey the truth, they are set free and come out from under the control of these demonic influences around them.

There are zero – not just a few, not one, but zero – New Testament precedents for the "spiritual warfare" and intercessory battles that are being promoted in the body of Christ today. Jesus never sent His disciples out to do "spiritual warfare" before He came into an area. He did send them out at times to announce His coming, but this was mainly just publicity.

Paul never called upon or encouraged the believers to do "spiritual warfare" as it's being promoted today. He's the one the Holy Spirit wrote 2 Corinthians 10:3-5 and Ephesians 6:11 through. Second Corinthians 10 reveals that our weapons are for taking every thought captive to Christ. Ephesians 6:11 tells us to stand against the wiles of the devil. The wrestling mentioned in the very next verse takes place in our thoughts (Eph. 6:12).

INFLUENCED THROUGH THOUGHTS

In our country, morals have decreased significantly in the last generation. The sexual immorality that's being promoted today couldn't have even been imagined thirty years ago.

One of the main reasons for this decline is because our culture has become so addicted to radio, television, and movies. Through these mediums, our morals have been steadily polluted and diluted.

Satan has touched individuals who have been raised up and who control the media. Both Christians and non-Christians alike are watching the same ungodly media. Therefore, the devil is exercising influence through the thoughts he is planting in people. Satan has to flow through physical things to control the way people think (Rom. 8:6, Prov. 23:7, and Is. 26:3).

Romans 12:2 says,

Be not conformed to this world: but be ye transformed...

How? By "spiritual warfare" and binding demons? No...

By the renewing of your mind, that ye may prove what is that good, and acceptable, and perfect, will of God.

Demons influence us through thoughts. They can't just give those thoughts directly; they have to influence a person, and then that person yields to Satan. He begins to educate them – putting his lies and deception into their life – so they can influence other people. The reason we see such a dominance of ungodly perspectives and principles today is because, as a whole, the news media, television, radio, and the movie industry is controlled by people who are under the influence of Satan. They are demonic in their attitudes and thoughts.

I read an article in which a prominent movie/television producer admitted that one of his goals is to change our country's morals. He is purposefully using his influence to change the Judeo-Christian ethic and morality of our culture. Satan is gaining control and exerting influence because he's fighting for people's minds, while the church is in their prayer closet trying to bind demonic powers. There is zero scriptural precedent for that. It's not the way they approached this in the Bible.

"LORD, GRANT US BOLDNESS"

The Apostle Paul went into terrible demonic places like Corinth and Athens. They had many different pagan gods and idols. He didn't counter all this idolatry by doing "spiritual warfare" – getting a bunch of Christians together and binding something. In Athens, he went into the marketplace and spoke to these people who did nothing but sit around trying to learn something new. Once he had their attention, he preached the Gospel and told them about the unknown God, the One they didn't truly understand. Paul declared, "He's the One, the only true God."

Paul went into Ephesus and shared God's Word. As I mentioned in chapter 14, back then, Ephesus was the location of the famous Diana of the Ephesians. In this temple, there was a statue that they believed fell down from heaven. Paul countered these deceptions and lies by telling people the truth. So many folks responded to the truth that the worship of Diana of the Ephesians literally ceased to be. They closed the temple down, and there has never been any demonic power operating through Diana of the Ephesians until the late 1900s when the "intercessors" resurrected her and made her the demonic power operating behind Islam.

A few years ago, they had over 20,000 people travel to Ephesus to do "spiritual warfare" and "bind" these demonic powers. Neither Jesus, Peter, nor Paul ever did that. They didn't encourage it. They never gathered people together to bind all the demonic powers in an area. They put their effort into preaching the Gospel and sharing God's Word.

They prayed like the early believers in Acts 4:

> **Lord, behold their threatenings: and grant unto thy servants, that with all boldness they may speak thy word, by stretching forth thine hand to heal; and that signs and wonders may be done by the name of thy holy child Jesus.**
>
> Acts 4:29-30

Then the place was shaken by the power of the Holy Spirit, and they went out boldly sharing the Gospel (Acts 4:31). Peter's shadow fell on people as he walked by on the street, and they were healed (Acts 5:15-16). Signs and wonders confirmed their preaching of the Word (Acts 5:12 and Mark 16:20). They saw their world changed not through "spiritual warfare" and "intercession" but through the preaching of the Gospel.

DE-CLAW SATAN

There are some Christians today who claim to be called to the "ministry of intercession." This is their whole life. They don't do anything else. They don't share the truth. They don't witness. They don't talk to people. They don't support social action. All they do is stay in their closets and pray.

Now, every believer ought to pray. It's an important part of an intimate relationship with God. I'm not against prayer, but there isn't any such thing as a "ministry of intercession." We're all supposed to pray, but we're all supposed to go out and do something too. Some people are using "intercession" as a cop-out to keep from sharing the Word of God.

The way people are born again is through a seed of God's Word being planted (1 Pet. 1:23). If Satan can deceive us and keep us from sharing God's Word, this is to his advantage. The Enemy's strategy is to keep us in prayer closets begging the Lord to do what He's told us to do. Instead of boldly sharing the Word and preaching the Gospel, we're afraid to tell anyone the truth because we might offend somebody.

The devil doesn't mind you praying as long as you're into this "spiritual warfare" and "intercession" stuff. Satan himself has inspired much of it. He has people out there fighting a ghost figure.

It's as if the devil is projecting a hologram and causing people to see an enemy coming. So people marshal all of their forces to fight this enemy that doesn't even exist. They exert a tremendous amount of effort and resources battling this ghost figure – and it makes them vulnerable in the areas that do exist. That's exactly what Satan is doing. He has the body of Christ busy fighting battles and tearing things down that don't even exist. Sure, Satan exists and his power exists, but he's not this all-powerful force that the intercessors have made him out to be.

> **Your adversary the devil, as a roaring lion, walketh about, seeking whom he may devour.**
>
> 1 Peter 5:8

Satan doesn't have the power to control us; he's using nothing but the same human power and authority that was given to mankind. Therefore, he can't do anything to us without our consent and cooperation. Yes, we have an Enemy who would like to destroy mankind as a whole, and each of us individually. How do we deal with this? Do we go directly to the devil and bind him? No. We deal with our thoughts. Satan can only influence us and gain our consent and cooperation through our thoughts.

That's the reason Jesus said,

Ye shall know the truth, and the truth shall make you free.

John 8:32

The only power Satan has is in lies and deception. That's the reason the truth makes you free. Once you know the truth, deception no longer has any power. It's de-clawed. The church's strength is in preaching the Gospel and sharing God's Word.

DEMONS WERE PRESENT

You do need to pray so you can be sensitive to God, yield to Him, hear clearly, and be bold to speak, but you don't need to do fifteen to twenty hours worth of "spiritual warfare" to prepare things before you get there. Just go in and preach the Gospel. The Word of God will change the atmosphere. As you preach the truth, the truth will cause demons to flee. Jesus would walk into a place, and the demons would literally cry out, run out, and come out of people. Now, if Jesus had been doing "spiritual warfare" the way it's promoted today, there wouldn't have been any demons crying out or coming out. He would have already dealt with them in prayer, and they would have already been gone. But the truth is, demons were present.

Demons were even present at the Last Supper. How else could Satan have entered into Judas Iscariot if he wasn't already there?

And after the sop Satan entered into him.

John 13:27

That's what the Bible says. Jesus didn't do "spiritual warfare" the way it's being promoted today. It's been given a status and a position that it never should have had. There's a lot of weirdness going on in the body of Christ today in the name of "spiritual warfare."

If Jesus couldn't keep Satan out of His last supper with His disciples, then you can't keep the devil out of your church or city by your "spiritual warfare."

If the Lord were to tarry another hundred years, people would look back on the "spiritual warfare" and "intercession" teachings of our day and think, *Surely that was one of the greatest errors that has ever crept into the body of Christ.* We're so close to it right now – and it's so prevalent and popular in the body of Christ – many people don't see it for what it is.

There is no New Testament model for this "spiritual warfare" and "intercession" stuff. Some of this is being taught from Scripture, but they're using Old Testament scriptures – and there's a huge difference between the way things were done in the Old Testament and the way they are done in the New.

NO NEW TESTAMENT MODEL
Lesson 23 – Outline

I. The warfare we face today is in enforcing the Lord's victory.

   A. It's fighting against the wiles of the devil – his deception, lies, trickery, cunningness, and craftiness (Eph. 6:11).

   B. All the warfare scriptures in the New Testament reveal that the battle is in our minds.

   > *For though we walk in the flesh, we do not war after the flesh: (For the weapons of our warfare are not carnal, but mighty through God to the pulling down of strong holds;) Casting down imaginations, and every high thing that exalteth itself against the knowledge of God, and bringing into captivity every thought to the obedience of Christ.*
   > 2 Corinthians 10:3-5

   C. Satan is fighting us with thoughts, and we counter him with the thoughts God gives us.

   D. As people believe and obey the truth, they are set free and come out from under the control of these demonic influences around them.

II. Satan has to flow through physical things to control the way you think (Rom. 8:6, Prov. 23:7, and Is. 26:3).

   > *Be not conformed to this world: but be ye transformed by the renewing of your mind, that ye may prove what is that good, and acceptable, and perfect, will of God.*
   > Romans 12:2

   A. Demons influence us through thoughts.

   B. They have to influence a person, and then that person yields to Satan.

   C. He begins to educate them – putting his lies and deception into their life – so they can influence other people.

III. Neither Jesus, Peter, nor Paul ever gathered people together to do "spiritual warfare" and "bind" demonic powers – they put their effort into preaching the Gospel and sharing God's Word.

   A. They prayed like the early believers in Acts 4:

> *Lord, behold their threatenings: and grant unto thy servants, that with all boldness they may speak thy word, By stretching forth thine hand to heal; and that signs and wonders may be done by the name of thy holy child Jesus.*
>
> Acts 4:29-30

- B. Then the place was shaken by the power of the Holy Spirit, and they went out boldly sharing the Gospel (Acts 4:31, 5:12-16; and Mark 16:20).

- C. They saw their world changed not through "spiritual warfare" and "intercession" but through the preaching of the Gospel.

- D. Some people are using "intercession" as a cop-out to keep from sharing the Word of God.

- E. The way people are born again is through a seed of God's Word being planted (1 Pet. 1:23).

IV. Satan can only influence us and gain our consent and cooperation through our thoughts.

> *Your adversary the devil, as a roaring lion, walketh about, seeking whom he may devour.*
>
> 1 Peter 5:8

- A. Once you know the truth, deception no longer has any power.

> *Ye shall know the truth, and the truth shall make you free.*
>
> John 8:32

- B. The church's strength is in preaching the Gospel and sharing God's Word.

- C. We do need to pray so we can be sensitive to God, yield to Him, hear clearly, and be bold to speak, but we don't need to do fifteen to twenty hours worth of "spiritual warfare" to prepare things before we get there.

- D. As you preach the truth, the truth will cause demons to flee.

- E. Demons were even present at the Last Supper (John 13:27).

V. Jesus didn't do "spiritual warfare" the way it's being promoted today.

- A. There is no New Testament model for this "spiritual warfare" and "intercession" stuff.

- B. Some of this is being taught from Scripture, but they're using Old Testament scriptures – and there's a huge difference between the way things were done in the Old Testament and the way they are done in the New.

NO NEW TESTAMENT MODEL
Lesson 23 – Teacher's Guide

1. The warfare we face today is in enforcing the Lord's victory. It's fighting against the wiles of the devil – his deception, lies, trickery, cunningness, and craftiness (Eph. 6:11). All the warfare scriptures in the New Testament reveal that the battle is in our minds (2 Cor. 10:3-5). Satan is fighting us with thoughts, and we counter him with the thoughts God gives us. As people believe and obey the truth, they are set free and come out from under the control of these demonic influences around them.

2. Satan has to flow through physical things to control the way we think (Rom. 8:6, Prov. 23:7, Is. 26:3, and Rom. 12:2). Demons influence us through thoughts. They have to influence a person, and then that person yields to Satan. He begins to educate them – putting his lies and deception into their life – so they can influence other people.

3. Neither Jesus, Peter, nor Paul ever gathered people together to do "spiritual warfare" and "bind" demonic powers – they put their effort into preaching the Gospel and sharing God's Word. They prayed like the early believers in Acts 4:29-30. Then the place was shaken by the power of the Holy Spirit, and they went out boldly sharing the Gospel (Acts 4:31, 5:12-16; and Mark 16:20). They saw their world changed not through "spiritual warfare" and "intercession" but through the preaching of the Gospel. Some people are using "intercession" as a cop-out to keep from sharing the Word of God. The way people are born again is through a seed of God's Word being planted (1 Pet. 1:23).

1. A. Read Ephesians 6:11 and 2 Corinthians 10:3-5. Where do all the warfare scriptures in the New Testament reveal that the battle is? (In our minds)
   B. How are people set free, and how do they come out from under the control of these demonic influences that are around them? (As they believe and obey the truth)
2. A. Read Romans 8:6, Proverbs 23:7, Isaiah 26:3, and Romans 12:2. How do demons influence us? (Through thoughts)
   B. When someone yields to Satan and he begins to educate them, what does he put into their life so they can influence other people? (His lies and deception)
3. A. Read Acts 4:29-31, 5:12-16; Mark 16:20; and 1 Peter 1:23. What did Jesus, Peter, and Paul put their effort into? (Preaching the Gospel and sharing God's Word)
   B. How are people born again? (Through a seed of God's Word being planted)

4. Satan can only influence us and gain our consent and cooperation through our thoughts (1 Pet. 5:8). Once we know the truth, deception no longer has any power (John 8:32). The church's strength is in preaching the Gospel and sharing God's Word. We do need to pray so we can be sensitive to God, yield to Him, hear clearly, and be bold to speak, but we don't need to do fifteen to twenty hours worth of "spiritual warfare" to prepare things before we get there. As we preach the truth, the truth will cause demons to flee. Demons were even present at the Last Supper (John 13:27).

5. Jesus didn't do "spiritual warfare" the way it's being promoted today. There is no New Testament model for this "spiritual warfare" and "intercession" stuff. Some of this is being taught from Scripture, but they're using Old Testament scriptures – and there's a huge difference between the way things were done in the Old Testament and the way they are done in the New.

4. A. Read 1 Peter 5:8;, John 8:32, and 13:27. When does deception no longer have any power? (Once we know the truth)
   B. What is the church's strength in? (Preaching the Gospel and sharing God's Word)
5. A. There is no New Testament model for what? (This "spiritual warfare" and "intercession" stuff)
   B. What is there between the way things were done in the Old Testament and the way they are done in the New? (A huge difference)

NO NEW TESTAMENT MODEL
Lesson 23 – Discipleship Questions

1. According to Ephesians 6:11-12, what don't we wrestle against?

2. Second Corinthians 10:3-5 reveals that the weapons of our warfare are not what?

3. What does Romans 8:6 say produces life and peace?

4. Romans 12:2 commands us not be conformed to what?

5. What are we transformed by?

6. After the early believers prayed in Acts 4:29-31, how did they speak the Word of God?

7. According to Acts 5:12-16, how many of the sick and demonised people brought to the apostles were healed?

8. Mark 16:20 reveals that the Lord confirmed what with signs following?

9. What does 1 Peter 1:23 say lives and abides forever?

10. First Peter 5:8 compares our adversary, the devil, to what?

11. Who does John 13:27 reveal entered into Judas after the sop?

12. Then Jesus told him to do what he was going to do how?

NO NEW TESTAMENT MODEL
Lesson 23 – Answer Key

1. Flesh and blood.

2. Carnal.

3. Spiritual-mindedness.

4. This world.

5. The renewing of our minds.

6. With boldness.

7. Every one.

8. The Word.

9. The Word of God.

10. A roaring lion.

11. Satan.

12. Quickly.

NO NEW TESTAMENT MODEL
Lesson 23 – Scriptures

Put on the whole armour of God, that ye may be able to stand against the wiles of the devil. For we wrestle not against flesh and blood, but against principalities, against powers, against the rulers of the darkness of this world, against spiritual wickedness in high places.

Ephesians 6:11-12

For though we walk in the flesh, we do not war after the flesh: (For the weapons of our warfare are not carnal, but mighty through God to the pulling down of strong holds;) Casting down imaginations, and every high thing that exalteth itself against the knowledge of God, and bringing into captivity every thought to the obedience of Christ.

2 Corinthians 10:3-5

For to be carnally minded is death; but to be spiritually minded is life and peace.

Romans 8:6

For as he thinketh in his heart, so is he: Eat and drink, saith he to thee; but his heart is not with thee.

Proverbs 23:7

Thou wilt keep him in perfect peace, whose mind is stayed on thee: because he trusteth in thee.

Isaiah 26:3

And be not conformed to this world: but be ye transformed by the renewing of your mind, that ye may prove what is that good, and acceptable, and perfect, will of God.

Romans 12:2

And now, Lord, behold their threatenings: and grant unto thy servants, that with all boldness they may speak thy word, By stretching forth thine hand to heal; and that signs and wonders may be done by the name of thy holy child Jesus. And when they had prayed, the place was shaken where they were assembled together; and they were all filled with the Holy Ghost, and they spake the word of God with boldness.

Acts 4:29-31

And by the hands of the apostles were many signs and wonders wrought among the people; (and they were all with one accord in Solomon's porch)...Insomuch that they brought forth the sick into the streets, and laid them on beds and couches, that at the least the shadow of Peter passing by might overshadow some of them. There came also a multitude out of the cities round about unto Jerusalem, bringing sick folks, and them which were vexed with unclean spirits: and they were healed every one.

Acts 5:12 and 15-16

And they went forth, and preached every where, the Lord working with them, and confirming the word with signs following. Amen.

Mark 16:20

Being born again, not of corruptible seed, but of incorruptible, by the word of God, which liveth and abideth for ever.

1 Peter 1:23

Be sober, be vigilant; because your adversary the devil, as a roaring lion, walketh about, seeking whom he may devour.

1 Peter 5:8

And ye shall know the truth, and the truth shall make you free.

John 8:32

And after the sop Satan entered into him. Then said Jesus unto him, That thou doest, do quickly.

John 13:27

ONE MEDIATOR
Lesson 24

Exodus 32 is an Old Testament passage that is often cited when people teach "spiritual warfare" and "intercession." Moses had been up on the mount receiving the Ten Commandments. He'd been up there fasting for forty days and forty nights in the presence of God. Afterward, he'd been given two tablets that had literally been written on by the finger of God:

> **The LORD said unto Moses, Go, get thee down; for thy people, which thou broughtest out of the land of Egypt, have corrupted themselves.**
>
> Exodus 32:7

It's interesting how the Lord told Pharoah, "Let *My* people go." Yet once they came out and started worshiping this golden calf, He told Moses, "This is *your* people." When a child does something good and wins an award, their parents say, "*My* child." But when they do something stupid, they say, "Look what *your* child did." God said, "Your people." He was willing to forsake them and let them go. God was ticked off at them because they had corrupted themselves.

> **They have turned aside quickly out of the way which I commanded them: they have made them a molten calf, and have worshipped it, and have sacrificed thereunto, and said, These be thy gods, O Israel, which have brought thee up out of the land of Egypt. And the LORD said unto Moses, I have seen this people, and, behold, it is a stiffnecked people: Now therefore let me alone, that my wrath may wax hot against them, and that I may consume them: and I will make of thee a great nation.**
>
> Exodus 32:8-10

POWER WITH GOD

God was mad at these people. He was going to destroy them and start over with Moses, making a brand-new nation out of him. Notice how He said this:

> **Now therefore let me alone, that my wrath may wax hot against them, and that I may consume them.**
>
> Exodus 32:10

The Lord was saying, "Moses, don't try to hinder Me. Don't try to talk Me out of this. Don't plead for mercy, because I want to give total vent to My wrath and destroy these people." By saying it this way, God meant, "Moses, you have so much power and influence with Me that if you plead with Me, you'll keep Me from venting my anger on these people."

It's amazing that Almighty God would be moved by any physical human being. It's not because we are greater in power or authority; it's because of His great love for us. Moses wasn't perfect. He had killed a man thinking he was bringing God's will to pass. He had failed. However, God loves us so much that when He finds someone who has a heart for Him, He respects them. By doing so, that gives them power and authority in His life. That's awesome!

And Moses besought the LORD his God, and said, LORD, why doth thy wrath wax hot against thy people, which thou hast brought forth out of the land of Egypt with great power, and with a mighty hand?

Exodus 32:11

"THEY'RE YOUR PEOPLE"

Moses put it back on God, saying, "Lord, these are Your people. They aren't my people. Remember, You're the One who redeemed them. They're Your people."

Wherefore should the Egyptians speak, and say, For mischief did he bring them out, to slay them in the mountains, and to consume them from the face of the earth? Turn from thy fierce wrath, and repent of this evil against thy people. Remember Abraham, Isaac, and Israel, thy servants, to whom thou swarest by thine own self, and saidst unto them, I will multiply your seed as the stars of heaven, and all this land that I have spoken of will I give unto your seed, and they shall inherit it for ever.

Exodus 32:12-13

Moses was reasoning with God, saying, "Lord, the Egyptians are going to hear about this. They'll say it was because You were too weak to bring these people into the Promised Land." Then Moses had the audacity to say:

Turn from thy fierce wrath, and repent of this evil against thy people.

Exodus 32:12

It's amazing that a man would tell God to repent. However, what's even more amazing is...

The LORD repented of the evil which he thought to do unto his people.

Exodus 32:14

A CLASSIC EXAMPLE

This is a classic example of Old Testament intercession. Moses confronted God, told Him to turn from His fierce wrath, and He did. Moses stood in between the people who were about to be destroyed and pled with an angry God to repent.

People take this example and use it to teach "spiritual warfare" and "intercession." Thinking this is how we need to pray to God today, they say, "O Lord, don't destroy our country. Have mercy on our city. Repent, and turn from Your fierce wrath!" That was appropriate for Moses to pray, because Christ hadn't come yet and suffered the punishment for our sin. However, under the New Covenant, everything has changed. Jesus became the intercessor to end all of that kind of intercession.

There is one God, and one mediator between God and men, the man Christ Jesus.

1 Timothy 2:5

In the New Testament, Jesus became the mediator that stood between us and God.

ANTICHRIST

God was holy, and man was not. We deserved the wrath of God. There needed to be mediation between God and man. So before Jesus came, Moses was a mediator. Speaking of Moses, Galatians 3 says that the Old Testament Law…

Was ordained by angels in the hand of a mediator.

Galatians 3:19

Moses served as a mediator between God and man. A mediator is someone who stands in between two parties who are in conflict with each other and tries to bring them into harmony and agreement. God was opposed to man because of our sin, so under the Old Covenant, Moses served as a mediator. He said "God, repent. Turn from Your fierce wrath," and He did. However, if Moses were to pray that way today – on this side of the cross – he'd be antichrist.

Antichrist means "against or instead of Christ." If Moses were to plead with God to turn from His fierce wrath today, he'd be acting against Jesus' mediation. By thinking *What Christ did is not enough. I need to add to it*, he'd be trying to take Jesus' place. It was appropriate for Moses to pray the way he did under the Old Covenant because Jesus hadn't come yet. But now that Jesus has come and we're under the New Covenant, there's only *one* mediator between God and man – the Lord Jesus Christ (1 Tim. 2:5).

That's why you're wrong to "intercede," begging and pleading with God for His mercy today. God's mercy has already been poured out to us through the Lord Jesus Christ. He's no longer angry with us over sin.

A MAJOR DIFFERENCE

I understand that the truths I'm sharing are contrary to what's been popularly accepted, but I encourage you to go to the Word and see for yourself. Many people think that God is angry at a certain country and that He's about to bring judgement upon a specific city. So they pray, "O Lord, have mercy and don't destroy." If you're praying that way, you're trying to take the place of the Lord Jesus Christ. Jesus has already satisfied God's anger and secured His mercy for these people and places.

Since God's wrath toward sin has been appeased through the sacrifice of Christ, does that mean we don't have any problems? Of course not! Through sin and unbelief, we're in the process of destroying ourselves. We've opened up doors to the devil, and he's taking full advantage of it. It's very appropriate to pray, "Father, I thank You that Jesus has already secured Your mercy and grace on our behalf. Thank You that You aren't out to destroy our city and country. However, we're giving place to the devil. We're about to destroy ourselves. So, Father, please give me wisdom and boldness to share Your Word and demonstrate Your power to others."

That's the reason I'm on radio, television, and the internet. That's why I'm putting out so many books, tapes, and CDs. I'm not just praying, "O God, do something. Change these places and have mercy on us." God has already had mercy on us. We just don't know what He's done. We've been lied to.

Most people are more moved by television, news programs, and movies than they are by the Word of God. They don't know the truth, so I'm using every medium I can to come across people's paths and share the Word with them. These truths are changing people's lives and facilitating revival. Revival comes through people as the Gospel is preached, the Word is taught, and the Holy Spirit confirms it.

There is a major difference between the Old and New Covenants. In the Old Testament, people like Moses pled with God, saying, "Lord, turn from Your fierce wrath." But in the New Testament, there's only one mediator between God and man, the man Christ Jesus. He has forever satisfied the demands and wrath of God. If we don't seek God, there will be plenty of problems. But that's because we're yielding ourselves to Satan, and he's going to steal, kill, and destroy whomever, whenever, and wherever he can (John 10:10). Yes, our city needs to change. Yes, our country needs to repent and turn to God. But it's not so we won't be judged. Since God has already placed upon His Son the judgement our sins deserved, we don't have to be judged.

APOLOGISE TO WHOM?

I didn't understand these truths when I first started out in ministry. So I liked to say, "If God doesn't judge our country, He's going to have to apologise to Sodom and Gomorrah." From my perspective, America deserved judgement because of our sin as much or more than these two Old Testament cities that went up in smoke. However, since then, God has revealed Himself and His Word to me in such a way that I now say, "If God were to judge our country, He'd have to apologise to Jesus." Why? Because Christ bore our punishment, judgement, and separation so that we wouldn't have to. God has already placed His wrath upon His own Son at the cross, so He's not about to judge us.

Our country is perilously close to being destroyed – not because of God's judgement but because of Satan's inroads. When you yield yourself to the devil through sin, you become his defenseless servant. He comes for no other purpose but to steal, kill, and destroy (John 10:10). It's stupid to yield to Satan. We need to submit ourselves to God.

"WILL YOU SPARE THE CITY?"

Let's take a closer look at when God judged these two cities. First, the Lord appeared to Abraham and told him He was sending two angels down to Sodom and Gomorrah to check them out. God wanted to see if they were as bad as He had heard, because He planned to judge them. As soon as Abraham heard about this, he...

> *Drew near, and said, Wilt thou also destroy the righteous with the wicked? Peradventure there be fifty righteous within the city: wilt thou also destroy and not spare the place for the fifty righteous that are therein? That be far from thee to do after this manner, to slay the righteous with the wicked: and that the righteous should be as the wicked, that be far from thee: Shall not the Judge of all the earth do right? And the LORD said, If I find in Sodom fifty righteous within the city, then I will spare all the place for their sakes.*
>
> Genesis 18:23-26

Here's Abraham pleading with God and saying, "Lord, You aren't going to destroy the righteous people that live in this city, too, are You? That's not the way a righteous God would act. If there's fifty righteous people there, will You spare the city?"

And God answered, "If there's fifty righteous people, I'll spare the city."

Then Abraham said, "What if there's forty-five righteous people? Will You spare the city?"

"If there's forty-five, I'll spare the city."

Abraham negotiated with God all the way down to ten people. If there were ten righteous people, God would spare the city. Abraham could have gone all the way down to one righteous person, and that would have been Lot (2 Pet. 2:7-8). There was one righteous person in the city, and God would have spared it for that one.

Without even factoring Jesus' atonement into the equation and forgetting about the New Covenant – which most Christians tend to do anyway – this passage shows us that God won't destroy a city or country if there are righteous people therein. It doesn't matter what country it is, there are things in it that are completely contrary to the kingdom of God. Nobody's country is living totally the way God wants it to. Yet, despite all this, there are righteous people now in every country of the world. That alone ought to debunk much of this "God's going to judge this country" teaching that's floating around the body of Christ today.

NEW TESTAMENT REALITY

In America alone, there are hundreds of thousands of righteous, born-again people who love God and are seeking Him. They may not be dominating in every area of society yet, but they're here. Therefore, God will not destroy America.

However, we also need to factor into this equation the truth of 1 Timothy 2:5. Jesus is now the one and only mediator between God and man. He forever satisfied God's wrath. In light of these truths, this whole pattern of Old Covenant intercession – begging God not to pour out His wrath and pleading with Him for mercy – doesn't fit the New Testament reality.

Most of the "spiritual warfare" and "intercession" stuff that people are promoting comes from the Old Covenant. They're taking Old Testament scriptures and teaching them as if Jesus Christ had never come. Basically, they're saying, "You be a mediator. You stand between God and man. You plead with Him to turn from His wrath. Don't allow Him to judge this land." Well, the truth is that Jesus Christ has already done all those things. He is the *only* New Testament mediator.

If you're trying to pray the same as Abraham in Genesis 18, you're standing against what Jesus has already done. If you're praying the same as Moses in Exodus 32, then you're trying to take Christ's place. You are acting as if Jesus hasn't come and His atonement wasn't enough. You're believing that His intercession wasn't enough, and you have to add to it. That's antichrist.

ONE MEDIATOR
Lesson 24 – Outline

I. Exodus 32 is an Old Testament passage that is often cited when people teach "spiritual warfare" and "intercession" (Ex. 32:7-10).

> *Moses besought the LORD his God, and said, LORD, why doth thy wrath wax hot against thy people, which thou hast brought forth out of the land of Egypt with great power, and with a mighty hand? Wherefore should the Egyptians speak, and say, For mischief did he bring them out, to slay them in the mountains, and to consume them from the face of the earth? Turn from thy fierce wrath, and repent of this evil against thy people. Remember Abraham, Isaac, and Israel, thy servants, to whom thou swarest by thine own self, and saidst unto them, I will multiply your seed as the stars of heaven, and all this land that I have spoken of will I give unto your seed, and they shall inherit it for ever. And the LORD repented of the evil which he thought to do unto his people.*
>
> Exodus 32:11-14

    A. This is a classic example of Old Testament intercession.

    B. Moses confronted God, told Him to turn from His fierce wrath, and He did.

    C. That was appropriate for Moses to pray, because Christ hadn't come yet and suffered the punishment for our sin.

    D. However, under the New Covenant, everything has changed.

    E. Jesus became the Intercessor to end all of that kind of intercession.

II. In the New Testament, Jesus became the mediator that stood between us and God.

> *There is one God, and one mediator between God and men, the man Christ Jesus.*
>
> 1 Timothy 2:5

    A. A mediator is someone who stands in between two parties who are in conflict with each other and tries to bring them into harmony and agreement.

    B. *Antichrist* means "against or instead of Christ."

    C. Now that Jesus has come and we're under the New Covenant, there's only *one* mediator between God and man – the Lord Jesus Christ (1 Tim. 2:5).

    D. God's mercy has already been poured out to us through the Lord Jesus Christ – He's no longer angry with us over sin.

III. Through sin and unbelief, we're in the process of destroying ourselves.

　　A.　We've opened up doors to the devil, and he's taking full advantage of it.

　　B.　There is a major difference between the Old and New Covenants.

　　C.　Since God has already placed upon His Son the judgement our sins deserved, we don't have to be judged.

　　D.　Our country is perilously close to being destroyed – not because of God's judgement but because of Satan's inroads.

　　E.　When you yield yourself to the devil through sin, you become his defenseless servant – and he comes for no other purpose but to steal, kill, and destroy (John 10:10).

IV. Let's take a closer look at when God judged Sodom and Gomorrah.

> **Abraham drew near, and said, Wilt thou also destroy the righteous with the wicked? Peradventure there be fifty righteous within the city: wilt thou also destroy and not spare the place for the fifty righteous that are therein? That be far from thee to do after this manner, to slay the righteous with the wicked: and that the righteous should be as the wicked, that be far from thee: Shall not the Judge of all the earth do right? And the LORD said, If I find in Sodom fifty righteous within the city, then I will spare all the place for their sakes.**
>
> Genesis 18:23-26

　　A.　Abraham negotiated with God all the way down to ten people.

　　B.　Without even factoring Jesus' atonement into the equation and forgetting about the New Covenant – which most Christians tend to do anyway – this passage shows us that God won't destroy a city or country if there are righteous people therein.

　　C.　Nobody's country is living totally the way God wants it to, but there are righteous, born-again people now in every country of the world.

V. This whole pattern of Old Covenant intercession – begging God not to pour out His wrath and pleading with Him for mercy – doesn't fit the New Testament reality.

　　A.　Most of the "spiritual warfare" and "intercession" stuff that people are promoting comes from the Old Covenant – taking Old Testament scriptures and teaching them as if Jesus Christ had never come.

　　B.　The truth is that Jesus Christ is the *only* New Testament mediator.

ONE MEDIATOR
Lesson 24 – Teacher's Guide

1. Exodus 32 is an Old Testament passage that is often cited when people teach "spiritual warfare" and "intercession" (Ex. 32:7-14). This is a classic example of Old Testament intercession. Moses confronted God, told Him to turn from His fierce wrath, and He did. That was appropriate for Moses to pray, because Christ hadn't come yet and suffered the punishment for our sin. However, under the New Covenant, everything has changed. Jesus became the Intercessor to end all of that kind of intercession.

2. In the New Testament, Jesus became the mediator that stood between us and God (1 Tim. 2:5). A mediator is someone who stands in between two parties who are in conflict with each other and tries to bring them into harmony and agreement. *Antichrist* means "against or instead of Christ." Now that Jesus has come and we're under the New Covenant, there's only *one* mediator between God and man – the Lord Jesus Christ (1 Tim. 2:5). God's mercy has already been poured out to us through the Lord Jesus Christ – He's no longer angry with us over sin.

3. Through sin and unbelief, we're in the process of destroying ourselves. We've opened up doors to the devil, and he's taking full advantage of it. There is a major difference between the Old and New Covenants. Since God has already placed upon His Son the judgement our sins deserved, we don't have to be judged. Our country is perilously close to being destroyed – not because of God's judgement but because of Satan's inroads. When we yield ourselves to the devil through sin, we become his defenseless servant – and he comes for no other purpose but to steal, kill, and destroy (John 10:10).

---

1. A. Read Exodus 32:7-14. This is a classic example of what? (Old Testament intercession)
   B. Why was this appropriate for Moses to pray? (Because Christ hadn't come yet and suffered the punishment for our sin)
2. A. Read 1 Timothy 2:5. What is someone who stands in between two parties who are in conflict with each other and tries to bring them into harmony and agreement? (A mediator)
   B. Now that Jesus has come and we're under the New Covenant, who is the only mediator between God and man? (The Lord Jesus Christ)
3. A. Read John 10:10. We're in the process of destroying ourselves how? (Through sin and unbelief)
   B. Why is our country perilously close to being destroyed? (Because of Satan's inroads)

4. When God judged Sodom and Gomorrah, Abraham negotiated with Him all the way down to ten people (Gen. 18:23-26). Without even factoring Jesus' atonement into the equation and forgetting about the New Covenant – which most Christians tend to do anyway – this passage shows us that God won't destroy a city or country if there are righteous people therein. Nobody's country is living totally the way God wants it to, but there are righteous, born-again people now in every country of the world.

5. This whole pattern of Old Covenant intercession – begging God not to pour out His wrath and pleading with Him for mercy – doesn't fit the New Testament reality. Most of the "spiritual warfare" and "intercession" stuff that people are promoting comes from the Old Covenant – taking Old Testament scriptures and teaching them as if Jesus Christ had never come. The truth is that Jesus Christ is the *only* New Testament mediator.

4. A. Read Genesis 18:23-26. Without even factoring Jesus' atonement into the equation and forgetting about the New Covenant – which most Christians tend to do anyway – what does this passage show us? (That God won't destroy a city or country if there are righteous people therein)
   B. Where are there righteous, born-again people living now? (In every country of the world)
5. A. This whole pattern of Old Covenant intercession – begging God not to pour out His wrath and pleading with Him for mercy – doesn't fit what? (The New Testament reality)
   B. Most of the "spiritual warfare" and "intercession" stuff that people are promoting comes from the Old Covenant – taking Old Testament scriptures and teaching them how? (As if Jesus Christ had never come)

ONE MEDIATOR
Lesson 24 – Additional Information

For additional study on this topic, I refer you to my teaching entitled *The War Is Over*. The New Testament is clear. Jesus bore the wrath of God for our sin. That's why God's not mad at you – He isn't even in a bad mood!

ONE MEDIATOR
Lesson 24 – Discipleship Questions

1. According to Exodus 32:7-14, Moses told the Lord to turn from His fierce wrath and do what?

2. How did the Lord respond?

3. Who does 1 Timothy 2:5 reveal as the one New Testament mediator between God and man?

4. According to Galatians 3:19, why was the Law added?

5. Until whom should come?

6. John 10:10 shows us that Jesus has come so that we might have what more abundantly?

7. In Genesis 18:23-26, Abraham was negotiating with God over which city?

8. Lot was described as a just and _____ kind of man in 2 Peter 2:7-8.

9. What did he see and hear from day to day that vexed his righteous soul?

ONE MEDIATOR
Lesson 24 – Answer Key

1. Repent of this evil He planned to do against His people.

2. He repented.

3. The man Christ Jesus.

4. Because of transgressions.

5. The seed to whom the promise was made (Jesus).

6. Life.

7. Sodom.

8. Righteous.

9. The filthy conversation (conduct) of the wicked with their unlawful deeds.

ONE MEDIATOR
Lesson 24 – Scriptures

And the LORD said unto Moses, Go, get thee down; for thy people, which thou broughtest out of the land of Egypt, have corrupted themselves: They have turned aside quickly out of the way which I commanded them: they have made them a molten calf, and have worshipped it, and have sacrificed thereunto, and said, These be thy gods, O Israel, which have brought thee up out of the land of Egypt. And the LORD said unto Moses, I have seen this people, and, behold, it is a stiffnecked people: Now therefore let me alone, that my wrath may wax hot against them, and that I may consume them: and I will make of thee a great nation.

Exodus 32:7-10

And Moses besought the LORD his God, and said, LORD, why doth thy wrath wax hot against thy people, which thou hast brought forth out of the land of Egypt with great power, and with a mighty hand? Wherefore should the Egyptians speak, and say, For mischief did he bring them out, to slay them in the mountains, and to consume them from the face of the earth? Turn from thy fierce wrath, and repent of this evil against thy people. Remember Abraham, Isaac, and Israel, thy servants, to whom thou swarest by thine own self, and saidst unto them, I will multiply your seed as the stars of heaven, and all this land that I have spoken of will I give unto your seed, and they shall inherit it for ever. And the LORD repented of the evil which he thought to do unto his people.

Exodus 32:11-14

For there is one God, and one mediator between God and men, the man Christ Jesus.

1 Timothy 2:5

Wherefore then serveth the law? It was added because of transgressions, till the seed should come to whom the promise was made; and it was ordained by angels in the hand of a mediator.

Galatians 3:19

The thief cometh not, but for to steal, and to kill, and to destroy: I am come that they might have life, and that they might have it more abundantly.

John 10:10

And Abraham drew near, and said, Wilt thou also destroy the righteous with the wicked? Peradventure there be fifty righteous within the city: wilt thou also destroy and not spare the place for the fifty righteous that are therein? That be far from thee to do after this manner, to slay the righteous with the wicked: and that the righteous should be as the wicked, that be far from thee: Shall not the Judge of all the earth do right? And the LORD said, If I find in Sodom fifty righteous within the city, then I will spare all the place for their sakes.

Genesis 18:23-26

And delivered just Lot, vexed with the filthy conversation of the wicked: (For that righteous man dwelling among them, in seeing and hearing, vexed his righteous soul from day to day with their unlawful deeds.)

2 Peter 2:7-8

THE BATTLE IS IN YOUR MIND
Lesson 25

Concerning the believer's authority, we need to recognise that Satan has already been dealt with by God. Since Jesus endured God's wrath at the cross, He isn't pouring it out upon us today. Our job is to stand in faith and enforce what the Lord has already done through His death, burial, and resurrection. The way we do this is by telling people the truth.

The battle is in your mind. Satan isn't controlling people through some demonic power. He's controlling them through lies and deceptions. By telling the truth, lies are exposed and people are set free. So much of this "spiritual warfare" and "intercession" teaching denies the ministry of the Lord Jesus Christ. That's not smart.

Jesus is the New Testament Intercessor who ended all Old Covenant intercession. There's now no need to beg for mercy or to tell God to repent. A New Testament believer praises God for what He's already done and offers oneself as a vessel for the Lord to work through.

However, the real focus needs to be on the way we think. We shouldn't just pray for someone and wait on God to touch them without human intervention. God flows through us. He uses us. We must preach the Gospel.

> *How then shall they call on him in whom they have not believed? and how shall they believe in him of whom they have not heard? and how shall they hear without a preacher? And how shall they preach, except they be sent?... So then faith cometh by hearing, and hearing by the word of God.*
>
> Romans 10:14-15 and 17

You can't just pray and get a person saved, healed, or anything. You must speak God's Word. Faith for salvation, healing, and everything else comes by hearing the Word of God.

"STOP THE PLAGUE!"

Numbers 16 is another Old Testament example that is often used to teach "spiritual warfare" and "intercession." People say, "You must stand in the gap, begging and pleading with God, for your loved ones to be saved, healed, or whatever." This passage of Scripture is right after Korah, Dathan, and Abiram rebelled against Moses. The earth opened up and swallowed all three of these men and all that they possessed (Num. 26:10-11). Of course, the people just screamed and ran for fear.

> *But on the morrow all the congregation of the children of Israel murmured against Moses and against Aaron, saying, Ye have killed the people of the LORD. And it came to pass, when the congregation was gathered against Moses and against Aaron, that they looked toward the tabernacle of the congregation: and, behold, the cloud covered it, and the glory of the LORD appeared. And Moses and Aaron came before the tabernacle of the congregation. And*

> *the LORD spake unto Moses, saying, Get you up from among this congregation, that I may consume them as in a moment. And they fell upon their faces.*
>
> Numbers 16:41-45

God was upset because the people had come against Moses and Aaron.

> *Moses said unto Aaron, Take a censer, and put fire therein from off the altar, and put on incense, and go quickly unto the congregation, and make an atonement for them: for there is wrath gone out from the LORD; the plague is begun. And Aaron took as Moses commanded, and ran into the midst of the congregation; and, behold, the plague was begun among the people: and he put on incense, and made an atonement for the people. And he stood between the dead and the living; and the plague was stayed. Now they that died in the plague were fourteen thousand and seven hundred, beside them that died about the matter of Korah.*
>
> Numbers 16:46-49

This is another example of where God became angry with the children of Israel. Moses recognised it and told Aaron to take a censer and put coals from off of the altar on it (symbolic of prayer). He took this censer – prayer – and stood, or interceded, between those who had already died of the plague and those who hadn't. Once the plague reached where he stood – the prayers and intercession – it stopped. However, 14,700 people died before Aaron could run in there with the censer and stop the plague.

I've literally heard people teaching on "intercession" say, "This is the way it is. God is holy and man isn't. He's so angry at people that He's about to destroy them. God is sending hurricanes, tornadoes, tsunamis, AIDS, and all kinds of tragedies. God's wrath has begun, and we as intercessors need to pray and stand between God and these people who are deserving of His wrath. We need to plead for mercy, calm Him down, and beg Him to sit back down on the throne so He won't destroy the human race." People are preaching such nonsense.

A MUCH BETTER JOB

Jesus is the only mediator now between God and man (1 Tim. 2:5). There's no other mediator and no other mediation that needs to be done. When Jesus died, He forever satisfied the wrath of God. The Lord isn't ready to destroy this nation, or any other. I'm not saying we don't deserve it; I'm saying God placed the punishment for our rebellion and sins upon Jesus. He's not giving us what we deserve. It's not God that is about to destroy this nation or city.

As an individual, you may feel like you deserve the wrath of God. You don't doubt that God exists. You just don't think He'll do anything for you, because you know you aren't living life the way you should. God is speaking to you right now, saying, "Jesus has already borne your punishment. He's already suffered your pain. He's not the one bringing tragedy into your life." You might be thinking, *But I have all kinds of problems. Surely, God is judging me.* No, you yielded yourself to Satan, and he has come to steal, kill, and destroy (John 10:10). So, yes, your life is a mess, but it's not because God's wrath is upon you and He's judging you.

God placed His wrath over your sins upon Jesus, and all you must do is humble yourself and receive the forgiveness He offers as a free gift. You don't have to beg and plead with the Lord to save you; He's already done it. He's already dealt with your sin through the atoning sacrifice of His Son.

You don't need to beg and plead on an individual basis or on a collective basis (for a city or country). God's wrath has been satisfied. If you're trying to tell God to repent and have mercy, then you're trying to improve upon the work that the Lord Jesus Christ has already done. I guarantee that Jesus did a much better job at it than what you could ever do.

POWERFUL PROOF

You don't need to plead with God to turn His heart toward you. His heart is already toward you because He loves you. This country is in the process of being destroyed because of its own wickedness and yielding to Satan. However, God wants to redeem this country and see its people wholeheartedly turn back to Him. He needs Christians to come out of their prayer closets and stop begging Him for what Jesus has already provided. He needs believers to stand up in faith and start taking this good news to others. "God isn't mad. He's not even in a bad mood. God isn't ticked off. He loves you and wants you to be free." Tell people the truth because it's the truth that will set them free (John 8:32).

It's not up to God whether the lost get saved or not. He's already made the atonement and paid for their sins. He's extended forgiveness and abundant life, but they aren't receiving it. He's sent the Holy Spirit to deal with people and convict them, but they're resisting Him. One of the biggest reasons people aren't making the right choice is because they aren't hearing the good news of the Gospel. They're being lied to by the devil. Although Satan is inspiring it, people are the ones who are saying "There are no absolutes. Sexual immorality isn't wrong. There are many roads to heaven" and so forth. Through these lies, people have dropped their guard and stopped resisting evil. They've embraced sin and, because of it, have welcomed Satan right into their lives. He's blinded their hearts from the light of Christ (2 Cor. 4:4), but the antidote isn't doing "spiritual warfare," binding demons, and begging God. It's us standing up, preaching the Gospel and telling people the truth.

God always backs up His truth with power (Mark 16:20). We need to believe the Word and trust the Holy Spirit to demonstrate it. Jesus had to have miracles to validate what He was saying. He told the religious Jews that if they couldn't believe because of His words that they should believe because of His miracles (John 10:38). If Jesus needed proof that He was sent from God and speaking the truth, then we do too. We need to start sharing God's Word and demonstrating His supernatural power. Then people will turn to the Lord.

SHARE THE TRUTH

I met a woman before a meeting in Birmingham who had just been in the hospital. She'd been lying flat on her back watching me say these things on television. The doctors had given her up to die. Just a year before, her mother had passed away from the same exact thing – cancer. This woman wasn't only sick in her body, but she was also sick in her heart and mind. She was hopeless and fearful because she'd seen other people die, and the doctors had told her there was nothing they could do. As she lay there on the hospital bed, she saw that I was going to be in Birmingham. So she pulled the tubes out, checked herself out of the hospital, and came to receive prayer.

I prayed with her, and she was instantly healed. Every bit of pain and all the cancer's symptoms were gone. At the end of the service, I gave an invitation for people to be born again. Since she'd never received the Lord, she came forward and was born again. She got healed, delivered of cancer, born again, baptised in the Holy Spirit, and spoke in tongues all in one night. She checked into the hotel and stayed for the next three days of meetings, getting built up in her faith. All this came to pass because she heard the truth and saw the power of God in demonstration.

Some of the doctrines that are held most dear in the body of Christ today have been established by the devil (1 Tim. 4:1). These lies have been rendering us ineffective. This woman in Birmingham didn't get healed through somebody interceding for her in some closet; she heard a believer speaking the truth and giving testimonies of what God had done. The Holy Spirit used these things to quicken her faith. A woman – who wasn't even born again yet – pulled the tubes out of her body, walked out of the hospital, and came to where the believers were meeting.

Faith came to her by hearing, and hearing by the Word of God (Rom. 10:17). When the truth comes to people, it begins to tear down the lies, deceptions, and strongholds of the devil. Faith can't rise in someone's heart unless the truth is shared with them.

God told Jeremiah,

> **Behold, I will make my words in thy mouth fire, and this people wood, and it shall devour them…Is not my word like as a fire? saith the LORD; and like a hammer that breaketh the rock in pieces?**
>
> Jeremiah 5:14 and 23:29

This is the reason we must speak the Word. Somehow or another, we've gotten away from this. We've been diverted and distracted, putting so much of our energy into begging God to do what He's already done. That's ineffective. We've been in prayer closets binding Satan and commanding him to let people go, thinking that if we pray hard enough, people will be born again. That's not true. The Word says that people must be born again by the incorruptible seed of God's Word (1 Pet. 1:23).

THE BATTLE IS IN YOUR MIND
Lesson 25 – Outline

I. A New Testament believer praises God for what He's already done and offers oneself as a vessel for the Lord to work through.

    A.   The real focus needs to be on the way we think.

    B.   We must preach the Gospel.

> *How then shall they call on him in whom they have not believed? and how shall they believe in him of whom they have not heard? and how shall they hear without a preacher? And how shall they preach, except they be sent? ... So then faith cometh by hearing, and hearing by the word of God.*
>
> Romans 10:14-15 and 17

    C.   Faith for salvation, healing, and everything else comes by hearing the Word of God.

II. Numbers 16 is another Old Testament example that is often used to teach "spiritual warfare" and "intercession."

    A.   People say, "You must stand in the gap, begging and pleading with God, for your loved ones to be saved, healed, or whatever."

> *But on the morrow all the congregation of the children of Israel murmured against Moses and against Aaron, saying, Ye have killed the people of the LORD. And it came to pass, when the congregation was gathered against Moses and against Aaron, that they looked toward the tabernacle of the congregation: and, behold, the cloud covered it, and the glory of the LORD appeared. And Moses and Aaron came before the tabernacle of the congregation. And the LORD spake unto Moses, saying, Get you up from among this congregation, that I may consume them as in a moment. And they fell upon their faces.*
>
> Numbers 16:41-45

    B.   God was upset because the people had come against Moses and Aaron.

> *Moses said unto Aaron, Take a censer, and put fire therein from off the altar, and put on incense, and go quickly unto the congregation, and make an atonement for them: for there is wrath gone out from the LORD; the plague is begun. And Aaron took as Moses commanded, and ran into the midst of the congregation; and, behold, the plague was begun among the people: and he put on incense, and made an atonement for the people. And he stood between the dead and the living; and the plague was stayed. Now they that died in the plague were fourteen thousand and seven hundred, beside them that died about the matter of Korah.*
>
> Numbers 16:46-49

III. Jesus is the only mediator now between God and man (1 Tim. 2:5).

A. God placed His wrath over your sins upon Jesus, and all you must do is humble yourself and receive the forgiveness He offers as a free gift.

B. He's already dealt with your sin through the atoning sacrifice of His Son.

C. If you're trying to tell God to repent and have mercy, then you're trying to improve upon the work that the Lord Jesus Christ has already done.

D. God's heart is already toward us because He loves us.

IV. God always backs up His truth with power (Mark 16:20).

A. If Jesus needed proof that He was sent from God and speaking the truth, then we do too (John 10:38).

B. We need to start sharing God's Word and demonstrating His supernatural power – then people will turn to the Lord.

C. Some of the doctrines that are held most dear in the body of Christ today have been established by the devil (1 Tim. 4:1).

D. Faith can't rise in someone's heart unless you share the truth with them.

> **Behold, I will make my words in thy mouth fire, and this people wood, and it shall devour them…Is not my word like as a fire? saith the LORD; and like a hammer that breaketh the rock in pieces?**
> Jeremiah 5:14 and 23:29

E. The Word says that people must be born again by the incorruptible seed of God's Word (1 Pet. 1:23).

THE BATTLE IS IN YOUR MIND
Lesson 25 – Teacher's Guide

1. A New Testament believer praises God for what He's already done and offers oneself as a vessel for the Lord to work through. The real focus needs to be on the way we think. We must preach the Gospel (Rom. 10:14-15 and 17). Faith for salvation, healing, and everything else comes by hearing the Word of God.

2. Numbers 16 is another Old Testament example that is often used to teach "spiritual warfare" and "intercession." People say, "You must stand in the gap, begging and pleading with God, for your loved ones to be saved, healed, or whatever." God was upset because the people had come against Moses and Aaron (Num. 16:41-49).

3. Jesus is the only mediator now between God and man (1 Tim. 2:5). God placed His wrath over our sins upon Jesus, and all we must do is humble ourselves and receive the forgiveness He offers as a free gift. He's already dealt with our sin through the atoning sacrifice of His Son. If we're trying to tell God to repent and have mercy, then we're trying to improve upon the work that the Lord Jesus Christ has already done. God's heart is already toward us because He loves us.

4. God always backs up His truth with power (Mark 16:20). If Jesus needed proof that He was sent from God and speaking the truth, then we do too (John 10:38). We need to start sharing God's Word and demonstrating His supernatural power – then people will turn to the Lord. Some of the doctrines that are held most dear in the body of Christ today have been established by the devil (1 Tim. 4:1). Faith can't rise in someone's heart unless we share the truth with them (Jer. 5:14 and 23:29). The Word says that people must be born again by the incorruptible seed of God's Word (1 Pet. 1:23).

1. A. Read Romans 10:14-17. What does a New Testament believer praise God for? (What He's already done)
   B. How does faith for salvation, healing, and everything else come? (By hearing the Word of God)
2. A. Read Numbers 16:41-49. Why was God upset? (Because the people had come against Moses and Aaron)
3. A. Read 1 Timothy 2:5. Where did God place His wrath over our sins? (Upon Jesus)
   B. How has God already dealt with our sin? (Through the atoning sacrifice of His Son)
4. A. Read Mark 16:20; 1 Timothy 4:1; 1 Peter 1:23; Jeremiah 5:14, and 23:29. What does God always back up with power? (His truth)
   B. Who established some of the doctrines that are held most dear in the body of Christ today? (The devil)

THE BATTLE IS IN YOUR MIND
Lesson 25 – Discipleship Questions

1. According to Romans 10:14-17, what comes by hearing, and hearing by the Word of God?

2. Numbers 26:10-11 says that the fire devoured how many men?

3. Whose children did not die?

4. Who fell on their faces in Numbers 16:41-45?

5. In Numbers 16:46-49, what did Moses tell Aaron to use to make an atonement for the people?

6. Whom did Aaron stand between?

7. Jesus said in John 10:38 to believe what?

8. So that we may know and believe that the Father is in Me and what?

9. According to 1 Timothy 4:1, what does the Spirit warn that some shall depart from in the latter times?

10. What will they give heed to instead?

11. What did God say His words in the mouth of the prophet in Jeremiah 5:14 would become?

12. What would be the wood that his words would devour?

13. In addition to fire, what is described as a hammer in Jeremiah 23:29?

14. What does that hammer break?

THE BATTLE IS IN YOUR MIND
Lesson 25 – Answer Key

1. Faith.

2. Two hundred and fifty.

3. Korah.

4. Moses and Aaron.

5. A censer.

6. The dead and the living.

7. The works He did.

8. I (Jesus) am in Him.

9. The faith.

10. Seducing spirits and doctrines of demons.

11. Fire.

12. People.

13. God's Word.

14. The rock in pieces.

THE BATTLE IS IN YOUR MIND
Lesson 25 – Scriptures

How then shall they call on him in whom they have not believed? and how shall they believe in him of whom they have not heard? and how shall they hear without a preacher? And how shall they preach, except they be sent? as it is written, How beautiful are the feet of them that preach the gospel of peace, and bring glad tidings of good things! But they have not all obeyed the gospel. For Esaias saith, Lord, who hath believed our report? So then faith cometh by hearing, and hearing by the word of God.

Romans 10:14-17

And the earth opened her mouth, and swallowed them up together with Korah, when that company died, what time the fire devoured two hundred and fifty men: and they became a sign. Notwithstanding the children of Korah died not.

Numbers 26:10-11

But on the morrow all the congregation of the children of Israel murmured against Moses and against Aaron, saying, Ye have killed the people of the LORD. And it came to pass, when the congregation was gathered against Moses and against Aaron, that they looked toward the tabernacle of the congregation: and, behold, the cloud covered it, and the glory of the LORD appeared. And Moses and Aaron came before the tabernacle of the congregation. And the LORD spake unto Moses, saying, Get you up from among this congregation, that I may consume them as in a moment. And they fell upon their faces.

Numbers 16:41-45

And Moses said unto Aaron, Take a censer, and put fire therein from off the altar, and put on incense, and go quickly unto the congregation, and make an atonement for them: for there is wrath gone out from the LORD; the plague is begun. And Aaron took as Moses commanded, and ran into the midst of the congregation; and, behold, the plague was begun among the people: and he put on incense, and made an atonement for the people. And he stood between the dead and the living; and the plague was stayed. Now they that died in the plague were fourteen thousand and seven hundred, beside them that died about the matter of Korah.

Numbers 16:46-49

For there is one God, and one mediator between God and men, the man Christ Jesus.

1 Timothy 2:5

The thief cometh not, but for to steal, and to kill, and to destroy: I am come that they might have life, and that they might have it more abundantly.

John 10:10

And ye shall know the truth, and the truth shall make you free.

John 8:32

In whom the god of this world hath blinded the minds of them which believe not, lest the light of the glorious gospel of Christ, who is the image of God, should shine unto them.

2 Corinthians 4:4

And they went forth, and preached every where, the Lord working with them, and confirming the word with signs following. Amen.

Mark 16:20

But if I do, though ye believe not me, believe the works: that ye may know, and believe, that the Father is in me, and I in him.

John 10:38

Now the Spirit speaketh expressly, that in the latter times some shall depart from the faith, giving heed to seducing spirits, and doctrines of devils.

1 Timothy 4:1

Wherefore thus saith the LORD God of hosts, Because ye speak this word, behold, I will make my words in thy mouth fire, and this people wood, and it shall devour them.

Jeremiah 5:14

Is not my word like as a fire? saith the LORD; and like a hammer that breaketh the rock in pieces?

Jeremiah 23:29

Being born again, not of corruptible seed, but of incorruptible, by the word of God, which liveth and abideth for ever.

1 Peter 1:23

FIGHT TO WIN!
Lesson 26

I've received many benefits through understanding the believer's authority. I've realised that Satan doesn't have the power to make me do anything. This old saying "The devil made me do it" is absolutely wrong. Satan can't make you do anything. All he can do is lie to you. Then, if you believe his lie, you empower him to accomplish his will. But he can't do anything to you without your consent and cooperation. This is the reason the battle isn't against demonic powers directly. Satan has been stripped. His only power is deception.

That's how he came against Adam and Eve. Satan didn't come in the form of some intimidating animal like a tiger, bear, or mammoth; he chose the most subtle, cunning, crafty animal and came against them with words – deception. Satan chose the snake because he knew he had no power to force Eve into doing anything. He used words to deceive her.

If Eve would have evaluated those words and refused to allow those ungodly thoughts to influence her, she wouldn't have been tempted. If she would have refused to listen to or think anything that countered what God had said, she wouldn't have committed that sin and plunged the whole human race under the authority and dominion of the devil. This all happened through words, and it's still happening today. Satan is fighting us with words and thoughts.

CHOOSE WISELY

The battle is right between your ears. It's not out there somewhere in the heavenly places. It's in your head. Every word you hear either releases life or death. Words based on and in line with the Word of God release life. Words that are inconsistent with what God says minister death.

> **Death and life are in the power of the tongue.**
>
> Proverbs 18:21

It's either life or death, one or the other. What are you listening to? What are you saying?

> **But I say unto you, That every idle word that men shall speak, they shall give account thereof in the day of judgement. For by thy words thou shalt be justified, and by thy words thou shalt be condemned.**
>
> Matthew 12:36-37

Every word you speak and every word you hear are either producing life or death. Everything you listen to on radio, television, or in movies is ministering either life or death. If you disagree with these truths from God's Word, you're deceived.

> **Be not deceived: evil communications corrupt good manners.**
>
> 1 Corinthians 15:33

I'm not suggesting that you move into a monastery and take a vow of silence; I'm encouraging you to recognise life and death and to exercise more self-control in what you're choosing. Every television and radio I've ever seen had an on/off knob and multiple stations to choose from. You don't have to sit in front of the set and just passively take whatever is offered to you. Choose wisely.

I have to deal with this the same as anybody else. There have been times when I've had nothing specific to do. I've wanted to kick back and relax a bit, so I turned on the television. I've flipped through the channels and nothing was on (What's new?), but I ended up watching something just for the sake of watching it, not realising that it was pouring junk into me.

You need to recognise that Satan is fighting you with negative words. You can't change the fact that every word you hear is either releasing death or life, but you can choose whether to listen to it or not. You don't have to swallow it and believe it. You can get to where you're constantly listening to words that minister life, but the choice is up to you.

RENEW YOUR MIND

Grace and peace be multiplied unto you through the knowledge of God, and of Jesus our Lord.

2 Peter 1:2

It's through the knowledge of God that grace and peace are multiplied unto us. Satan knows this, which is why he battles us in our minds.

Be not conformed to this world: but be ye transformed by the renewing of your mind.

Romans 12:2

Metamorphoo is the Greek word rendered "transformed." It's where we get the English word *metamorphosis*. If you want to change from being something creepy, crawly, and earthbound into something beautiful that can fly, then you need to renew your mind.

Many people are trying to take a shortcut. They keep their minds in the gutter, listening to all the things of the world. They allow the sewage of this world to flow through them, but they want the results that God produces. They think, *If I just pray and ask, I can receive.* There's more to it than just praying and believing. They must also cooperate with God's spiritual laws. The way God operates through people is when they get their hearts and minds stayed upon Him. However, Satan hinders God through their thoughts.

WORD MINDED

To be carnally minded is death; but to be spiritually minded is life and peace.

Romans 8:6

If you want to experience life and peace, then you need to become spiritually minded. Jesus said,

The words that I speak unto you, they are spirit, and they are life

John 6:63

Being spiritually minded is being Word minded. It's thinking on what God has to say about your situation instead of what the world has to say. If you are Word minded, you'll have life and peace. Grace and peace will be multiplied to you as you continually think on the knowledge of God. You can't just think negatively – adopting the mindset of the world – and then experience the life, grace, and peace of God. It doesn't work that way.

I get nearly all of my news off the little three-minute news bites on the radio. I hardly watch any television. I figure if something is really that important, it'll make the radio news bites. I've gotten to where I can pretty much handle three minutes of anything negative that the world has to say. But even in those three little minutes, so much of what is said is based on fear, doubt, and unbelief. If you swallow all of that, you'll be in turmoil. But if you listen to and go by the Word of God, you'll have life, grace, and peace.

Through God's Word, I know I'm protected.

> *No weapon that is formed against thee shall prosper; and every tongue that shall rise against thee in judgement thou shalt condemn. This is the heritage of the servants of the LORD and their righteousness is of me, saith the LORD.*
>
> Isaiah 54:17

Notice that you aren't automatically protected. This verse says that you have to condemn the words that come against you. If you just passively sit there and let these ungodly things be spoken, then they will impact you (1 Cor. 15:33). But when you hear something contrary to God's Word, if you will condemn it – recognise it as being wrong, and counter it with the truth of the Word. Then it becomes powerless.

My wife will tell you that there are many times when I talk back to the television and radio. We'll be listening to the news, and they'll say, "It's flu season." I'll declare, "There is no season where the Word of God doesn't work. By His stripes, I have been healed. I'm not getting the flu!" This is what it means to condemn the words that come against us. Even if many people around me are affected, I'll be safe and sound.

> *A thousand shall fall at thy side, and ten thousand at thy right hand; but it shall not come nigh thee. Only with thine eyes shalt thou behold and see the reward of the wicked.*
>
> Psalm 91:7-8

In addition to protection, God's Word promises prosperity, healing, and deliverance. If you will keep your mind fixed on Him, these things will work for you. Remind yourself of how God protected, prospered, healed, and delivered other people in the Word. Keep those thoughts in the forefront of your thinking, and you'll have peace. But if you allow your mind to go the way the world is thinking – fear, doubt, and unbelief – you'll have all those things instead. It really is this simple.

THE ANTIDOTE TO ANY PROBLEM

Grace and peace come through the way you think. Think properly and then you'll have grace, joy, life, and peace. They don't come by prayer but through the knowledge of God.

> *According as his divine power hath given unto us all things that pertain unto life and godliness, through the knowledge of him that hath called us to glory and virtue.*
>
> 2 Peter 1:3, emphasis mine

All things that pertain to life and godliness come through the knowledge of God. It's not "some things" or "a few things" but "all things." This means that if you are sick in your body, you have a knowledge problem. If you're poor, you have a knowledge problem. If you're depressed, you have a knowledge problem. The antidote to any problem is the knowledge of God.

Most people don't believe that. They think that if you have an emotional problem, you take a pill for it. "This problem has nothing to do with me and my choices. I don't have any responsibility whatsoever. It's just the way my hormones are – my chemistry. It's what so-and-so did to me." All of these excuses are wrong in light of God's Word. You need to accept responsibility, go to the Bible, and start thinking according to the Word (Is. 26:3).

The key is how you think.

> **Whereby are given unto us exceeding great and precious promises: that by these ye might be partakers of the divine nature, having escaped the corruption that is in the world through lust.**
>
> 2 Peter 1:4

Through the knowledge of God, we are given exceedingly great and precious promises. The Word of God is the knowledge of God. It's God's thoughts. These promises are the knowledge of God. We become partakers of God's divine nature and escape the corruption that is in the world through lust by the knowledge of God – not by begging for it in prayer or pleading for God to move. You must get your thinking straightened out (Prov. 23:7).

WHAT IS YOUR MIND FULL OF?

You can't be tempted with something you don't think.

> **Truly, if they had been mindful of that country from whence they came out, they might have had opportunity to have returned.**
>
> Hebrews 11:15

This scripture is talking about Abraham and Sarah. They used to live in Ur of the Chaldees, which was in the area of Babylon. God told them to leave there and come over into the land we now call Israel. He told them that someday, they would inherit that land. Abraham actually entered into the Promised Land when he was about 75 years old. He lived to be 175 and never did inherit that promise in his lifetime. He had to buy a parcel of that land just to be able to bury his wife, but it was generations later that the Israelites actually came in and possessed the land.

How did Abraham remain faithful to God's promise – His word to him – for all those years? Hebrews 11:15 says that if they had been mindful – thinking – of the country they came out of, they might have had opportunity to have returned. For them, an opportunity to go back to Ur of the Chaldees would have been a temptation to sin. It would have been rebellion against God for them to have returned to their homeland. Their opportunity to sin – temptation – was linked to what they thought.

If you think on things that provide you with temptation, then an opportunity to sin will come. But if you refuse to think on things that generate temptation, you won't be tempted.

That's good news! Another way of saying this is: You can't be tempted with what you don't think about.

Our culture has convinced us that we need to be "informed" about all of the junk, rottenness, and perversion going on in the world. God's Word teaches us otherwise.

> **I would have you wise unto that which is good, and** simple **concerning evil.**
> Romans 16:19, emphasis mine

We are to be simple, or ignorant, of evil. The Lord doesn't want us to be well versed in these things. The original temptation Adam and Eve fell for was the desire to know more – to know good and evil. God had already given them all the knowledge they needed. Everything He told them was good. God doesn't want us to know evil.

Yet today we feel like we need to know all kinds of evil – what everyone else is doing. By doing so, we open ourselves up to temptation. We can't be tempted by what we don't think. We need to win the battle for our minds. We need to quit exposing ourselves to all of the junk Satan is offering through this world, and we need to get to where all we do is think on God's Word. If the Word of God is all we meditate on, then God's Word is all we'll be tempted with. That's the way it works.

NAÏVE IN NEW YORK

I'm a living example of this truth in action. I was raised in a Christian home and just believed what I was told. I don't remember hearing much about adultery, fornication, or sexual immorality, except that they were wrong. So I never really thought about it.

When I was eighteen years old, my mother took me to a Billy Graham youth event in Bern, Switzerland. Since we were traveling as part of a group, I stayed with a bunch of guys while Mom was with the other women. Our first stop was New York City. I was plucked out of my controlled environment and planted downtown in a very ungodly city. I was exposed to things I had never seen or heard of before. I didn't even know they existed. But because I was naïve, I wasn't tempted.

I remember walking around 42nd and Broadway, where there was a tremendous amount of prostitution. There must have been about a hundred women lined up along this wall. I didn't have a clue. It never even dawned on me what was going on. I never even wondered why they were there. I just thought, *What a great opportunity!* So I took some tracts and went down the row passing them out and witnessing to each of these prostitutes. I didn't know who they were or why they were standing there, so I wasn't tempted. There I was, out on the streets of downtown New York City at two in the morning, witnessing to people. I'd never seen that many folks in my life. As a little country boy from Texas, I was pretty shocked.

While out there, a pimp tried to sell me one of his girls. He came up to me and started speaking in street language. I didn't know what he was talking about. Nobody I knew talked that way. This guy tried to sell me for ten minutes, but I didn't understand what he was trying to communicate. Finally, he just looked at me, turned around, threw up his hands, and walked off shaking his head. He was probably wondering, *What rock did this hick crawl out from?*

Back at the hotel, I told my roommates some of the things this guy had said. They had to explain to me that he was a pimp trying to sell me a prostitute. I was so naïve, I didn't even know what he was talking about. I hadn't thought that way before. I wasn't aware of the terminology. Therefore, I wasn't tempted.

YOU CAN WIN

Are you someone who has to fight temptation tooth and nail? Are you holding on with white knuckles, yet you can't understand why it's so hard to live for God? It's because you allow so much junk to be planted in you. You're trying to rebuke lust, sexual addiction, and pornography by doing "spiritual warfare" against these demons, yet you're sitting there listening to and watching stuff every day on television that encourages sin.

Today's television programs will expose you to more sex in an hour's time than your great-grandparents saw their entire lifetime. Even if you find a decent show, the commercials will kill you. The average magazine and newspaper isn't much better. They show all kinds of nudity and sexual content. The media bombards with it on all sides.

The sad thing is that most Christians allow this stuff into their homes. They expose their children to it, and then they wonder why they're having problems. They're doing "spiritual warfare" and "intercession" so that their kids will grow up to be godly people, but then they just allow Satan to deposit his perversion and unbelief in them. The devil loves it when people use the television as a babysitter so they don't have to pay any attention to their kids.

We've allowed things into our lives and then wondered, *Why am I so tempted? Why is the Christian life so hard to live?* It's hard because Satan comes at us through the way we think. He can do nothing to us without our consent and cooperation. We need to start being selective about what we let into our eyes, ears, and hearts.

Your life will go in the direction of your dominant thoughts. Don't let the junk of this world fill your mind. Set your heart to seek the Lord, and meditate on His Word. The battle truly is in your mind. You can win this fight, but you must fight to win!

FIGHT TO WIN!
Lesson 26 – Outline

I. Satan is fighting us with words and thoughts.

   A. The battle is right between your ears.

   B. Words based on and in line with the Word of God release life.

   Death and life are in the power of the tongue.

   Proverbs 18:21

   C. Words that are inconsistent with what God says minister death.

   But I say unto you, That every idle word that men shall speak, they shall give account thereof in the day of judgement. For by thy words thou shalt be justified, and by thy words thou shalt be condemned.

   Matthew 12:36-37

   D. Every word you speak and every word you hear are either producing life or death.

   Be not deceived: evil communications corrupt good manners.

   1 Corinthians 15:33

   E. I'm encouraging you to recognise life and death and to exercise more self-control in what you're choosing.

II. It's through the knowledge of God that grace and peace are multiplied unto us.

   Grace and peace be multiplied unto you through the knowledge of God, and of Jesus our Lord.

   2 Peter 1:2

   A. Satan knows this, which is why he battles us in our minds.

   Be not conformed to this world: but be ye transformed by the renewing of your mind.

   Romans 12:2

   B. If you want to change from being something creepy, crawly, and earthbound into something beautiful that can fly, you need to renew your mind.

   C. The way God operates through us is when we get our hearts and minds stayed upon Him.

   D. Satan hinders God through our thoughts.

III. If you want to experience life and peace, you need to become spiritually minded.

> *To be carnally minded is death; but to be spiritually minded is life and peace.*
>
> Romans 8:6

A. Being spiritually minded is being Word minded.

> *The words that I speak unto you, they are spirit, and they are life.*
>
> John 6:63

B. It's thinking on what God has to say about your situation instead of what the world has to say.

C. In addition to protection, God's Word promises prosperity, healing, and deliverance (Is. 54:17 and Ps. 91:7-8).

D. Think properly and then you'll have grace, joy, life, and peace.

> *According as his divine power hath given unto us all things that pertain unto life and godliness, through the knowledge of him that hath called us to glory and virtue: Whereby are given unto us exceeding great and precious promises: that by these ye might be partakers of the divine nature, having escaped the corruption that is in the world through lust.*
>
> 2 Peter 1:3-4

E. The antidote to any problem is the knowledge of God, and the Word of God is the knowledge of God – it's God's thoughts.

IV. You can't be tempted with something you don't think.

> *Truly, if they had been mindful of that country from whence they came out, they might have had opportunity to have returned.*
>
> Hebrews 11:15

A. If you think on things that provide you with temptation, then an opportunity to sin will come. But if you refuse to think on things that generate temptation, you won't be tempted.

B. We are to be simple – ignorant – of evil (Rom. 16:19).

C. We need to quit exposing ourselves to all of the junk that Satan is offering through this world, and we need get to where all we do is think on God's Word.

FIGHT TO WIN!
Lesson 26 – Teacher's Guide

1. Satan is fighting us with words and thoughts. The battle is right between our ears. Words based on and in line with the Word of God release life (Prov. 18:21). Words that are inconsistent with what God says minister death (Matt. 12:36-37). Every word we speak and every word we hear are either producing life or death (1 Cor. 15:33). Let's recognise life and death and exercise more self-control in what we're choosing.

2. It's through the knowledge of God that grace and peace are multiplied unto us (2 Pet. 1:2). Satan knows this, which is why he battles us in our minds (Rom. 12:2). If we want to change from being something creepy, crawly, and earthbound into something beautiful that can fly, then we need to renew our minds. The way God operates through us is when we get our hearts and minds stayed upon Him. Satan hinders God through our thoughts.

3. If we want to experience life and peace, then we need to become spiritually minded (Rom. 8:6). Being spiritually minded is being Word minded (John 6:63). It's thinking on what God has to say about our situation instead of what the world has to say. In addition to protection, God's Word promises prosperity, healing, and deliverance (Is. 54:17 and Ps. 91:7-8). We need to think properly, and then we'll have grace, joy, life, and peace (2 Pet. 1:3-4). The antidote to any problem is the knowledge of God, and the Word of God is the knowledge of God – it's God's thoughts.

4. We can't be tempted with something we don't think (Heb. 11:15). If we think on things that provide us with temptation, then an opportunity to sin will come. But if we refuse to think on things that generate temptation, we won't be tempted. We are to be simple – ignorant – of evil (Rom. 16:19). We need to quit exposing ourselves to all of the junk that Satan is offering through this world, and we need to get to where all we do is think on God's Word.

1. A. Read Proverbs 18:21, Matthew 12:36-37, and 1 Corinthians 15:33. What is Satan fighting us with? (Words and thoughts)
   B. What is every word we speak and every word we hear producing? (Either life or death)
2. A. Read 2 Peter 1:2 and Romans 12:2. How is grace and peace multiplied unto us? (Through the knowledge of God)
   B. How does Satan hinder God? (Through our thoughts)
3. A. Read Romans 8:6, John 6:63, Isaiah 54:17, Psalm 91:7-8, and 2 Peter 1:3-4. Being spiritually minded is being what? (Word minded)
   B. What is the antidote to any problem? (The knowledge of God)
4. A. Read Hebrews 11:15 and Romans 16:19. We can't be tempted with what? (Something we don't think)
   B. We need to quit exposing ourselves to all of the junk that Satan is offering through this world, and we need to get to where all we do is think on what? (God's Word)

FIGHT TO WIN!
Lesson 26 – Discipleship Questions

1. Proverbs 18:21 reveals that the tongue has what power?

2. What does 1 Corinthians 15:33 say corrupts good manners?

3. According to 2 Peter 1:2, how is grace and peace multiplied unto us?

4. As we prove God's will – make it manifest to our natural senses – Romans 12:2 tells us that we'll find it to be what?

5. According to John 6:63, what are spirit and life?

6. Isaiah 54:17 says that no weapon formed against us shall what?

7. This is the heritage of whom?

8. And our _____ is of Him.

9. Psalm 91:7-8 says that even though ten thousand may fall at _____, it shall not come nigh us.

10. Only with our eyes will we see what?

11. Through the knowledge of Him, 1 Peter 1:3-4 says that we are given exceeding great and precious what?

12. By them, we are partakers of what?

13. According to Romans 16:19, God would have us wise concerning what?

14. He would also have us simple concerning what?

FIGHT TO WIN!
Lesson 26 – Answer Key

1. Death and life.
2. Evil communications.
3. Through the knowledge of God and of Jesus Christ our Lord.
4. Good, acceptable, and perfect.
5. Jesus' words.
6. Prosper.
7. The servants of the Lord.
8. Righteousness.
9. Our right hand.
10. The reward of the wicked.
11. Promises.
12. The divine nature.
13. That which is good.
14. Evil.

FIGHT TO WIN!
Lesson 26 – Scriptures

Death and life are in the power of the tongue: and they that love it shall eat the fruit thereof.

Proverbs 18:21

But I say unto you, That every idle word that men shall speak, they shall give account thereof in the day of judgement. For by thy words thou shalt be justified, and by thy words thou shalt be condemned.

Matthew 12:36-37

Be not deceived: evil communications corrupt good manners.

1 Corinthians 15:33

Grace and peace be multiplied unto you through the knowledge of God, and of Jesus our Lord.

2 Peter 1:2

And be not conformed to this world: but be ye transformed by the renewing of your mind, that ye may prove what is that good, and acceptable, and perfect, will of God.

Romans 12:2

For to be carnally minded is death; but to be spiritually minded is life and peace.

Romans 8:6

It is the spirit that quickeneth; the flesh profiteth nothing: the words that I speak unto you, they are spirit, and they are life.

John 6:63

No weapon that is formed against thee shall prosper; and every tongue that shall rise against thee in judgement thou shalt condemn. This is the heritage of the servants of the LORD, and their righteousness is of me, saith the LORD.

Isaiah 54:17

A thousand shall fall at thy side, and ten thousand at thy right hand; but it shall not come nigh thee. Only with thine eyes shalt thou behold and see the reward of the wicked.

Psalm 91:7-8

According as his divine power hath given unto us all things that pertain unto life and godliness, through the knowledge of him that hath called us to glory and virtue: Whereby are given unto us exceeding great and precious promises: that by these ye might be partakers of the divine nature, having escaped the corruption that is in the world through lust.

2 Peter 1:3-4

Thou wilt keep him in perfect peace, whose mind is stayed on thee: because he trusteth in thee.

Isaiah 26:3

For as he thinketh in his heart, so is he: Eat and drink, saith he to thee; but his heart is not with thee.

Proverbs 23:7

And truly, if they had been mindful of that country from whence they came out, they might have had opportunity to have returned.

Hebrews 11:15

For your obedience is come abroad unto all men. I am glad therefore on your behalf: but yet I would have you wise unto that which is good, and simple concerning evil.

Romans 16:19

CONCLUSION

Now that you realise the spiritual dynamics behind what's happening in the physical realm, you recognise that we're truly in a spiritual battle! You understand the spiritual significance of your choices, words, and actions. And you recognise that the battlefield is in your mind. Whom you yield to – God or Satan – is whom you empower to work in and through your life (Rom. 6:16). Therefore, submit to God, resist the devil – and he will flee from you (James 4:7)!

I pray this newfound awareness will motivate you to meditate daily on the truths of God's Word. Let them penetrate your heart and renew your mind. Then you'll find yourself thinking God's thoughts, speaking His Word, and acting in faith. You'll discover more of God's laws and how to cooperate with them. And as you take responsibility to exercise your God-given authority, you'll enjoy more and more of the abundant life Jesus died and resurrected to provide.

RECEIVE JESUS AS YOUR SAVIOUR

Choosing to receive Jesus Christ as your Lord and Saviour is the most important decision you'll ever make!

God's Word promises, **"That if thou shalt confess with thy mouth the Lord Jesus, and shalt believe in thine heart that God hath raised him from the dead, thou shalt be saved. For with the heart man believeth unto righteousness; and with the mouth confession is made unto salvation"** (Rom. 10:9-10). **"For whosoever shall call upon the name of the Lord shall be saved"** (Rom. 10:13).

By His grace, God has already done everything to provide salvation. Your part is simply to believe and receive.

Pray out loud, *"Jesus, I confess that You are my Lord and Saviour. I believe in my heart that God raised You from the dead. By faith in Your Word, I receive salvation now. Thank You for saving me!"*

The very moment you commit your life to Jesus Christ, the truth of His Word instantly comes to pass in your spirit. Now that you're born again, there's a brand-new you!

Please contact me and let me know that you've prayed to receive Jesus as your Saviour or to be filled with the Holy Spirit. I would like to rejoice with you and help you understand more fully what has taken place in your life. I'll send you a free gift that will help you understand and grow in your new relationship with the Lord. *Welcome to your new life!*

RECEIVE THE HOLY SPIRIT

As His child, your loving heavenly Father wants to give you the supernatural power you need to live this new life.

> *For every one that asketh receiveth; and he that seeketh findeth; and to him that knocketh it shall be opened ... how much more shall your heavenly Father give the Holy Spirit to them that ask him?*
>
> Luke 11:10-13

All you have to do is ask, believe, and receive!

Pray, *"Father, I recognise my need for Your power to live this new life. Please fill me with Your Holy Spirit. By faith, I receive it right now! Thank You for baptising me. Holy Spirit, You are welcome in my life!"*

Congratulations – now you're filled with God's supernatural power!

Some syllables from a language you don't recognise will rise up from your heart to your mouth (1 Cor. 14:14). As you speak them out loud by faith, you're releasing God's power from within and building yourself up in your spirit (1 Cor. 14:4). You can do this whenever and wherever you like.

It doesn't really matter whether you felt anything or not when you prayed to receive the Lord and His Spirit. If you believed in your heart that you received, then God's Word promises that you did. **"Therefore I say unto you, What things soever ye desire, when ye pray, believe that ye receive them, and ye shall have them"** (Mark 11:24). God always honours His Word – believe it!

Please contact me and let me know that you've prayed to receive Jesus as your Saviour or to be filled with the Holy Spirit. I would like to rejoice with you and help you understand more fully what has taken place in your life. I'll send you a free gift that will help you understand and grow in your new relationship with the Lord. *Welcome to your new life!*

Other Teachings by Andrew Wommack

Spirit, Soul & Body
Understanding the relationship of your spirit, soul, and body is foundational to your Christian life. You will never truly know how much God loves you or believe what His Word says about you until you do. In this series, learn how they're related and how that knowledge will release the life of your spirit into your body and soul. It may even explain why many things are not working the way you had hoped.

Spirit, Soul & Body CDs and DVDs
Item Code: 1027-C   4-CD album

Spirit, Soul & Body Books
Item Code: 318   **Paperback**
Item Code: 318E   **Ebook (pdf, mobi, epub)**

Spirit, Soul & Body Study Guides
Item Code: 418   **Spiral-bound Book**
Item Code: 418E   **Ebook (pdf)**

Living in the Balance of Grace and Faith
This book explains one of the biggest controversies in the church today. Is it grace or faith that releases the power of God? Does God save people in His sovereignty, or does your faith move Him? You may be surprised by the answers as Andrew reveals what the Bible has to say concerning these important questions and more. This will help you receive from God in a greater way and will change the way you relate to Him.

Living In The Balance of Grace and Faith Books
Item Code: 228   **Hardback**
Item Code: 328E   **Ebook (pdf, mobi, epub)**

Living In The Balance of Grace and Faith Study Guides
Item Code: 428   **Spiral-bound Book**
Item Code: 428E   **Ebook (pdf)**

The True Nature of God
Are you confused about the nature of God? Is He the God of judgment found in the Old Testament or the God of mercy and grace found in the New Testament? Andrew's revelation on this subject will set you free and give you a confidence in your relationship with God like never before. This is truly nearly-too-good-to-be-true news.

The True Nature of God CDs and DVDs
Item Code: 1002-C   5-CD album

The True Nature of God Books
Item Code: 308   **Paperback**
Item Code: 308E   **Ebook (pdf)**

Grace, The Power of The Gospel

The vast majority of Christians believe their salvation is at least in part dependent on their performance. Paul's revelation of grace in Romans settles the issue. It's not what you do, but what Jesus did.

Grace, The Power Of The Gospel Books

Item Code: 322   **Paperback**
Item Code: 322E   **Ebook (pdf, mobi, epub)**

Grace, The Power Of The Gospel Study Guide

Item Code: 422   **Spiral-bound Book**
Item Code: 422 E   **Ebook (pdf)**

A Year of Devotions

Want to see progressive change in your life, effortless change? Take the time to begin or end your day with devotions. Most of these were written by Andrew Wommack, but also feature authors Bob Yandian and Bob Nichols.

Item Code: 319   **Paperback**
Item Code: 319E   **Ebook (pdf)**

Harnessing Your Emotions

Emotions: Can't live with them; can't live without them. So how do you bring them under control? You need to know.

Item Code: 313   **Paperback**
Item Code: 313E   **Ebook (pdf)**

The New You & The Holy Spirit

What really happened when you were saved and filled with the Holy Spirit? Read as Andrew gives you the specifics of your new life in Christ and the baptism of the Holy Spirit.

The New You & The Holy Spirit Books

Item Code: 323   **Paperback**
Item Code: 323E   **Ebook (pdf)**

You've Already Got It!
So Quit Trying To Get It

God has already blessed, healed, and prospered you. Don't struggle under feelings of condemnation and unworthiness anymore. Everything has already been given to you as a gift from God.

You've Already Got It! Books

Item Code: 320   **Paperback**
Item Code: 320E   **Ebook (pdf)**

The Believer's Authority

Like it or not, every one of us is in a spiritual war. You can't be discharged from service, and ignorance of the battlefield only aids the enemy. In war, God is always for us, and the devil is against us; whichever one we cooperate with will win. And there's only one way the enemy can get your cooperation—that's through deception. In this teaching, Andrew exposes this war and the enemy for what he is.

The Believer's Authority CDs and DVDs

Item Code: 1045-C   6-CD album
Item Code: 1045-D   6-DVD album (as recorded from television)

The Believer's Authority Books

Item Code: 327   Paperback
Item Code: 327E   Ebook (pdf, mobi, epub)

The Believer's Authority Study Guides

Item Code: 427   Spiral-bound Book
Item Code: 427   Ebook (pdf)

The Effects of Praise

Every Christian wants a stronger walk with the Lord. But how do you get there? Many don't know the true power of praise. It's essential. Listen as Andrew teaches biblical truths that will not only spark understanding but will help promote spiritual growth so you will experience victory.

The Effects of Praise CDs and DVDs

Item Code: 1004-C   3-CD album

The Effects of Praise Books

Item Code: 309   Paperback

God Wants You Well

Health is something everyone wants. Billions of dollars are spent each year trying to retain or restore health. So why does religion tell us that God uses sickness to teach us something? It even tries to make us believe that sickness is a blessing. That's just not true. God wants you well!

God Wants You Well CDs and DVDs

Item Code: 1036-C   4-CD album
Item Code: 1036-D   6-DVD album (as recorded from television)

God Wants You Well Books

Item Code: 102   Booklet
Item Code: 330   Paperback
Item Code: 330E   Ebook (pdf, mobi, epub)

God Wants You Well Study Guide

Item Code: 430   Study Guide
Item Code: 330E   Ebook (pdf)

The War Is Over

Many have not heard the news that the longest conflict in history ended in a decisive victory nearly 2,000 years ago, continuing to fight the battle of sin and judgment. The message in this book will set you free from condemnation, judgment, and fear so you can receive the blessings of God.

The War Is Over Books
Item Code: 326 Paperback
Item Code: 326E   Ebook (pdf, mobi, epub)

The War Is Over Study Guides
Item Code: 426 Spiral-bound Book
Item Code: 426E   Ebook (pdf)

Discover The Keys To Staying Full of God

Staying full of God is not a secret or mysterious; it's simple. For that reason, few people recognise the keys, and even less practice them. Learn what they are and put them into practice; they will keep your heart sensitive.

Discover the Keys to Staying Full of God Books
Item Code: 324 Paperback
Item Code: 324E   Ebook (pdf, mobi, epub)

Discover the Keys to Staying Full of God Study Guides
Item Code: 424   Spiral-bound Book
Item Code: 424E   Ebook (pdf)

Mini Booklets

Insights Into Faith

For many, faith is elusive. Some seem to have it and others don't. The Bible says we all have "the measure of faith" (Rom. 12:3). Read and Andrew will explain.

Item Code: 100

Self-Centredness: The Root of All Grief

It's not other people. It's not your circumstances. And it's not the devil. It's the only thing you have the power to change.

Item Code: 315

ABOUT THE AUTHOR

For over four decades, Andrew Wommack has traveled America and the world teaching the truth of the Gospel. His profound revelation of the Word of God is taught with clarity and simplicity, emphasising God's unconditional love and the balance between grace and faith. He reaches millions of people through the daily *Gospel Truth* radio and television programs, broadcast both domestically and internationally. He founded Charis Bible College in 1994 and has since established CBC extension schools in other major cities of America and around the world. Andrew has produced a library of teaching materials, available in print, audio, and visual formats. And, as it has been from the beginning, his ministry continues to distribute free audio materials to those who cannot afford them.

Andrew Wommack Ministries – Europe

PO Box 4392, WS1 9AR, Walsall, England

E-mail: enquiries@awme.net

UK Helpline Phone (orders and prayer):

+44 (0)1922 473300

Hours: 7:30 AM to 4:00 PM GMT

Web: www.awme.net